Youth Violence

Interventions for Health Care Providers

Robert
Public H

American Public Health Association
Washington, DC

American Public Health Association
800 I Street, NW
Washington, DC 20001–3710
www.apha.org

Georges C. Benjamin, MD, FACP
Executive Director

Printed and bound in the United States of America
Set in: New Baskerville and Gil Sans
Interior Design and Typesetting: Terence Mulligan
Cover Design: Jennifer Strass
Printing and Binding by Port City Press, Baltimore, Maryland

ISBN: 978-0-87553-188-5

800 06/08

Table of Contents

Acknowledgements

The preparation of this manuscript was made possible through a grant from the National Institutes of Health, National Library of Medicine to Public Health Management Corporation (PHMC) (formerly called Philadelphia Health Management Corporation); Principal Investigator Robert Ketterlinus, Ph.D. This grant, *Youth Violence: Interventions in Emergency Departments* (G13 LM007638), provided support to develop Chapters 1, 2, 3, 4 and 7. We would also like to acknowledge the funding support provided to PHMC by the William Penn Foundation that enabled us to work with a broad array of individuals and organizations to help implement and coordinate youth violence interventions in both community and hospital settings. In addition to the generous grant support we received, we also thank Karen Fulbright-Anderson, PhD, Robin M. Ikeda, MD, MPH, and Nancy Guerra, EdD, who reviewed drafts of these chapters and shared their expertise. Thanks also go to Nicole Dreisbach and Frances Schulz of PHMC for their research and administrative assistance, respectively, as well as Margaret E. Caracappa for editorial assistance. We also thank the authors of all of the chapters for their cooperation and patience during the production of this book. Lastly, we extend our gratitude for the support provided by Ellen Meyer, APHA Director of Publications and Terence Mulligan, APHA Book Production Manager.

Preface

Since 2002 the murder rate in Philadelphia climbed steadily, from just under 300 to 406 in 2006, and 392 in 2007; there was a parallel increase in the number of gunshot-wound victims among ages 7 to 24. Additionally, part one major crimes—in which a juvenile is the victim—are becoming more violent. Of the 4,523 juvenile victims of part one major crimes, 79% were victims of murder, rape, robbery, or aggravated assault. The murder rate in Philadelphia is higher than larger cities including New York City, Los Angeles, and Chicago. However, wherever youth violence occurs, even if it involves a small number of youth, everyone should be concerned because violence affects us all in a myriad of ways.

In 1985, former Surgeon General C. Everett Koop articulated the need for a public health approach to tackle youth violence. Harvard Professor Dr. Deborah Prothrow-Stith has reduced this to the simple question: What if we treated violence as a preventable disease? If we did, then all health care professionals would be promoting the prevention of violence by employing scientific theory and data collection, problem identification, surveillance, program development and implementation research, and program effectiveness research.

Emergency department and allied health professionals are well-positioned to intervene with young victims of violence using a public health approach. In addition to providing needed physical care to violently injured youth, there is a range of opportunities, based on over 20 years of public health and developmental research, for intervening in recurring or escalating cycles of violence among youth and young adults.

Youth Violence is the first book to address theory, current research, and operational guidance on the ways hospitals, especially Emergency Departments (EDs), might utilize a public health approach to respond to intentional violence involving youth. The book includes reviews of current research and practice relevant to healthcare providers. The authors discuss the theoretical and operational components of ED-based prevention interventions in three cities, specific examples of program operations and outcomes, case studies, and directions for further research and program development. In keeping with a comprehensive public health approach to youth violence, the book intends to inform a broad audience of public health and healthcare planners, hospital-based providers (from medicine, social worker, pastoral care, and administration), and community-based youth service professionals.

In sum, *Youth Violence* contains information for building a strong foundation for hospital-initiated youth violence prevention and intervention programs. Hopefully, the information and insights provided in the following chapters will inspire others to begin, or increase, their efforts to reduce violence among one of our most valuable assets—our youth.

Robert D. Ketterlinus, PhD

Introduction

Robert D. Ketterlinus, PhD

Despite a significant decline since the 1990s in the occurrence of violent crimes nationwide (Bureau of Justice Statistics, 2004), homicide is the second-leading cause of death among people ages 10–24. Young adults and adolescents are disproportionately victimized by firearm-related homicide, and gunshot wounds are the second leading cause of death for all people aged 10-34. From 1981 to 1999, 20- to 24-year-olds were most likely to be victims of homicide, especially by firearms, but victimization rates among 15- to 19-year-olds rose and fell more dramatically than other age groups between 1985 and 1999. Adolescent victimization rates surpassed the rates for those 25 and older by 1990 and did not fall back below the rate for persons in their late 20s until 1998. Blacks have historically been at high risk of victimization by firearm-related homicide (Wellford, Pepper, and Petrie, 2004). Youth and young adults are not only victimized by violent crimes, but also perpetrate these crimes. In 1999, there were 2.4 million arrests of youths with 104,000 of these arrests for violent crimes (USDHS, 2001).

In 1985, former Surgeon General C. Everett Koop articulated the need for a public health approach to tackle youth violence (Koop and Lundberg, 1992). After 20 years of efforts by different Federal agencies, each with their own focus and expertise around youth violence and injury, the Surgeon General reported that there are still several myths about youth violence that had the potential to impede progress in reducing youth violence and its consequences (U.S. DHHS. 2001). The myths and the research findings that contradict them include:

- *The epidemic of youth violence that marked the early 1990s is over, and young people—as well as the rest of society—are much safer today than a decade ago.* Although the number of lethal acts performed by youths has declined, the overall number of violent acts committed by youths has not fallen. For example, arrest rates for aggravated assault are 70 percent higher today than they were in 1983, the first year of a decade that witnessed dramatic increases in rates of violence by young people. Studies of self-report data, in particular, support the conclusion that the epidemic has not ended. In addition, the number of young females involved in serious violent acts has increased significantly.
- *Most future violent offenders can be identified in early childhood.* Exhibiting uncontrollable behavior or being diagnosed with a conduct disorder as a young child is not a predictor of violence in adolescence. Most violent offenders at age 16 and 17 have no history of conduct disorders such as

antisocial behavior or aggressive behavior. One major study, for example, demonstrated that signs of these types of disorders did not appear until after the onset of puberty.

- *Most children who are abused and neglected will become violent offenders.* Physical abuse and neglect are relatively weak predictors of violence. Most children who are abused and neglected do not become violent offenders.
- *African-American and Hispanic youths are more likely to become involved in violence than other racial or ethnic groups.* Although there are racial and ethnic differences in homicide arrest rates, data from self-reports indicate that race and ethnicity have little bearing on the overall proportion of nonfatal violent behavior. There are differences in the timing and continuity of violence over the life span, which account in part for the over-representation of these groups in U.S. jails and prisons.
- *Getting tough with juvenile offenders by trying them in adult criminal courts reduces the likelihood that they will commit more crimes.* Youths transferred to adult criminal courts have significantly higher rates of re-offending and a greater likelihood of committing subsequent felonies than youths who remain in the juvenile justice system. They are also more likely to be victimized physically and sexually.
- *Weapons-related injuries in schools have increased dramatically in the past 5 years.* Weapons-related injuries have not changed significantly in the past 20 years. In comparison to other environments, including neighborhoods and homes, schools are relatively safe places for young people.

The Federal government has responded by promoting a public health approach to the continuing problem of youth violence. The public health approach promotes prevention by employing scientific theory and data collection, problem identification, surveillance, program development and implementation research, and program effectiveness research. The public health approach also promotes inter- and intra-agency collaboration and dissemination of prevention research and programs. The creation of Healthy People 2010 (HP 2010) has been one such method of the public health approach. HP 2010, which established national health objectives, advocates tracking and identification of trends in public health outcomes. Youth violence and injury prevention are included in HP 2010 national health objectives, making the prevention of youth violence a national goal. Furthermore, the Centers for Disease Control recently created The National Center for Injury Prevention (NCIP) to develop surveillance systems to identify, measure, and monitor trends in youth violence; to identify effective prevention and intervention programs; and to disseminate these programs in real world settings.

By the early 1990s, healthcare professionals began articulating the need to adopt a public health approach to Emergency Medicine, including intentional injuries (Berstein et al. 1994). Medical staff stationed in the emergency department (ED) were witnessing both the effects and frequency of violently injured youth passing through the ED (Prothrow-Stith and Spivak, 2004). While protocols for identifying cases of intimate partner violence, child abuse, and substance abuse have all been implemented in the ED, protocols for identifying cases of youth violence lag behind these other public health issues. However, several hospital- and ED-based violence intervention/prevention programs have been developed out of the recognition that EDs provide an opportunity for medical staff to identify violently injured youth and refer them for community-based services. This book describes ED-based youth violence and intervention programs created across the country over the past 15 years.

Purpose of the Book

Youth Violence addresses theory, current research, and operational guidance on the ways hospitals, especially Emergency Departments (EDs), might respond to intentional violence involving youth. The book includes reviews of current research and practice relevant to healthcare professionals, especially ED providers in urban areas. The theoretical and operational components of ED-based prevention interventions, specific examples of program operations and outcomes, and directions for further research and program development are included, with a focus on the problem of youth violence in urban areas and appropriate hospital initiated interventions.

The book is designed to fill a gap in the literature on youth violence prevention, specifically a description of ED-based interventions. A second purpose is to provide emergency department (ED) and allied healthcare staff with a practical guide to the implementation of a collaborative, community-based youth violence prevention initiative.

Several chapters in *Youth Violence* were developed as part of Philadelphia's Healthcare Collaborative: Youth Violence Prevention initiative (HCC), funded over a four-year period by the William Penn Foundation. The Collaborative comprised four university hospital EDs: Albert Einstein Medical Center (AEMC), Thomas Jefferson University Hospital (TJUH), The Children's Hospital of Philadelphia (CHOP), and the Hospital of the University of Pennsylvania (HUP). The Philadelphia Health Management Corporation (PHMC), a non-profit public health agency, managed the project and provided technical assistance to the hospitals and to the Philadelphia based Anti-Violence/Anti-Drug Network (PAAN). PAAN provided community-based crisis intervention services for HCC participants and their families (A more detailed description of the HCC project and youth served is included in Chapters 1–4). PHMC also applied for, and was awarded a grant (Robert D. Ketterlinus, Ph.D., Principal Investigator) from the National Institutes of Health (NIH), National Library of Medicine (NLM) to produce the draft chapters for this book, produced and published by the American Public Health Association.

The specific aims of this book are to:

- *Advance the field of youth violence prevention* by summarizing research and operational experiences for an interdisciplinary understanding of ED-based violence prevention and intervention programs.

- *Inform a healthcare audience* of ED providers and their referral resources about the potential opportunities, benefits, and challenges of addressing violence among injured young patients. This audience includes all members of the ED team (medicine, social work, mental health, pastoral care) as well as administrators, advocates, and community service providers who serve as referrals.
- *Provide readers with an empirical and practical understanding* of the issues that need to be addressed when developing an ED-based collaborative program.
- *Illustrate tested program models* that can be replicated or adapted by ED and other healthcare staff seeking to initiate some or all of these model components or researchers seeking to corroborate intervention effectiveness.

In sum, the book contains information for building a strong foundation for ED-initiated youth violence prevention and intervention programs in urban areas.

Emergency Departments' Potential to Implement a Public Health Approach to Youth Violence Intervention and Prevention

Emergency departments, especially those in large urban hospitals, are well positioned to intervene with young victims of violence using a public health approach. In addition to providing needed physical care to violently injured youth, there is a range of opportunities for intervening in recurring or escalating cycles of violence among youth and young adults. ED staff are strategically positioned to:

- *Identify, contact, and track high-risk youth.* The ED provides both opportunities and challenges to establishing contact with youth at high risk for continued violence. The ED offers the opportunity to serve youth with a wide range of characteristics, needs and risks. Typically, ED social workers and other staff respond to emergency health issues by diagnosing the specific risks to the patient's well-being, tailoring an emergency response and suggesting longer-term referral and follow-up. Such responses also are appropriate to the risk of retaliatory violence. The book includes examples of effective procedures and instruments for identifying and tracking youth.
- *Implement a multifaceted intervention.* Young victims of intentional injury vary widely in 1) their type and level of risk for repeat or retaliatory violence; 2) their intervention needs; 3) their levels of cooperation; and 4) their potential assets and resiliency. This broad, heterogeneous risk group requires a broad range of community-based interventions. Depending on the risks and target population specified, ED based interventions can include:
- *Emergency and crisis intervention:* immediate intervention for youth at risk to self or others. This can include deescalating peer, family, or community violence.
- *Debriefing:* helps youth reframe the incident and articulate and validate concerns for safety.

- *Prevention counseling or programs (generic or faith-based):* provide specific advice for improving safety, such as household firearm storage or lifestyle adjustments, including modification of behaviors, attitudes, or interpersonal skills.
- *Psychological counseling:* monitor and reduce impact of post-traumatic stress.
- *Increasing adult support:* builds resiliency to risk exposure.
- *Case management*: provides specific problem solving, advocacy for systems changes and facilitation of referrals to community resources. Outreach and home visits help strengthen the intervention, using community members, the faith community, and the family as resources.

Overview of the Book

While each chapter can be read on its own in no particular order, we recommend that the reader begin with Chapter 1 by Ketterlinus and Cheney, who provide context for the program examples described in the book by reviewing the literature on intentional youth violence. The chapter is divided into two parts. In Part I the literature on several interrelated topics is summarized, including the extent and nature of youth violence, the causes and consequences of youth violence, violence and mental health, and disparities in youth violence. In Part II, model and promising evidence-based prevention, intervention, and treatment programs in the area of violence are summarized. An overview of resources focuses on approaches to implementing evidence-based programs and resources for providing health providers with the competencies needed to address violence prevention.

The first three program examples are drawn from Philadelphia HealthCare Collaborative project. Datner, Lee-Ibarra, Kassam-Adams, and Fein open Chapter 2 with a description of *The Violence Intervention Project (VIP) of The University of Pennsylvania.* The authors address the relationship between youth exposure to violence and Acute Stress Disorder and Post-Traumatic Stress Disorder, as well as implications for emergency physicians. They also include case studies of several VIP participants who successfully completed the program.

In Chapter 3, Ginsburg discusses the development of a theoretical framework for assessing behavioral change that emerged from his work on the VIP project at the University of Pennsylvania. He provides guidelines for assessing the needs, resources, and potential to change behaviors for young violently injured patients, using actual examples of methods he and his colleagues have used to help youth change behaviors that could lead to violent outcomes.

In Chapter 4, Corbin and colleagues describe a faith-based approach to the care of violent youth operated at the Thomas Jefferson University (TJU) Hospital emergency department. This approach was incorporated into TJU's emergency department-based Jefferson Community Violence Prevention Program (JCVPP), a multidisciplinary collaboration amongst physicians, nurses, social workers, and chaplains that provided support and a referral service to violently injured youth and young adults.

In the next two chapters, examples of hospital-based youth violence intervention/prevention programs in two other cities are presented. These programs were still in operation at the time this book was published, while the Philadelphia HealthCare Collaborative project had expired.

Melzer-Lange and her colleagues describe in Chapter 5 the history and implementation of Project Ujima, a hospital- and community-based youth violence intervention/prevention program in Milwaukee, Wisconsin. The chapter also includes a client case history, followed by a summary of outcome and cost analyses of the program and lessons learned during its implementation.

In Chapter 6, Calhoun and Becker describe the creation of *Caught In The Crossfire*, a hospital-based peer intervention program for violently injured youth serving the East Oakland, California community. The authors also summarize findings from a previously published outcomes study and present an 11-step plan to design and implement a successful peer intervention. They conclude with several case studies of youth who participated in the intervention.

In the closing Chapter 7, Ketterlinus summarizes Chapters 2–6 and suggests areas for further program development and research. The chapter includes a description of a new Trauma Center/ED-based youth firearms surveillance and intervention project being implemented in three major hospitals in Philadelphia which builds on the lessons learned by the Philadelphia HealthCare Collaborative project and other programs described in this book.

References

Bernstein E., Goldfrank, L.R., Kellerman, A.L., and Hargarten, S.W. (1994). A public health approach to emergency medicine: Preparing for the twenty-first century. *Acad. Emerg. Med.*, 227-236.

Bureau of Justice Statistics. (2004). Criminal Victimization - 2004. Washington, DC: U.S. Department of Justice.

Koop, C. E., & Lundberg, G. (1992). Violence in America: a public health emergency. *JAMA*, 22: 3075-3076).

Prothrow-Stith, D., and Spivak, H.R. (2004). Murder is no accident; Understanding and preventing youth violence in America. San Francisco: Jossey-Bass.

U.S. Department of Health & Human Services. (2001). Youth Violence: A Report of the Surgeon General. Rockville, MD: U.S. Department of Health and Human Services, Centers for Disease Control and Prevention, National Center for Injury Prevention and Control; Substance Abuse and Mental Health Services Administration, Center for Mental Health Services; and National Institutes of Health, National Institute of Mental Health.

Wellford, C. F., Pepper, J. V., & Petrie, C. V. (2004). *Firearms and Violence: A Critical Review.* Washington, DC: The National Academies Press.

Chapter 1

Literature Review

Robert D. Ketterlinus, PhD, and Rose Cheney, PhD

Introduction

This chapter includes a series of literature reviews that together provide a broad context for the specific emergency department (ED)-based youth violence intervention and prevention program examples provided in this book. The literature review is divided into two parts. In Part I the literature reviews focus on current knowledge regarding the extent and nature of youth violence; the causes and consequences of youth violence; violence and mental health; and disparities in youth violence and related behavioral health outcomes. Part II includes a broad summary of evidence-based prevention, intervention and treatment programs in the area of violence, and approaches to implementing evidence-based programs in different settings, including hospital EDs and trauma centers. The chapter ends with a brief overview of resources for providing health providers with the competencies needed to prevent youth violence.

Part I: Community and Youth Violence

In this section we summarize the literature on several interrelated topics including the extent and nature of youth violence, the causes and consequences of youth violence, violence and mental health, and disparities in youth violence.

Extent and Nature of Community and Youth Violence: National and Local Data

Community Violence

Community violence is defined as exposure to acts of interpersonal violence committed by individuals who are not intimately related to the victim, including violence that occurs in schools. Acts that fall under the community violence umbrella include sexual assault, use of weapons, muggings, etc. Community violence may also include the sounds of bullet shots, as well as social disorder issues such as the presence of teen gangs, drugs, and racial divisions.

While it is true that the risk of exposure to community violence is higher among poor, nonwhite individuals living in densely populated urban areas, studies on rates of community violence are beginning to demonstrate that community violence affects a wide range of people. In a national survey of girls and boys 10–16 years old, over one-third reported being the direct victim of violence including aggravated assault, attempted kidnapping, and sexual assault (Boney-McCoy and Finkelhor, 1995). Another study compared the rate of exposure to violence of urban elementary school children living in low-violence neighborhoods to the rate of those living in high-violence neighborhoods (Hill and Jones, 1997). Results indicated that over 75% of the total sample witnessed violent acts such as homicide, stabbings, physical assault, and gang violence. The only difference between the rates of exposure in the two groups was in exposure to homicide. Whereas 9% of the children living in the low-violence neighborhoods reported witnessing homicide, 32% of the children living in high-violence neighborhoods reported exposure to homicide. Interestingly, despite these high rates, more than 50% of the parents in both groups stated that their children had not been exposed to violence in the community.

Richters and Martinez (1993) examined rates of exposure to community violence as compared to being the direct victim of violence. They found that 59% of fifth and sixth grade children living in a moderately violent neighborhood in Washington, D.C., reported being the victim of violence while 97% reported witnessing violence such as a shooting, mugging, or drug trade. Other research suggests that between 39% and 70% of adults have experienced a traumatic event and that a large segment of these traumas are serious crimes (Resnick and Kilpatrick, 1994). One large general population study of more than 4,000 adult women found that 36% of the sample reported exposure to rape, other sexual assault, aggravated assault, or the homicide of someone close to them. More than 12 million women, or 12.7% of the sample, lived through a completed rape (Resnick, Kilpatrick, Dansky, Saunders, and Best, 1993).

Children in neighborhoods where community violence is high may witness or experience street violence (shootings, stabbings, beatings) directly. Community violence is most prevalent in urban neighborhoods that are poor, lack resources, and have inadequate housing (Covell, 2005). Youth can also be exposed to community violence in community workplaces (restaurants, grocery or convenience stores) that are at increased risk of victimization from robberies and related homicides. Other venues for community violence include sports activities, where aggression levels and verbal bullying are elevated. Urban minority children who are exposed to community violence are at increased risk for increases in aggressive behavior and depression over at least a one-year period, even after controlling for lifetime degree of exposure (Gorman-Smith and Tolan, 1998).

Children who are homeless are most vulnerable to community violence victimization as "through their survival strategies they are exposed to a wide range of dangerous practices and persons," making them particularly vulnerable to physical and sexual abuse (Covell, 2005).

Youth Violence

According to the National Crime and Victimization Survey (2004), there were an estimated 5.2 million violent crime victimizations (assault, rape, violent robbery) of U.S. residents age 12 and older (Catalano, 2005). Historically, males and youths have been most vulnerable to violent victimization, and in 2004, 49.7 per 1,000 youth aged 12–15 were victims of violent crime, whereas 11.0 and 2.1 per 1,000 adults aged 50–64 and 65+, respectively, were violently victimized (Catalano, 2005).

Despite a significant decline since the 1990s in the occurrence of violent crimes nationwide (Bureau of Justice Statistics, 2004; Butts and Snyder, 2006), homicide is the second-leading cause of death among people 10–24. Young adults and adolescents are disproportionately victimized by firearm-related homicide, and gunshot wounds are the second leading cause of death for all people aged 10–34 (U.S. Department of Health and Human Services, 2001). From 1981 to 1999, 20- to 24-year-olds were most likely to be victims of homicide, especially by firearms, but victimization rates among 15- to 19-year-olds rose and fell more dramatically than other age groups between 1985 and 1999. Adolescent victimization rates surpassed the rates for those 25 and older by 1990 and did not fall back below the rate for persons in their late 20s until 1998. Blacks have historically been at high risk of victimization by firearm-related homicide (Wellford, Pepper, and Petrie, 2004).

Youth and young adults are not only victimized by violent crimes, but also perpetrate these crimes. In 1999, there were 2.4 million arrests of youths with 104,000 of these arrests for violent crimes (U.S. Department of Health and Human Services, 2001).

While violent incidents occur throughout the day and night, in 2004 aggravated assaults were slightly more likely to occur during daytime hours (6:00 p.m.– 6:00 a.m.) than nighttime (52.4% versus 45.8%, respectively). Sexual assaults were considerably more likely to occur during nighttime hours (6:00 p.m.–6:00 a.m.) than during daytime hours (62.9% versus 34.8%) (Catalano, 2005). Crimes perpetrated by youth tend to occur most frequently in the afterschool (3:00 p.m.–6:00 a.m.) hours.

Violence in Schools

Peer bullying is the most common form of school violence among both boys and girls. Children most vulnerable for victimization of peer bullying are those who are obese, of minority sexual orientation, and those with disabilities. Boys who bully tend to be physically aggressive, while girls are more likely to engage in social or verbal bullying (Covell, 2005).

The federal No Child Left Behind law signed in 2002 requires school safety data reporting to identify "persistently dangerous schools" so that parents can then have the option of transferring their child(ren) to a safer school.

Gang Violence

Gang activity is responsible for a large percentage of serious violent crimes in the United States. Prevalence estimates suggest the existence of at least 26,000 gangs in the U.S with more than 840,500 active gang members (USDHHS, 2001). Violence plays a large role in gang life, as it is used to control and expand drug distribution (turf protection), ensure adherence to gang code of conduct, and prevent members from leaving the gang (U.S. Department of Justice, 2005).

Nationwide surveys have found that school-aged children are exposed to gangs, such that in 1998, 7% of boys and 4% of girls reported having belonged to a gang in the past year, and in 2000, more than one-quarter (28%) of surveyed students from urban schools reported a street gang presence (U.S. Department of Justice, 2005).

The 2001 National Youth Gang Survey (NYGS) results regarding gang constitution showed that approximately one-half of all gang members (49%) are Hispanic/Latino, 34% are African American, 10% are Caucasian, and 6% are Asian (U.S. Department of Justice, 2005).

There are several community factors or conditions that enable gangs to take root, and which may also be critical in addressing the design of interventions to combat gangs and gang violence. Gangs are able to take root in communities where socializing agents (families, schools) are ineffective and alienating, adult supervision is largely absent, and there is limited access to good, conventional career and employment opportunities.

Intentional Firearm Violence and Youth

Firearm injury accounted for 2,900 deaths and 13,000 injuries for persons under age 20 in 2002 (Fingerhut and Christoffel, 2002), with older adolescents at particularly high risk. While other weapon types contribute to homicide and suicide deaths, firearms are particularly lethal (Zimring, 1998). For youth 15–19, gunshots are the second and third leading causes of death, accounting for 83% of homicides and 49% of suicides. The cumulative risk of firearm death before age 20 is estimated to be 1 out of every 869 white males and one out of every 248 black males (Fingerhut and Christoffel, 2002).

Among youth, the characteristics associated with higher firearm-related mortality include older ages (17–19); male; black or Hispanic ethnicity; and residence outside the Northeast region of the country. Residence in a core urban neighborhood raises the risk for firearm homicide, while rural residence raises the risk for firearm suicide (Fingerhut and Christoffel, 2002). Data on firearm offending suggest that the characteristics of youth committing firearm homicides resemble those of their victims (Hemenway, 2004).

Weapons Carrying by Youth

Analysis of the dramatic increase in homicide rates in the late 1980s and early 1990s reveals that this increase was due primarily to the increase in youth homicide with handguns (Blumestein, 2002). The subsequent decline in the late 1990s also was dominated by a decline in handgun homicides by young people. Understanding the factors affecting weapon choice and impact is difficult, confounded by interactions between instrumental lethality (the weapon and ammunition) and intent (Reiss and Roth, 1993).

Disentangling the issue of intent is complex, since there are many scenarios for firearm use and information, when available, is uncertain and imprecise. Firearms can be used with specific intent to kill a victim, to threaten as part of a robbery, to communicate threats or inflict harm on family or acquaintances, for self-defense, or seemingly with no strategy at all (Reiss and Roth, 1993). While drug markets may have been important for the increase in gun prevalence in urban communities, they also may have furthered the diffusion of gun carrying throughout the larger community (Blumstein, 2002). A survey of inner city, African American youth found that intention to carry a gun was independently associated both with fear of victimization and with a history of delinquency (Lane, Cunnigham, and Ellen, 2004). Regarding suicide, the availability of guns in the home is associated with an increased risk for firearm suicide by youth, even those without suicidal risk factors (Maris, Berman, and Silverman, 2000). The issue of intent and substitution, for homicides, suicides, injury and threats, remains a key question for future firearm violence research (National Research Council, 2005).

Federal law, with few exceptions, prohibits the sale of handguns to persons under the age of 21 and the sale of long guns to persons under the age of 18. Despite these restrictions, youth in this country have had easy access to firearms. Between 1980 and 1987, just over half of homicides by a juvenile offender were committed with a firearm. The percent of homicides by firearm peaked in 1994 at 82% nationally and then began to decline (Snyder and Sickmund, 1999). Youth acquire guns from a variety of sources. Firearm trafficking investigations have demonstrated that guns are illegally diverted to youth through a number of trafficking sources, including unlicensed dealers, corrupt dealers, and straw purchases (Braga and Kennedy, 2001). Criminally involved youth report acquiring first guns through friends, family, and finds, and their more recent, new high caliber guns from known sources, often connected to high volume trafficking (Webster, Freed, Frattaroli, and Wilson, 2002). Youth are involved in either buying or selling guns, through informal networks of family, acquaintances or street sources (National Research Council, 2005).

Relationship Between Weapon Carrying and Fighting Among Youth

Among youth, weapon carrying is associated with increased involvement in physical fighting and a greater likelihood of injury among those who do fight. Lowry et al. (1998) used data from the Youth Risk Behavior Survey supplement to the 1992 National Health Interview Survey to examine relationships among weapon carrying, physical fighting, and fight-related injury among U.S. adolescents aged 12–21 years (N = 10,269). Weapon carrying (15%) and physical fighting (39%) were common among adolescents. One out of 30 (3.3%) adolescents reported receiving medical care for fight-related injuries. Controlling for demographic characteristics, youth who carried weapons were more likely than those who did not to have been in a physical fight (Odds Ratio = 3.3). The association between weapon carrying and physical fighting was stronger among females (OR = 5.0) than among males (OR = 2.9), but did not vary significantly by age, race/ethnicity, or place of residence (urban, suburban, rural). Controlling for frequency of physical fighting and demographics, adolescents who carried a handgun (OR = 2.6) or other weapon (OR = 1.6) were more likely than those who did not carry a weapon to have had medical care for fight-related injuries.

In a study of over 3,000 urban high school students, Durant, Kahn, Beckford, and Woods (1997) found that weapon carrying at school was more strongly associated with use of violence and the use of substances at school than with previous victimization and fear of attending school. The data analysis also revealed a subgroup of students who reported being victimized at school, feared attending school, used alcohol at school, and carried weapons at school.

Estimates obtained in the late 1990s suggest that 10% of male high school students have carried a gun in the past 30 days, with gun carrying even more common (25%) in high crime areas. More than 80% of male juvenile offenders report having possessed a gun (Freed, Webster, and Longwell, 2001).

The presence of illegal drug markets (especially crack cocaine) has been historically a strong factor in the prevalence of youth gun homicide, especially among African American youth in urban areas, a vast majority of whom are engaged in the use of illegal drugs (Blumstein, 2002). As drug markets grow, more youth are recruited as sellers and younger children are engaged in other roles in the drug selling culture. Following the example of adults involved in drug markets, youth commonly carry handguns for protection and dispute resolution. In one national survey 43% of urban high school students who reported carrying a gun within the past 12 months claimed they carried it primarily for protection (Sheley and Wright, 1998).

It has been hypothesized that the increase in gun carrying by youth involved in drugs results in the diffusion of guns in the community and the conversion of ordinary youth fighting and other violent encounters into homicides and attempted homicides (Cork, 1999). Research suggests that, historically, when drug markets decline there is a concomitant reduction in the number of young drug sellers, a reduced associated need for handguns, and a general reduction in community violence involving youth.

Costs of Violence

Violent behavior imposes many types of costs on society. The economics of crime literature has traditionally distinguished between three types of costs (Demmert, 1979): 1) those caused directly by violence (i.e., external costs imposed by the offender); 2) those costs society incurs in its attempt to deter or prevent future incidents (through deterrence, incapacitation, or rehabilitation of offenders as well as preventive measures taken by potential victims); and

3) those costs incurred by the offender (such as the opportunity cost of the offender's time while either engaging in the offense or being punished).

There are two types of costs: monetary and nonmonetary. Monetary costs consist of out-of-pocket expenditures, such as medical treatment, property damage and loss, and emergency police or ambulance response. They also consist of lost wages and productivity. In addition to these monetary costs, injury victims and their families may endure pain, suffering, and reduced quality of life. Since pain, suffering, and quality of life are not normally exchanged in the marketplace, there is no direct method of observing their monetary value. Indeed, the term "cost" is more difficult to conceptualize for nonmonetary losses because one cannot simply "buy" or "sell" pain and suffering.

Violence costs the United States an estimated $425 billion in direct and indirect costs each year (Illinois Center for Violence Prevention, 1998). Of these costs, approximately $90 billion is spent on the criminal justice system, $65 billion on security, $5 billion on the treatment of victims, and $170 billion on lost productivity and quality of life. The annual costs to victims are approximately $178 billion (Illinois Center for Violence Prevention, 1998). One approach to reducing these costs is to prevent violence as much as possible. Preventing a single violent crime not only averts the costs of incarceration, it also prevents the short- and long-term costs to victims, including material losses and the costs associated with physical and psychological trauma.

The direct medical costs for firearm injuries range from $2.3 billion to $4 billion, and additional indirect costs, such as lost potential earnings, are estimated at $19.0 billion (Gunderson, 1999). Total economic loss to victims of violent crimes averages $221 per victim (Catalano, 2005). In 2004, economic loss was higher for black victims than for white, highest among 25- to 34-year-olds and lowest among young adolescents aged 12–15. Average economic loss did not vary greatly by gender (Catalano, 2005).

The national costs of gun violence are roughly $100 billion per year, with $15 billion or more attributable to gun violence against youth. The medical costs, including immediate and lifetime care, of approximately 135,000 firearm injuries that occurred in 1994 is estimated at $2.3 billion (Cook and Ludwig, 2002). The tangible costs to the victims from medical expenses and lost productivity are only a small part of the overall problem. The real burden of gun violence comes from the cost of public and private efforts to reduce the risks and the fear of victimization that remains despite these efforts (Cook and Ludwig, 2002). Nonfatal firearm injury may result in lifetime disabilities, including traumatic brain or spinal cord injury. Costs of firearm violence, however, are not limited to medical costs. The individual and community impacts of firearm violence affect future productivity, public resources, property values, freedom of movement, residential inequalities, psychological health, and lifestyle choices (Richmond et al., 2004). The community impact of endemic firearm violence interferes with healthy youth development. These more intangible costs, combined with medical costs, suggest a national burden of gun violence against youth on the order of $15 billion per year (Cook and Ludwig, 2002).

Model violence prevention programs can be expensive, but the benefits accrued from these programs can offset these costs, and even provide modest monetary benefits to society. Below is a list of program costs for several model youth violence and risk prevention programs (Elliott, 1998).

Cost of Evidence-Based Violence Prevention Programs:

- Functional Family Therapy: $1,350–$3,750 per family for 90 days (average 12 visits per family).
- Multidimensional Treatment Foster Care: $2,691 per youth per month for an average of 7 months.
- Multisystemic Therapy: $4,500 per youth.
- Prenatal and Infancy Home Visitation by Nurses: $3,200 per family per year during the first three years of program operation; $2,800 per family per year when the program is fully operational.

Cost of Evidence-Based Risk Prevention Programs:

- Life Skills Training: $7 per student per year, plus a one-time minimum of $2,000 per day for one to two days of training.
- The Midwestern Prevention Project: $28 per student per year for school and parent programs.

Table 1 summarizes the monetary benefits (net costs) of several model violence prevention programs targeting children and youth in different stages of development and in different community settings (USDHHS, 2001). These findings suggest that programs targeting youth already involved in the juvenile justice system provide larger monetary benefits than those targeting other, less at-risk children and youth.

A comprehensive review of the literature on the costs and benefits of violence prevention and intervention programs for children, adolescents and adults, including those with behavioral health components (often subsumed under the rubric of "crime prevention"), is beyond the scope of this chapter (see comprehensive reviews of the literature by Aos, Phipps, Barnoski, and Lieb, 2001; Aos, Lieb, Mayfield, Miller, and Pennucci, 2004; Aos, Lieb, Mayfield, Miller, and Pennucci, 2006). It should be noted that research suggests that the public is willing to pay more in taxes to pay for programs to reduce gun violence. For example, when asked if they would vote for a program to reduce gunshot injuries by 30%, 76% of the respondents said they would vote for a program for which they would pay $50 more per year in income taxes, 69% would pay $100 more per year, and 64% would pay $200 more per year (Cook and Ludwig, 2000).

It is important to educate and engage communities in discussions about the role of the behavioral health system in violence prevention and intervention activities. Furthermore, it is important to use rigorous methods to track program costs, and to invest in program evaluations that include economic

Table 1

Age	Program	Estimated Cost per Participant (S)	Benefits per Dollar Cost (S): Benefits to the Taxpayer (Criminal Justice System Benefits)	Benefits per Dollar Cost (S): Benefits to the Taxpayer and Victim
Early Childhood	Perry Preschool Program	13,938	0.66	1.50
	Syracuse Family Development Research Program	45,092	0.19	0.34
	Prenatal and Infancy Home Visitation by Nurses	7,403	0.83	1.54
Middle Childhood	Seattle Social Development Project	3,017	0.90	1.79
Adolescent: Non-Juvenile Offender	The Quantum Opportunities Program	18,292	0.09	0.13
	Big Brothers Big Sisters of America	1,009	1.30	2.12
Adolescent: Juvenile Offender	**Community Based**			
	Multisystemic Therapy	4,540	8.38	13.45
	Functional Family Therapy	2,068	6.85	10.99
	Multidimensional Treatment Foster Care*	1,934	14.07	22.58
	Intensive supervision (probation)**	1,500	0.90	1.49
	Institution-Based			
	Boot camps**	-1,964	0.42	0.26

Source: Washington State Institute for Public Policy, 1999.
* Costs calculated relative to costs of treatment in a regular group home.
** Costs calculated relative to costs of regular probation.

analysis to begin to build a knowledge base that identifies violence prevention programs, interventions, and initiatives that are cost-effective.

Developmental Pathways and Risk of Violence

Despite the high-profile nature of community and predatory violence, especially gunshot incidences among youth, the major setting for violence in America is the home (Straus, 1974). Interfamilial abuse, neglect, and domestic battery account for the majority of physical and emotional violence suffered by children in this country (see Koop and Lundberg, 1992; Horowitz Weine, and Jekel, 1995; Carnegie Council on Adolescent Development, 1995). In order to understand the roots of community and predatory violence, the effects of interfamilial violence, abuse, and neglect on the development of the child must be considered. For example, the adolescents and adults responsible for community and predatory violence likely developed the emotional, behavioral, cognitive, and physiological characteristics that mediate these violent behaviors as a result of interfamilial violence during childhood (O'Keefe, 1995; Myers, Scott, Burgess, and Burgess, 1995; Mones, 1991; Loeber et al., 1993; Lewis, Mallouh, and Webb, 1989).

Research is proceeding in several biological-based areas including genetics, neurochemical mechanisms, neurotransmitters and receptors, brain mechanisms, and more recently, diet and nutrition (Reiss, Miczek, and Roth, 1994). For example, research on humans suggests that prenatal and perinatal traumas results in a significant percentage increase of adult substance abuse and violence that ranges from a 56% to 500% increase when compared to normal controls (Prescott, 1996). Also there is extensive scientific research in animals and humans documenting that mother infant/child separations (loss of bonding/mother love) during the most sensitive periods may result in permanent developmental brain abnormalities associated with juvenile and adult patterns of depression, and chronic stimulus-seeking behaviors including substance abuse, eating disorders, aggression, and violence (e.g., homicide and suicide; Prescott, 2002). Furthermore, the emerging neurodevelopmental literature is beginning to pinpoint the biological mechanisms and contexts under which the brain adapts to violent trauma and the consequences for the development of persistent serious violence (Perry, 1997; 2001).

While a review of the research on the factors that mediate the development of violence is beyond the scope of this chapter, the findings revealed from this literature should be considered in any efforts to address youth violence

Next an overview of the research on the age of onset and prevalence of serious violence is presented, followed by a summary of the literature on developmental pathways and risk of violence.

Age of Onset and Prevalence of Serious Violence

Eighty-five percent of people who become involved in serious violence by age 27 report that their first act occurred between age 12 and 20 (USDHHS, 2001). The onset of serious violence is negligible after age 23 and before age 10 (only 0.2% of arrests for serious violent crime in 1997 involved a child under age 10).

In Table 2 are data from the National Youth Survey that shows the hazard rate for serious violence during the first two decades of life.

The peak age of onset is 16, when about 5% of male adolescents report their first act of serious violence. The age of onset peaks somewhat later for white males (age 18) than for African American males (age 15). The hazard rate at the peak age also varies somewhat by race/ethnicity: 5% for white males and 8% for African American males. No comparable hazard rates have been published for female youths.

The proportion of youths at any given age who report having committed at least one serious violent act is also greatest in the second decade of life. Age-

Table 2

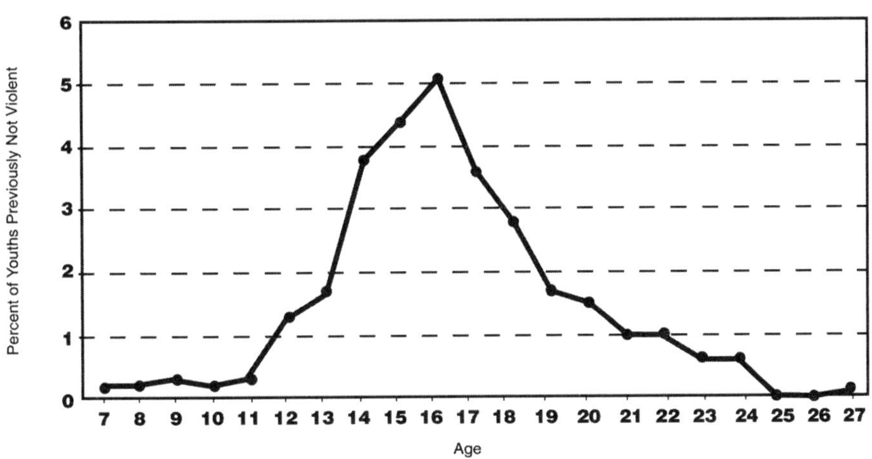

Source: Eliott, 1994. 95% confidence intervals are all less than or equal to ± 1.0%

specific prevalence among male youths ranges from about 8% to 20% between the ages of 12 and 20, and among females, it ranges from 1% to 18%. The rates for African American youths ages 14–17 are 36–50% higher than those for white youths. Rates among Hispanic youths are similar to or lower than those reported by African American youths.

Developmental Pathways

Research has identified discrete developmental pathways that can lead to serious violence and delinquent behavior during adolescence and young adulthood. For example, Loeber et al. (1993) have identified three pathways, each of which starts with milder behaviors and progresses to more serious behaviors. Each pathway also varies with respect to age of onset:

1) Authority conflict pathway: begins with defiant and disobedient behavior in early childhood with a progression to similar behaviors in adolescence such as truancy, running away, and staying out late.
2) Covert pathway: minor covert behaviors such as shoplifting and lying with progression to more serious behavior such as fire setting and vandalizing property, and further escalation to more serious offenses.
3) Overt pathway: starts with aggressive behaviors such as bullying and progresses to more serious violent behaviors.

Children who follow a developmental pathway towards serious violence and delinquency that begins before age 13 have been referred to as life-course persistent offenders, while those who begin after age 13 and older are called adolescent-limited offenders (Moffitt, 1993).

Life-course persistent offenders, who represent a relatively small proportion of the overall offender population, can be identified by characteristics that set them apart from other offenders. These include early onset of offending, active offending during adolescence, persistence of violence and crime during adulthood, and escalation of the seriousness of offending over time. Between 20% and 45% of males who are serious violent offenders at ages 16 or 17 are said to be on a life-course-persistent developmental pathway (Stattin and Magnusson, 1996; U.S. Department of Health and Human Services, 2001). Dalhberg and Simon (2002) summarized several longitudinal studies that have produced evidence of life-course persistent offending. This research shows that children who exhibit aggressive behavior as young as eight years old were more likely to score very high on aggression on the Minnesota Multiphasic Personality Inventory (MMPI) at age 30, to report high levels of physical aggression and spouse abuse as adults, to have more criminal convictions as adults ,and to engage in more serious criminal acts. Furthermore, the children of these individuals also tended to exhibit aggressive behavior. Other research found significant continuity in aggression and violence over a 40-year period beginning in childhood. Life-course persistent offenders also engage in other high-risk behaviors such as drinking, driving drunk, and using drugs, and have more criminal and noncriminal convictions. Findings from the Rochester Youth Development Study indicate that 40% of youth who committed a violent offense before age 9 became chronic offenders by age 16, and 30% continued to offend into early adulthood.

Adolescent-limited offenders, who make up the majority of the overall offender population, begin committing violent and other offenses at age 13 or older. Data from the National Youth Survey (a national probability sample of youth ages 11–17 who were followed until ages 27–33) indicated that adolescent-limited offenders have a shorter offending career than life-course-persistent offenders, primarily during the adolescent period of development, for a period of one to three years.

Most of the research on pathways of violent and other offending discussed above focuses on males. The few studies examining offending patterns of girls are mixed with respect to continuity of violence. For example, the Columbia County (New York) Study found that girls with an early history of high aggression scored significantly higher on aggression, punishment, and criminology 22 years later compared to girls in the low or medium aggression groups (Hauesmann et al., 1984), while findings from a Swedish study do not show a relationship between early aggression and later violent offenses among girls (Stattin and Magnusson, 1989). The Woodlawn (Chicago) study found a consistent pattern of relationships between early and later aggression and violence for both males and females, but a cross-national study found a high correlation between childhood physical aggression and violent and delinquent offending in adolescence for males but not for females. Finally, Elliott (1994) reports later onset and peak in the incidence of aggressive and delinquent behavior among girls than boys.

The epidemiological research summarized above indicates several clear developmental pathways to violent and other offending. However, we must turn to developmental research to help explain why some children exhibit patterns of behavior that fit the pathways outgrow early onset of aggressive, disobedient, and oppositional behavior, while others persist into adolescence and adulthood. Below is a summary of the developmental literature that has identified predictors of violent and delinquent offending

Developmental Research on Predictors of Violent and Delinquent Offending: Risk and Protective Factors

A risk factor is anything that increases the probability that a person will suffer harm. A protective factor is something that decreases the potential harmful effect of a risk factor. Risk factors increase the probability that a young person will become violent, while protective factors buffer the young person against those risks. The public health approach to youth violence involves identifying risk and protective factors, determining how they work, making the public aware of these findings, and designing programs to prevent or stop the violence. In the following sections we summarize the literature on risk and protective factors related to violent and delinquent offending,

Risk Factors

The large body of research on factors that increase the probability of violent and criminal behavior has been examined in detail in several papers and reports (Coie and Dodge, 1997; Farrington, 1998; Hawkins et al., 1998; Loeber and Hay, 1997; and USDHHS, 2001). In this section, we provide a summary of the major findings found in these reviews, divided into five key predictor domains: individual factors, peer factors, family factors, school factors, and community factors (a summary of literature reviews of these predictor domains by Dalhberg and Simon, 2002 and USDHHS, 2001 is provided below). We have also added a section on a relatively unstudied predictor domain—biological factors—based on emerging literature in this area.

Individual Risk Factors

Children who drink are not only more likely to be violent but also to be the victims of violence. Shepherd, Sutherland, and Newcombe (2006) asked 4,000 11- to 16-year-olds about their drinking and experience with violence. They found that drinkers were more likely to hit others, be hit by others, and engage in fighting, suggesting a direct link between alcohol misuse and vulnerability to injury.

Violent and delinquent behavior has been shown to be correlated to several childhood internalizing and externalizing behavioral factors including attention problems, hyperactivity, impulsiveness (poor behavioral control), and disruptive and oppositional behavior. For example, a meta-analysis concluded that hyperactivity, daring behavior, impulsiveness, and attention problems at ages 6–11 were the strongest predictors for violent and serious delinquent behavior from ages 15–25 (Lipsey and Derzon, 1998). Several individual studies have shown that persistent serious offenders were several times more likely than nondelinquents to have qualified for a disruptive behavior disorder diagnosis before age 14, and other research suggests that hyperactivity, oppositional behavior, and poor behavioral control may have strong links to persistent violent offending (as opposed to persistent nonviolent offending). There is also some evidence that attention deficit/hyperactivity disorder (ADHD) is higher among adolescent persistent offenders (any type) than among adolescents considered as "temporary" offenders. Of all the behavioral factors, early physical aggression is the most powerful predictor of involvement in violent and delinquent behavior before age 13.

While not as strong as the behavioral factors discussed above, several other individual level factors have been identified as helping predict stable patterns of violent and delinquent behavior, including certain personality traits and belief systems such as aggressive attitudes, high levels of distrust and social disconnection, lack of empathy and guilt, and sensation seeking.

Social-cognitive deficits have also been identified as predicting involvement in violent and aggressive behavior during adolescence, but the links to adult violent and criminal behavior have not be studied. Research suggests that children and adolescents with social-cognitive impairment have difficulty interpreting social situations, make premature social decisions, and often perceive the intentions and actions of others as hostile. When confronted with aggressive responses from others, highly aggressive youth are often unable to find nonaggressive solutions; instead they tend to use retaliatory tactics, thinking that is the best way to reduce adverse treatment by others.

Peer Risk Factors

Research has demonstrated that an individual's risk of serious delinquency and involvement in crime is increased greatly when an adolescent associates with delinquent peers. Reviews of longitudinal studies conclude that social ties and involvement with antisocial and delinquent peers were the strongest predictors for later offending among 12- to 14-year-olds, ranking higher than other individual and family factors. Research on adolescents without a prior history of problem behavior shows a relationship between exposure to deviant peers and the initiation of violent and other offending.

Family Risk Factors

Family demographic factors such as family size, low income, and disrupted families have long been identified as predictors of adolescent involvement in violence and other problem behaviors. Furthermore, a "weak family environment" is another important predictor variable. A weak family environment is characterized by poor family management and parenting practices, deficiencies in problem-solving and communication, family conflict, and parent problem behaviors (crime, drug and alcohol use).

Family violence, including intimate partner violence, child maltreatment, and a general family climate of conflict and hostility are also predictors of adolescent involvement in violent behavior, with one longitudinal study demonstrating a dose–response relationship between exposure to family violence and early involvement in violent behavior. These findings help explain why children with abuse histories are more likely to exhibit aggression in school and the community, are at increased risk for serious violent and delinquent behavior as adolescents, and are at increased risk for being arrested for a violent crime as an adult.

Findings from the Adverse Childhood Experiences (ACE) study have revealed that children exposed to a constellation of experiences within families ("ACE factors"—childhood abuse and neglect, household dysfunction; mom treated violently; household substance abuse and mental illness; parental separation and divorce; incarcerated household member) are at increased risk for a variety of adult health problems including risk for intimate partner violence and suicide attempts. As the number of ACE factors increase the risk for these outcomes also increases. The ACE factors are also related to health-related behaviors and outcomes during childhood and adolescence including illicit drug use and suicide attempt (Edwards et al., 2005; Felitti et al., 1998).

School Risk Factors

Poor academic performance, low commitment to school, and school failure are related to the onset, escalation, and seriousness of offending in adolescence and to persistence of offending in adulthood. Certain school settings can also contribute to the onset and persistence of violent behavior including undisciplined classrooms, lax enforcement of school rules and policies, tight physical space, and an environment that reinforces feelings of anger, resentment, and rejection. Also, school suspension and expulsion, which in most schools are routine responses to physical fighting, substance use, and weapons carrying increase the probability of further problem behaviors by reducing student supervision and creating opportunities for problem behaviors outside of school.

Schools are the primary setting for the phenomenon of bullying. Bullying includes harassment, intimidation to varying degrees, taunting, and ridicule (Geffner, Loring, and Young, 2002). Sometimes, bullies are motivated by hate and bias, sometimes by cultural norms, peer pressure, or the desire to retaliate. Bullying may occur within the context of initiation rituals and be labeled "hazing," or it can be overtly or implicitly about gender, constituting sexual harassment. Sometimes there is no readily identifiable reason for bullying; when kids are asked who school bullies target, their answers can be disturbing precisely because they are not extraordinary: bullies pick on kids who are "weaker," "smaller," "funny looking," or "dumb."

Although no standard or universally understood definition of bullying exists, certain elements usually are present. The first is a pattern of behavior over time-repeated exposure to intentional injury or discomfort inflicted by one or more students against another. This behavior may include physical contact, verbal assault, social ostracism, obscene gestures, or other aggressive acts that cause the victim to feel fearful or distraught. More serious instances of bullying can result in physical injury or emotional trauma. A second common element is a perceived imbalance of power, which allows one student, or group of students, to victimize others.

Depending on the frequency and intensity of bullying and on the social and personal characteristics of the victim, the consequences of being bullied range from minor psychological and physical problems to homicide and suicide. A national study funded by the federal government found that three-quarters of school shootings committed by students against other students involved acting out of anger or revenge for having been the victim of bullying at school (Vossekuil, Fein, Reddy, Borum, and Molzeleski, 2002). Victims of bullying are at increased risk for a variety of mental health problems including depression, somatic complaints, health problems, poor sleep, bed-wetting, feelings of loneliness, and social isolation. Depression is the most strongly related response to victimization (Hawker and Boulton, 2000).

While some victims of bullying experience consequences of victimization into adulthood, bullies suffer more serious consequences as they age. Compared to nonbullies, bullies are more likely to do poorly in school, drop out, cheat on tests, and have problems with the legal system. Bullies are also more likely to spend time unsupervised at home, drink alcohol and use drugs, and carry or have easy access to weapons (Berthold and Hoover, 2000).

Community Risk Factors

Developmental trajectories of violence and delinquent behavior must be considered in the context of social and economic influences on communities. A comprehensive review of these influences is beyond the scope of this report. To summarize, crime and violence are high in neighborhoods with concentrated disadvantage. In addition to having high concentrations of poor and unemployed people, these areas are characterized by high levels of residential instability; drug distribution networks; crowded housing; low community participation; diminished social controls and social capital; and high rates of school dropouts, substance abuse, and a disproportionate number of single-family households (Sampson, Radenbush, and Earls, 1997; Proctor and Dalaker, 2003). Many of these factors limit the ability and willingness of community residents to supervise and control children and adolescents, fostering interpersonal violence, delinquency, and crime. Over time, adolescents growing up in these types of communities are at increased risk for becoming involved in offender peer groups and to adopt lifestyles and behaviors that put them at risk for violent perpetration and victimization (Laub and Lauritsen, 1998; Sampson, Morenoff, and Gannon-Rowley, 2002).

Protective Factors

A comprehensive review of the literature on protective factors for youth violence concluded that evidence regarding protective factors against violence has not met the standards established for risk factors (USDHHS, 2001). Therefore, the report presents information about proposed protective factors. A summary of these findings is presented below.

Individual Protective Factors

An intolerant attitude toward deviance, including violent behavior, is the strongest proposed protective factor. It reflects a commitment to traditional values and norms as well as disapproval of activities that violate these norms. Young people whose attitudes are antithetical to violence are unlikely to become involved in activities that could lead to violence or to associate with peers who are delinquent or violent. Four other individual factors have not yet been shown to moderate violence, although they may buffer risks for antisocial behavior or general delinquency: high IQ, being born female, positive social orientation, and perceived peer disapproval of deviant behavior.

Family Protective Factors

A secure attachment in infancy to a parent or other adult who senses and responds to a baby's needs, and a warm, supportive relationship with parents or other adults has been shown to protect against antisocial behavior. However, studies so far have not found a significant buffering effect of these proposed protective factors on the risk of violence.

Several studies have pointed to monitoring or supervision of activities as a protective factor against delinquency and antisocial behavior, but this is essentially the opposite of failure to monitor, an adolescent-onset risk factor with a small effect size. To date, no evidence of moderating effects on the risk of violence has been presented.

School Protective Factors

Commitment to school is another proposed protective factor that has been found to buffer the risk of youth violence. Young people who are committed to school are unlikely to engage in violence, both because it is incompatible with their orientation and because it would jeopardize their achievement in school and their standing with adults.

Some studies have found that recognition for or involvement in conventional activities—whether family, school, extracurricular, religious, or community—is a protective factor against antisocial behavior. However, involvement in family, volunteer, and school club activities other than sports has an insignificant effect on risk for violence.

Peer Group Protective Factors

Having friends who behave conventionally is a proposed protective factor that seems to reduce the risk of delinquency, but there is no evidence of a true buffering effect on specific risk factors. However, researchers have found that associating with peers who disapprove of violence may inhibit violence in young people.

Community Protective Factors

No protective factors have been proposed yet in the community domain. In summary, the developmental literature has identified clear developmental pathways to different types of violence and has identified specific risk and protective factors for violence, although more research is needed especially in the area of protective factors. Prevention and intervention programs designed to impact the timing and progress of these pathways may provide an opportunity to reduce the prevalence of violent behavior or minimize its consequences. One of the specific implications of this research for the behavioral health system is the importance of using comprehensive standardized screening and assessments for the risk of interpersonal and other types of violence. Also, while few asset- or strength-based measures are available relative to the number of risk-based measures, it is none-the-less important that violence prevention and intervention programs attempt to incorporate existing individual, family, and community positive supports and resources in addition to using strategies to reduce risk of violence (Pollard, Hawkins, and Arthur, 1999).

Because of the important role of behavioral health services on violence prevention and intervention, it is essential to understand the relationship of violence and mental health and substance abuse. Summaries of the literature on these topics are presented next.

Exposure to Community Violence: Acute Stress Disorder (ASD) and Post Traumatic Stress Disorder (PTSD)

Exposure to community violence is a major underlying cause of much of the incidence of childhood and adolescent trauma including behavioral and emotional problems, and, especially in the case of exposure to gun violence, acute stress disorder (ASD) and Post Traumatic Stress Disorder (PTSD).

Living in communities where violence is common can negatively affect children's development, and the effects of direct and indirect exposure to violence are similar. The effects of exposure to community violence can include nervousness, sleep problems, intrusive thoughts, anxiety, stress, loneliness, grief, depression and antisocial behavior, and declines in school achievement and cognitive performance. Repeated trauma can lead to anger, despair, and severe psychic numbing, often resulting in major changes in behavior and perspectives (American Psychological Association, 1993; Jenkins and Bell, 1997). Youth living in violent communities may experience pathological adaptation such as hopelessness, fatalistic thoughts, desensitization to violence, and truncated moral development, all of which may lead to an increase in participation in high-risk behaviors (Garbarino, Dubrow, Kostelny, and Pardo, 1992).

Age and social and cognitive development mediate youths' reaction to community violence. The effects of gun violence can be severe if exposure occurs during early childhood through early adolescence that represents critical periods of neurological growth and development (Pynoos, Steinberg, Ornitz, and Goenjian, 1997). Children under age 11 exposed to traumatic events are up to three times more likely to develop PTSD than children over age 12 (Davidson and Smith, 1990; Schwarz and Kowalski, 1991). However, adolescents who witness a single violent episode (e.g., school or neighborhood shooting) often experience more stress than younger children because they may feel guilty about surviving and about not taking action to help other victims.

Youth who witness a single incident of gun violence may get caught in a cycle of violence that may involve exposure to other types of violence, higher levels of aggression, and less parental monitoring than their peers, and in some cases PTSD (Slovack and Singer, 2001). Exposure to gun violence can also desensitize youth to the effects of violence and increase the likelihood that they will use violence to solve problems or express emotions (Garbarino and Bedard, 2001).

Acute Stress Disorder (ASD)

Acute Stress Disorder (ASD) is a psychiatric diagnosis that was introduced into the *Diagnostic and Statistical Manual of Mental Disorders (DSM-IV)* in 1994. The current diagnostic criteria for ASD are similar to the criteria for PTSD, although the criteria for ASD contain a greater emphasis on dissociative symptoms and the diagnosis can only be given within the first month after a traumatic event. The inclusion of ASD in the *DSM-IV* was not accompanied by extensive research, and some debate exists regarding whether the diagnostic criteria accurately reflect pathological reactions to trauma that occur within the first month after a trauma (Bryant and Harvey, 2000). However, even though debate exists about the empirical basis of the diagnosis and the degree to which it represents a distinct diagnostic category (Brewin, Andrews, and Rose, 2003), it has been found to be highly predictive of subsequent PTSD (Fein et al., 2002; Shemesh et al., 2003).

Post Traumatic Stress Disorder (PTSD)

Exposure to community violence is a major risk factor for the development of PTSD in children and youth. Results from population studies indicate that 15%–43% of girls and 14%–43% of boys have experienced at least one traumatic event related to exposure to community violence in their lifetime. Of those children and adolescents who have experienced a trauma, 3%–15% of girls and 1%–6% of boys could be diagnosed with PTSD. Other studies have shown that as many as 100% of children who witness a parental homicide or sexual assault develop PTSD. Similarly, 90% of sexually abused children, 77% of children exposed to a school shooting, and 35% of urban youth exposed to community violence develop PTSD (American Academy of Child and Adolescent Psychiatry, 2005).

While many children and adolescents exposed to violence (i.e., witnessing or directly experiencing a violent event) express symptoms of PTSD, and a substantial minority develop clinically significant PTSD, the exposure to violence has a wider effect, including depression, behavioral problems, poor school performance, decreased IQ and reading ability, lower GPA, increased absence from school, and interference with developmental milestones in childhood in adolescence (Stein et al., 2003).

Individuals of all ages can experience PTSD as a result of community violence (Resnick and Kilpatrick, 1994). Studies have found post traumatic symptoms and disorders among infants and toddlers, although symptoms expressed by children look different from those expressed by adults (Osofsky, 1995). Children with PTSD display disorganized or agitated behavior and have nightmares, and they may become withdrawn, fearful, aggressive, or have difficulty paying attention. They may regress to earlier behaviors such as sucking their thumbs and bed-wetting, and they may develop separation anxiety. They may also engage in play that compulsively reenacts the violence.

Adolescents with PTSD can experience nightmares and intrusive thoughts about the trauma, may be easily startled, and often avoid reminders of the trauma. They can become depressed, angry, distrustful, fearful, and alienated, feel betrayed and may feel they do not have a future. These reactions are common among adolescents who are chronically exposed to community violence. Other trauma-related reactions can include impaired self-esteem and body image, learning difficulties, and acting out or risk-taking behaviors such as running away, drug or alcohol use, suicide attempts, and inappropriate sexual activities. Children and adolescents risks for developing PTSD increase with the severity of exposure, negative parental reactions to the exposure, and the child's physical proximity to the community violence.

A child's or adolescent's exposure to community violence also affects his or her family. Extreme anxiety concerning the child's health and well-being is a common parental reaction. Resources for parents may be limited, which may lead to frustration and anger. Many parents blame themselves for not protecting their child adequately. They may become overprotective or use punitive discipline in response to their child's trauma-related acting out behavior. Relationships among family members can become strained and many parents have to face the task of reassuring their child while trying to cope with their own fears, especially if there is a chronic risk for future community violence exposure.

Violence and Alcohol and Drug Use

Among people who have committed violence, drug users and those with drinking problems are more likely to repeat violence; and among those who have committed a violent act and use drugs, those who frequently use heroin or other opiates are more likely than others to commit violent acts at high rates. However, it should be noted that many people use drugs and many have drinking problems, but most of them are not violent (Reiss, Miczec, and Roth, 1994).

Alcohol consumption plays a major role in both the commission of violent crime and in victimization. The U.S. Department of Justice Report on Alcohol and Crime found that alcohol abuse was a factor in 40% of violent crimes committed in the United States. (Greenfield, 1998). About 6 in 10 convicted jail inmates said that they had been drinking on a regular basis during the year before the offense for which they were serving time. Nearly two out of three of these inmates, regardless of whether they drank daily or less often, reported having previously been in a treatment program for an alcohol dependency problem. Among violent offenders, 41% of probationers, 41% of those in local jails, 38% of those in state prisons, and 20% of those in federal prisons were estimated to have been drinking when they committed the crime.

Alcohol consumption is a major factor in admissions to hospital EDs. The connection between occasional drinking and injuries may be just as strong as the link between chronic drinking and getting hurt. For example, Spurling and Vinson's (2005) ED study of 2,517 patients with an acute injury and 1,856 age- and sex-matched controls found that about 4% of injuries occurred among those drinking at levels typically associated with safe consumption (less than four drinks for men and three drinks for women), about the same rate of injuries among patients having an alcohol dependency.

Ehrlich, Brown, and Drongowski (2006) tested 443 patients ages 14–17 who entered the emergency room at the school's hospital for treatment of severe injuries. Their study found that about 40% of injured teens treated in a hospital emergency rooms tested positive for alcohol or other drugs, including 29% testing positive for opiates, 11.2% for alcohol, and 20% for marijuana.

About three million violent crimes occur each year in which victims perceive the offender to have been drinking at the time of the offense. Among those victims who provided information about the offender's use of alcohol, about 35% of the victimizations involved an offender who had been drinking. Two-thirds of victims who suffered violence by an intimate partner (a current or former spouse, boyfriend, or girlfriend) reported that alcohol had been a factor. Among spouse victims, three out of four incidents were reported to have involved an offender who had been drinking. By contrast, an estimated 31% of stranger victimizations where the victim could determine the absence or presence of alcohol was perceived to be alcohol related.

Studies have generally revealed a positive association between criminal behavior (including violent crime), victimization, and abuse of alcohol and other drugs. For example, Kingery, Pruitt, and Hurley (1992) examined the relationships between violence, drug use, and victimization in a representative sample of American adolescents. The commonly used illegal drugs (marijuana, amyl/butyl nitrites, psychedelics, amphetamines, and cocaine) and alcohol were considered. Drug users, compared to nonusers, fought more, took more risks which predisposed them to assault, and were assaulted more both at school and outside school supervision. Adolescents who were victims at school were also more likely to be victimized outside of school supervision. This study demonstrates that the adolescent perpetrators of violence may also be victims of violence, and that illegal drug/alcohol use is related to victimization.

Recent research suggests that children who drink are not only more likely to be violent but also to be the victims of violence. Shepherd, Sutherland, and Newcombe (2006) surveyed 4,000 11- to 16-year-olds about their drinking and experience with violence. They found that drinkers were more likely to hit others, be hit by others, and engage in fighting. Clinical observation suggests that adolescents with alcohol use disorders often have complex histories that include childhood maltreatment and other traumas (Clark, Lesnick, and Hegedus, 1997).

Race, Ethnic and Gender Disparities in Violence

Race and Ethnic Disparities in Violence

Disadvantaged racial and ethnic minorities in the United States are overrepresented in the both the juvenile justice and adult criminal justice systems, largely because of the use of incarceration as a drug control tool (Bonzar, 2003; Leiber, 2002; Leiber and Mack, 2003). In particular, there is a significant disparity in the juvenile justice system's handling of black youths compared to its handling of non-Hispanic white and Hispanic drug offenders. (Sickmund, 2004). These disparities appear to lead to a spiral of other disparities in recidivism and health outcomes (Guerra and Smith, 2006).

African American and Hispanic youth have been disproportionately victimized by homicide. For example, the Healthy People 2010 report shows that African American youth (male and female) aged 15–24 experienced homicide rates in 1995 that were more than twice that of their Hispanic counterparts (74.4 per 100,000 and 34.1 per 100,000, respectively). Moreover, the African American youth homicide rate that year was nearly 14 times the rate of their white non-Hispanic counterparts (5.4 per 100,000).

Racial and gender disparities are highly evident in firearms-related fatalities. Males are disproportionately the victims of gun fatalities, with a 5.5 to 1 disparity with females, and males accounting for 85% of all firearm-related fatalities. A comparison of gun-related fatality rates and motor vehicle fatality rates found that for black families, "the chance of their male children dying from a gunshot wound is 62% higher than the chance of dying in a motor vehicle crash." In contrast, the chance of Hispanic youth dying as a result of firearm injury was about the same as the chance of dying in a motor vehicle accident, and white youths are more likely to die by motor vehicle accident than as a result of firearms. The racial, ethnic, and age patterns for female youth firearm-related fatalities follow the same patterns at a lower incidence level (Cook and Ludwig, 2002).

Gender Disparities in Violence

Female youth with co-occurring disorders in the juvenile justice system are a disparate population with unique needs to be met through "gender-specific, culturally and developmentally sensitive policy and practice" (Prescott, 1998).

Most adolescent girls involved with the juvenile justice system are arrested for nonviolent, drug-related offenses. Over one-half of arrests of adolescent girls are for running away from home. Many of these girls run away from home to escape domestic violence, and encounter more violence, sexual risk, and substance abuse while living on the streets, and are therefore entering the system with serious medical and psychological needs (Prescott, 1998).

Risk factors and personal histories of juvenile girls in the juvenile justice system include the following:

- Approximately 75% of juvenile girls adjudicated delinquent have a history of sexual abuse.
- Approximately 85% of juvenile girls with mental health needs have higher rates of depression than adolescent boys.
- Approximately 60%–85% need substance abuse treatment (Prescott, 1998).

The juvenile justice system is largely designed to accommodate the needs of boys, and as such, can negatively impact girls in the system. To begin, the act itself of running away from home, even if to escape abuse, can constitute "delinquent" behavior and result in juvenile justice involvement. Staff misunderstanding cues of female adolescents with traumatic pasts acting out can interpret behavior as delinquent rather than as symptomatic, and can potentially disqualify girls from receiving needed services. Some male service providers, monitors, and staff actually "reinforce for adolescent abused girls negative relationships with men, reinforcing traumatic stress, particularly standard crisis protocol, designed for male offenders, that require groups of men to surround and subdue adolescent girls in very physical and forceful ways" (Prescott, 1998).

Part II: Model and Promising Evidence-Based Programs

In this section we provide a summary of literature reviews and other sources of information on model and promising evidence-based prevention, intervention, and treatment programs in the area of violence. An overview of several ED and trauma center youth violence prevention and intervention programs are included in the section titled Nursing, Primary Care, and Hospital-Based Violence Prevention/Intervention, and the chapters that follow this chapter include specific program examples of other related programs.

We concluded with an overview of resources focused on approaches to implementing evidence-based programs, and resources for the competencies needed to address violence prevention. Our reviews relied on both published research as well as a growing number of compendiums of model and promising evidenced-based programs (a list of compendiums is included in the Appendix).

I. Model and Promising Violence Prevention and Intervention Programs

Since 1990, a number of major literature reviews have been published that identify model and promising prevention and intervention programs specifically targeting violence. A majority of these reports focus on programs that target children and adolescents in community and school settings involved in or at risk for a variety of types of intentional violence (e.g., guns, bullying, fighting). The reviews, some of which include benefit/cost analysis, are listed below (full citations can be found in the reference list):

- *Violence Prevention for Young Adolescents: A Survey of the State of the Art* (Wilson-Brewer, et al., 1991).
- *Bullying at School: What We Know and What We Can Do* (Olweus, 1993).
- *Preventing Crime: What Works, What Doesn't, What's Promising: A Report to the United States Congress* (Sherman et al., 1997).
- *Serious and Violent Juvenile Offenders: Risk Factors and Successful Interventions* (Loeber and Farrington, 1998).
- *Youth Violence Prevention, Intervention, and Social Policy: An Overview* (Elliott and Tolan, 1999).
- *Promising Strategies to Reduce Gun Violence* (Office of Juvenile Justice and Delinquency Prevention [OJJDP], 1999).
- *Violence Prevention Programs in Schools: State of the Science and Implications for Future Research* (Howard, Flora, and Griffin, 1999).
- *Best Practices of Youth Violence Prevention: A Sourcebook for Community Action* (Thorton et al., 2002).
- *Schools and Delinquency* (Gottfredson, 2001).
- *Youth Violence: A Report of the Surgeon General* (USDHHS, 2001).
- *The Comparative Costs and Benefits of Programs to Reduce Crime* (Aos et al., 2001).
- *Blueprints for Violence Prevention* (Mihalic et al., 2004).
- *Bullying in American Schools: A Social-Ecological Perspective on Prevention and Intervention* (Espelage and Swearer, 2004).

Thorton et al. (2002) provided a useful framework for describing evidenced-based primary and secondary prevention programs that have the potential to impact the behavioral health of children and adolescents, and many have the potential to benefit from the addition of behavioral health principles and practices. Later in this chapter the literature on evidence-based tertiary intervention programs is summarized.

Thorton et al. (2002) identified four main strategies to prevent violence among high-risk children and adolescents:

1) Parent- and family-based interventions improve family relations by combining parent training skills, education about child development and child risk factors for violent behaviors, practice in parent–child

communication, use of conflict resolution and nonviolent parenting.

2) Mentoring involves pairing a youth with a supportive, nonjudgmental adult. For youth involved in the juvenile justice system, community-based adult supervision has been found effective in preventing recidivism.
3) Home visiting strategies involve social workers or specially trained nurses visiting at-risk families in their homes in order to provide information, health care, psychological support and other services designed to improve parent and family functioning.
4) Social-cognitive strategies furnish children with effective skills to deal with difficult social situations through the use of didactic teaching, role-modeling, and role-playing to teach children positive, nonviolent social interactions, nonviolent conflict resolution techniques, and promote nonviolent beliefs.

Finally, it should be noted that while many behavioral interventions to reduce youth gun injury and violence have been developed, there is little or no evidence that any of these programs achieve their goals (Hardy, 2002).

Delinquency Prevention and Early Intervention Programs for Youth

Below are selected examples of effective primary violence prevention programs in school, community, health care, and criminal justice settings.

School-Based Programs

The most effective violence prevention, urban school-based programs are comprehensive, integrated, and incorporate multiple strategies at multiple levels in multiple settings. Four types of educational strategies have been found to be most effective in preventing youth violence: 1) conflict management skills training, 2) psychoeducational strategies, 3) family-based strategies, and 4) youth-oriented programs (Greene, 1998). Examples of effective programs that incorporate these strategies include the Seattle Social Development Project (SSDP) (Hawkins, Kosterman, Catalano, Hill, and Abbott, 2005) and the Olweus Bullying Prevention Program (OBPP) (Olweus, Limber, and Mihalic, 1999).

Community-Based Programs

In general, community-based youth violence prevention programs focus on fostering partnerships between providers in key areas including health, mental health, child welfare, childhood education, family support, substance abuse, domestic violence, crisis intervention, law enforcement, legal services, and courts to improve the provision of services to young children exposed to violence. Examples of promising programs include the Safe Start Program, which targets adolescents of all ages (11 programs funded by the Office of Juvenile

Justice and Delinquency Prevention); the Positive Adolescent Choices Training (PACT) Program, a culturally sensitive violence prevention program that targets African American adolescents (Yung and Hammond, 1998); and the Youth Relationships Project, which targets mid-adolescents 14 to 16 years old (Pittman, Wolfe, and Wekerle, 1998). A unique community-based program is the Oakland Men's Project that began in 1979. This program began as a small group of men seeking to support the growing coalition of rape crisis centers and battered women's shelters, but has since grown into a training center for men of all ages, working with groups and individuals to address the issues of how violence is socialized into American culture, particularly male violence against women and children (Kivel, 1998). The program has been widely replicated in schools, prisons, and homeless shelters and now targets both adults and adolescents. Project staff members conduct training sessions with social workers, nurses, counselors, physicians, attorneys, parole officers, and the police.

Community–Police Partnerships: Youth Exposed to Community Violence

Children who are witnesses to or victims of violence are of particular concern because of the increased risk of perpetrating future acts of violence, therefore perpetuating a cycle of violence that can become cross-generational. Several studies have found community–police partnership programs to be superior to other law enforcement approaches for dealing with individuals with mental illness (Daly, 2006). Below are descriptions of a promising community–police partnership program.

The Child Development Community Policing (CDCP) Program was developed by the Yale Child Study Center and New Haven Department of Police Services in 1991. CDCP works to reduce the negative consequences (emotional and behavioral problems, future aggression and delinquency) of youth's exposure to violence and to increase the community's capacity to reduce risk of violence. The CDCP Program is a collaborative alliance of community agencies including law enforcement, juvenile justice, domestic violence agencies, medical and mental health professionals, child welfare agencies, schools, and other community agencies (National Center for Children Exposed to Violence [NCCEV], 2005). For instance, police officers and mental health professionals are brought together "for mutual training, consultation, and support so that they may effectively provide direct interdisciplinary intervention to children and families who are victims, witnesses, or perpetrators of violent crimes"(OJJDP, 1999). The CDCP Program is considered a national model for police–mental health partnerships. Similar programs have been replicated in Baltimore, Maryland; Buffalo, New York; Portland, Oregon; and Italy (OJJDP, 1999).

Preventing and Mitigating Firearm Violence

Given the complex nature of firearm violence, there is no single solution to preventing firearm threats and injury, or for mitigating the individual or social consequences of gun violence. This means that researchers, policymakers, health care providers, law enforcement, communities, students, and parents all can have vital roles in addressing different aspects of the problem. Unfortunately, the number of proven prevention strategies is limited. Prevention partners need to be aware of the limitations of existing interventions and conduct ongoing evaluation of effectiveness in order to make best use of limited resources and to avoid potential, unintentional negative consequences. Interdisciplinary reviews of the factors associated with firearm violence and systematic reviews of specific interventions are excellent tools for informing the development of individual or community interventions (Zara, Briss, and Harris, 2005).

Behavioral Interventions

Little evidence exists on effective firearm prevention programs based upon behavioral change. Challenges in the design of behavioral change research, measurement of outcomes, understanding of childhood development constraints, and a general lack of theory-based intervention design have contributed to an overall lack of intervention effectiveness for behavioral change. More troubling is the potential that some approaches are counterproductive, increasing risky behaviors, enhancing the lure of firearms, establishing a false norm of gun carrying for adolescents, or reinforcing an overly optimistic assessment of personal risk. Promising practices are preventive programs built upon strong education, psychological, or sociological theories (National Research Council, 2005).

Environmental Interventions

Household storage of firearms as locked, unloaded, or separated from the ammunition has been found to be associated with significant reductions in risk of unintentional and intentionally self-inflicted firearm injury in adolescents and children (Grossman et al., 2005). On a community level, gun buybacks have not been found to be effective, since these programs, for the most part, do not focus on guns or populations with high risk of criminal use (Sherman, 2001).

Legislative and Enforcement Interventions

While some studies have found evidence that legislation such as local gun bans may have been effective, there is not enough evidence to determine the effectiveness of firearm laws (Zara, Briss, and Harris, 2005). Two enforcement policies that have been found to be effective are uniform targeted gun patrols and criminal history background checks (Sherman, 2001). Findings on punishment enhancements, which may have deterrent or incapacitation effects, remain mixed (National Research Council, 2005).

Comprehensive Community Programs

Comprehensive community programs are designed to either reduce youth firearm violence or mitigate the repercussions of community firearm violence for community members. Concentrated poverty, disorder, crime, gun violence. and social inequities can create environments where youth feel the need to be armed in order to be safe (Reich, Culross, and Behrman, 2002). Comprehensive interventions that target youth earlier in childhood also show promise of effectiveness (Zara, Briss, and Harris, 2005). Research has shown that rather than single factors, multiple factors are associated with violence and traumatic outcomes (Humphreys, Sharps, and Campbell, 2005). Community programs can engage multiple partners to address multiple factors, within a single overall goal of a safer community. To effectively use limited resources and to avoid unintended negative effects, these programs should develop strategies that are based on identified risks, incorporate best practices, monitor progress, and evaluate their results (Thorton, Craft, Dahlberg, Lynch, and Baer, 2002).

Finally, the federal Office of Juvenile Justice and Delinquency Prevention has published a list of promising comprehensive community-based gun violence prevention programs that include the following model programs:

- Baltimore Comprehensive Communities Program-Baltimore, MD
- Boston Strategy to Prevent Youth Violence-Boston, MA

See http://ojjdp.ncrjs.org for a complete listing and description of these and related gun violence prevention programs.

Nursing, Primary Care, and Hospital-Based Violence Prevention/Intervention

Despite increasing awareness of the potential role that health care professionals can play in youth violence prevention and intervention, few health-care-setting-based prevention/intervention programs have been implemented. In this section an overview of the most promising programs implemented in three types of settings is presented: nursing home visitation, primary care, and hospitals.

Prenatal and Infancy Home Visitation by Nurses

Prenatal and Infancy Home Visitation by nurses is a program targeting low-income, at-risk pregnant women beginning prior to the birth of their first child and continuing until the child is two years old. The program aims 1) "to improve pregnancy outcomes and child care, health, and development; (2) to build a social support network around family; and (3) to enhance mothers' personal development, including educational achievement, participation in the workforce, and personal competency skills and self-efficacy" (USDHHS, 2001).

Positive documented program outcomes include fewer arrests and less alcohol use by youths at age 15 who received home visits, lower rates of child abuse and neglect than among control groups, and lower incidence of running away from home (Olds et al., 1998; 1999; USDHHS, 2001). Olds et al. found that the program helped mothers defer rapid subsequent pregnancies, therefore enabling women more opportunity for employment and economic self-sufficiency. Household and economic stability is likely a factor in the benefits experienced by the children who were born into this program. (Olds et al., 1999).

Pediatric Primary Care

Primary health care providers represent a natural point of contact with young children and their families, especially regarding screening and early intervention to promote children's mental health and well-being, prevent or delay risk factors, promote protective factors, thus preventing the need for expensive care in later life (Rosman, Perry, and Hepburn, 2005). Pediatric primary care providers are in a unique position to reach a large number of families and to provide screening and follow-up.

It has been suggested that pediatricians can play a role in preventing firearm injuries by working with parents of children of all ages (Webster and Wilson, 1994), especially in urban areas where gun ownership (legal and illegal) is common (Kahn, Kazimi, and Mulvihill, 2001). Specific strategies that pediatricians can use include encouraging parents to remove guns from the home, or at minimum to keep guns unloaded and locked; advising parents to limit viewing of gun violence in the media, playing with toy guns, and playing with video games that involve shooting and being alert for early indicators of aggressive behavior. It is also important for pediatricians to become vocal advocates for laws that restrict gun availability, and many medical societies have adopted policies that can be used in gun injury prevention efforts (Longjohn and Christoffel, 2004).

An example of a gun violence prevention physician-directed parent education kit is the Steps to Prevent Firearm Injury (STOP 2) Program developed by the Brady Center to Prevent Gun Violence. The materials in the kit prepare health care providers to talk with parents about the dangers of keeping a gun in the home, with the ultimate goal of incorporating gun violence prevention into routine injury prevention counseling. Unfortunately, the one study of this program found there was not a statistically significant drop in gun ownership or improvement in safe gun storage among parents who received the information from their pediatricians (Wellford, Pepper, and Petrie, 2004).

Hospital-Based Programs for Adolescent Victims of Violence

By the early 1990s, health care professionals began articulating the need to adopt a public health approach to Emergency Medicine, including intentional injuries (Berstein et al.,1994). Medical staff stationed in the ED were witnessing both the effects and frequency of violently injured youth passing through the

ED (Prothrow-Stith and Spivak, 2004). While protocols for identifying cases of intimate partner violence, child abuse, and substance abuse have all been implemented in the ED, protocols for identifying cases of youth violence lag behind these other public health issues. However, several hospital- and ED-based violence intervention/prevention programs have been developed out of the recognition that EDs provide an opportunity for medical staff to identify violently injured youth and refer them for community-based services. Those interested in implementing violence prevention programs suited for hospital settings can access an extensive list of programs on the Internet at http://www.aast.org/VPG/index.html.

A majority of U.S. trauma and emergency departments offer counseling and referral services for victims of violence, however, there are fewer than a dozen that offer comprehensive counseling, intervention, and inpatient treatment to victims of gun violence (Bonderman, 2001). While much more research is needed, anecdotal evidence suggests that trauma and ED doctors working with social workers and counselors could turn an injury event and recovery period into an opportunity to intervene and disrupt the potential for repeat violence.

Several hospital and trauma center/emergency department youth violence surveillance and prevention programs have been implemented around the country, including Baltimore (Chang, Cornwell, and Phillips, 2003; Chang, Wright, Markakis, Copeland-Linder, and Menvielle, 2007), Chicago (Zun, 2004; Zun, Downey, and Rosen, 2006), Boston (Sege, Kharasch, and Perron, 2002), Flint, Michigan (available online at http://www.sph.umich.edu/yvpc/projects/er/index.shtml); Milwaukee (Marcelle and Melzer-Lange, 2001), Oakland, CA (Becker, Hall, Ursic, Jain, and Calhoun, 2004), and two programs in Philadelphia (Ketterlinus, 2002; Wyant, Thorton, Ketterlinus, Cheney, and Wiebe, 2006). The Milwaukee, Oakland, and one of the Philadelphia programs are described in detail in this book.

Baltimore, Maryland: Hospital-Based Injury Prevention Outreach Program

Responding to the American College of Surgeon's recommendation that level-one trauma centers should have "major activity in prehospital management, education, and injury prevention," the Adult Trauma Service at Johns Hopkins began gathering in-hospital patient data to identify patient demographic, injury, and community characteristics; this information is vital for violence prevention program development. Using mapping software, patient neighborhood locations were identified, enabling the trauma center to develop an injury prevention outreach program to meet the needs of patients and the community. This in-hospital assessment of patient and community characteristics revealed that, while the overall percentage of gunshot victims presenting to the trauma center significantly declined between 1995 and 2000, this decline was not mirrored in all age groups. Youth between the ages of 15 and 24 represented a greater proportion of the gunshot injuries. Additionally, mortality rates from firearms had not declined over the years.

The program that developed out of this assessment should be viewed as a prevention intervention program. This program relies on an outreach strategy to prevent firearm injuries. The components of this outreach prevention program entail:

- Disseminating videotapes, which present gunshot victims' testimonies of the violent incident;
- Slide show presentations, narrated by health care professionals, such as physicians or medical students, are shown to at-risk youth in the identified communities to depict the anatomical damage caused by gunshot wounds; and
- Hospital tours, conducted by a physician and/or medical students, which allow identified at-risk youth to meet with gun shot survivors.

This program is not hospital-based, although many aspects of this program are located in the hospital. In fact, the trauma center has forged partnerships with area agencies, such as the Police Athletic League, which conduct the bulk of the outreach in the identified communities. Thus, while the hospital was able to identify the target areas, it was only through community partnerships that the outreach prevention program could be implemented.

While the above-mentioned Baltimore program is prevention oriented, the project team recently conducted a randomized control trial of a pilot case management program for violently injured youth (Chang et al., 2007) that examined the impact of the program on service utilization and risk for reinjury. Youth ages 12–17 identified in the ED with intentionally violent injuries and their families received either case management services by phone or in person over a four month period, or received a list of community services (control group). Analyses of six-month follow-up interviews found that the case management program did not increase service utilization or significantly reduce risk factors for further violent injury. The authors suggest that more intensive ED-based case management programs may be needed to address the needs of youth victims of interpersonal violence and their families.

Like the Baltimore case management pilot project, the following ED-based programs are intervention oriented; that is, they are designed to identify intentionally injured youth and begin the process of intervention prior to ED discharge.

Chicago, Illinois: Within Our Reach

Within Our Reach primarily operates on a case management model, which seeks to address and meet the psychosocial needs of violently injured youth. This ED-based youth violence intervention program attempts to remedy the one-sided medical approach that addresses the physical needs of violently injured youth presenting to the ED without addressing their psychosocial needs as well. This collaborative program links violently injured youth to a social service agency, which provides them with services, through case management, for six months. The collaborative partners for this program include the Mt. Sinai Hospital Emergency Department, a hospital social worker, and the Boys and Girls Clubs of Chicago.

To be enrolled in this program, youth must meet certain criteria: they must be between the ages of ten and twenty-four and present to Mt. Sinai's Emergency Department with an interpersonal injury that is either life- or limb-threatening. Cases of child abuse and sexual assault are excluded. Youth must also reside in the hospital's service area.

The following protocol are used for program enrollment: youth deemed eligible, based on the above-mentioned criteria, are administered an assessment tool by either a social worker or some other health care professional—all of whom are trained in enrollment processes. This assessment tool, which has not been validated as of yet, was developed by a multidisciplinary team of staff from emergency medicine, social work, and public health. After the assessment, ED staff then alert the case manager that a youth is eligible for possible program enrollment. On weekdays, the case manager begins the evaluation for enrollment in the ED; at other times, the case manager locates the youth either in the hospital or at the youth's home for enrollment.

The case manager serves as a bridge from the health care system, the ED of Mt. Sinai Hospital, to a social service agency, the Boys and Girls Clubs of Chicago or other community-based services. The case manager schedules appointments, arranges transportation to and from services, and communicates with the referral services.

Boston, Massachusetts: Boston Violence Project

Boston's Violence Project has been in operation since the early 1990s as a response to the rising rates of violent injuries. This program recognized that few of its community efforts were catching the hardest-to-reach youth. In response, a violence trauma team was created within the hospital to capture these violently injured youth. The intent of this program is to provide integrated health services that address the immediate medical as well as future psychological needs of hospitalized youth; the aim is to engage youth in exploring alternative solutions to prevent future injury. The collaborative partners for this program include nurses, social workers, child or adolescent psychiatrists, and the Massachusetts Department of Public Health's Violence Prevention Project.

Criteria for program enrollment include youth between the ages of 12 and 17 who have presented to Boston City Hospital's ED—the area's only level-one trauma center—with an injury sustained from interpersonal violence; youth presenting to the ED with injuries sustained from sexual assault, intimate partner violence, and child abuse are excluded.

The protocol for program enrollment involves an ED nurse, trained in identifying program eligible youth, who summons an ED social worker or the project liaison; the social worker and liaison are always available by pager for the intervention. The actual intervention, which can take place either in the ED (outpatient) or on the hospital floor (inpatient), comprises six steps and is conducted in a one-on-one counseling session—lasting between 45 minutes to two hours—by either the social worker or the project counselor.

- Step 1 includes the counselor reviewing or assessing the incident with the youth; this moment allows the youth to provide a testimonial of the incident.
- Step 2 involves trying to ascertain the youth's future plans; at this point, the counselor begins to broach or introduce a nonviolent alternative.
- Step 3, the counselor tries to provide the youth with information about morbidity and mortality statistics of similar youth in similar situations; this tactic allows both the counselor and youth to understand the prevalence of certain risk factors present in the youth's life as well as to educate the youth as to his/her risk profile.
- Step 4 explores the coping skills and support systems available in the youth's life; the counselor may provide coping strategies or provide referrals to local agencies.
- Step 5, a post-hospital discharge safety plan is developed; the goal is to not only create a safety strategy but more importantly, to give youth some semblance of personal control in his/her life, which may allay feelings of helplessness.
- Step 6 refers youth to follow-up services; referrals may include both youth and family services.

This one-on-one session operates on the principle of the "teachable moment"—a psychoeductional framework. By temporarily removing youth from their violent environment, counselors are able to maximize their ability to capture the hardest-to-reach youth for counseling. It is believed that these youth are more malleable when situated outside of their violent confines.

Youth agreeing to participate in the program are then given a set of standardized assessment measures four months after the initial intervention; these measures include Stress Index, Youth Risk Behavior Survey, Teen Opinion Survey, among others. This program included the only published research examining the effectiveness of an ED-based program using an experimental design (Zun, Downey, and Rosen, 2003). Patients aged 10–24 years who were victims of interpersonal violence (excluding child abuse, sexual assault, and domestic violence) were randomly assigned in the study. The control group was given a list of services and the treatment group received an assessment, case management for six months, and referral to appropriate resources. One hundred eighty-eight youth were enrolled in the study; 82.5% were male, 65.4% were African American, and 31.4% were Hispanic, and the average age was just over 18 years old. At the end of six months, 78 of the 96 youth (81.3%) in the treatment group made one or more contacts with their case manager and made use of social service, health care, and other referrals. Education (21.6%), job readiness (19.1%), and mental health (11.9%) were the most frequently used services. Nine of the 92 (9.8%) in the control group used services; most of these referrals were for social services (seven of nine respondents) and the others were health care-related. The differences in utilization of services between the treatment and the control groups were found to be significantly different and there was a strong positive correlation of using services and case management.

Zun, Downey, and Rosen (2006) published a study that examined youth self-reported revictimization or arrest and state-reported incarceration and reinjury 6 and 12 months after their intake into the study. The findings revealed that the self-reported reinjury rate was significantly reduced over time in the treatment group, but there were no differences between the groups in the number of self-reported arrests, state-reported reinjuries via the trauma registry, or state-reported incarcerations.

Flint, Michigan: Brief Emergency Department Intervention

This project, located in Flint, Michigan's Hurley Hospital ED, has adapted an existing alcohol related intervention for youth violence prevention. The intervention is designed to include an interactive component addressing violence prevention. The program content is based on risk and resiliency factors associated with violence and includes connections between alcohol use and violence, as well as violence not associated with alcohol use.

Project staff developed a computer intervention in the form of a website for youth that have been treated in the Hurley Hospital ED. The website, http://www.saferflintteens.com, contains interactive youth-centered modules adapted from the CDC-endorsed Smart Talk Program as well as community violence resources and information for both youth and parents with links to other relevant Internet sites. A pilot study was conducted at Hurley Medical Center ED among adolescent patients to determine potential Internet access and utilization. Based on this survey, (n=30), 97% of youth indicated they have access to the Internet.

The computer modules utilize the prevention principles of social learning theory as well as the Aggression Replacement Training (ART) model. The ART model is based on the assumption that youth are deficient in prosocial behaviors including negotiating differences and responding effectively to teasing and anger. It includes anger control training and moral education in a psychoeducationally-based intervention for schools.

Milwaukee, Wisconsin: Project UJIMA

In the early 1990s, a trauma nurse at the Children's Hospital of Wisconsin convened a series of meetings among hospital staff, emergency physicians, and community leaders to address concerns over the increasing numbers of youth injured by firearms. Project UJIMA—a hospital- and community-based home visiting program, which provides individual and family services—developed out of those meetings. This collaborative intervention program is designed to address the physical injury as well as psychosocial issues that may arise from the violent incident. The collaborative partners of Project UJIMA include the

Children's Hospital of Wisconsin, the Family Services of Milwaukee, and the Medical College of Wisconsin.

The youth enrolled in the program range in age from ten to eighteen years. Youth who are intentionally injured are eligible for enrollment; self-inflicted injuries, child abuse, or those currently receiving psychosocial services are excluded.

The detailed protocol for program enrollment comprises the following steps: when a youth enters the ED of Children's Hospital of Wisconsin with an injury sustained from interpersonal violence, the ED social worker and UJIMA community liaison are called to the ED. The youth is administered the Trauma Symptoms Checklist for Children to assess the presence of Posttraumatic Stress Disorder. From there, the community liaison introduces program services and seeks parental consent. The community liaison develops a follow-up plan while in the ED, that is, before ED discharge. Youth follow-up plans are further developed with the help of Family Services after discharge; program enrollees receive services for up to one year. The liaison continues to serve as a conduit to community resources for both the youth and family. Project UJIMA provides home visitations, mental health services, and youth activities. The parental consent form, which was obtained in the ED, allows for the free flow of information among agencies without jeopardizing youth confidentiality or privacy.

Chapter 5 of this book provides a detailed description of this program, as well as a summary of findings from previously published research.

Oakland, California: Caught in the Crossfire

The Caught in the Crossfire Program in Oakland, California, is considered a model hospital-based violence prevention program (Becker, Hall, Ursic, Jain, and Calhoun, 2004). Adolescents admitted into the hospital with a violence-related injury are linked to an Intervention Specialist who helps the injured patient and his/her families and friends to cope with the injury and to start talking about alternatives to retaliation, identifying the youth's short-term needs, and developing a plan for staying safe. After discharge, the Intervention Specialist helps the youth transition back into the community through intensive case management consisting of personal and telephone follow-up contact, support, and mentoring, extending support to the youth's family as well. Intensive case management is ongoing for six months to a year. The Intervention Specialist coordinates assistance from social services providers; probation officers; school teachers, administrators, and guidance counselors; hospital medical social workers; and other youth service professionals. This results in a network of wraparound aid to the teenager. An evaluation of the program found that, compared to a comparison group, more of the program participants re-enrolled in school, received mental health counseling and job training, secured part-time and full-time employment, and found relief from crisis situations involving housing, food, transportation, and health care.

Chapter 6 of this book provides a detailed description of this program, as well as a summary of findings from previously published research.

Philadelphia, Pennsylvania: HealthCare Collaborative for Youth Violence Prevention

The HealthCare Collaborative to Prevent Youth Violence (HCC) provided a medical intervention point and links to community-based services for violently injured youth at risk for repeat or retaliatory violence. The Collaborative addressed the William Penn Foundation's goal to promote the healthy development of vulnerable youth in the Philadelphia region and narrow the opportunity gap between low-income children and their more advantaged peers.

Between 1997 and 2000, four emergency departments in Philadelphia, Pennsylvania and two EDs in Camden, New Jersey, designed and implemented systems for the identification and assessment of young victims of intentional injury as part of a larger grant program funded by the William Penn Foundation. Philadelphia Health Management Corporation (PHMC) played an important role in this effort (then known as the "Healthcare Connection") by monitoring and evaluating grantee progress and providing support, technical assistance, and coordination to the grantees.

Building on lessons learned during the first phase of the project, the second phase of the project (2001–2004) included the four Philadelphia hospital EDs as part of the newly named collaborative—HealthCare Collaborative (HCC). The four EDs were located at the Albert Einstein Medical Center, Thomas Jefferson University Hospital, the Children's Hospital of Philadelphia, and Hospital of the University of Pennsylvania. The Philadelphia Health Management Corporation (PHMC), a private nonprofit public health organization, coordinated the grantees' activities, facilitated communication and links between grantees and local resources, and helped develop and disseminate project findings to enhance future replication and sustainability. The final HCC partner was the Philadelphia Anti-Violence/Anti-Drug Network (PAAN), a community-based outreach organization that provided crisis intervention services for youth victims of intentional violence presenting in the HCC EDs, as well as organizing neighborhood antiviolence activities around incidents of youth violence in schools and neighborhoods.

A list of HCC publications and presentations are presented after this chapter's bibliography. Later in this book descriptions of two HCC programs are presented.

Philadelphia, Pennsylvania: Pennsylvania Injury Reporting and Intervention System (PIRIS)

In 2005, the Pennsylvania Department of Health, the Philadelphia Department of Public Health, in conjunction with Philadelphia Health Management Corporation (PHMC), the Firearm Injury Center at Penn (FICAP), the Hospital of the University of Pennsylvania, Temple University Hospital, Albert Einstein Medical Center, Pennsylvania Trauma Systems Foundation, Philadelphia Anti-Drug/Anti-Violence Network (PAAN), and other local partners, implemented the nation's only hospital-based, injury surveillance and intervention system to aid in violence prevention strategies.

PIRIS targets 15- to 24-year-old youth with intentional gunshot injuries. Trauma Center staff at each hospital refers the youth and their families to a PHMC Intervention Case Manager who attempts to recruit them into the program. Youth and family members who agree to participate receive crisis intervention services, and once the victim is medically stabilized a comprehensive needs assessment is conducted. The needs assessment is then used to develop a case management plan for treatment and other services (e.g., educational and employment services), and the case manager helps youth and their families' access funding for treatment and other services.

It is anticipated that the lessons learned from this pilot project will be used to support the implementation of the program in other trauma centers in Pennsylvania and in other states.

Program Commonalities and Differences

The ED-based violence intervention programs described above (Boston, MA, Chicago, IL, Flint, MI, Milwaukee, WI, and Philadelphia, PA) incorporated the following common approaches.

Like the Philadelphia HCC and PIRIS programs, the Boston, Chicago, and Milwaukee programs were not created solely to treat physical injuries. Instead, these programs also recognize the social/psychological consequences of interpersonal violence and seek to identify and reduce these effects.

Through collaborations with community-based organizations, these programs have sought to address the social mechanisms that may have contributed to the youth's involvement in intentional violence. As one program director noted, services are already available for victims of sexual and family violence, thus, the next step is to provide appropriate services for victims of youth violence.

These programs also commonly recognize the need to partner with other health care professionals within the hospital. Partnering with social workers, case managers, and community liaisons—and having them stationed in the ED or available by pager—allows someone more familiar with the social lives of youth to administer the psychosocial needs assessments and administer interventions. These programs typically rely on someone other than a physician to enroll youth and administer the assessment form and intervention.

While the reasons are unclear, all of the highlighted intervention and prevention programs rely on a single hospital to capture youth for enrollment in their respective violence prevention and intervention programs; there appear to be no collaborations with other hospitals. The Philadelphia-based HCC and PIRIS programs are the only known multihospital youth violence reduction programs. Perhaps these other ED-based programs are the only level-one trauma centers in their communities, and therefore, the only appropriate hospital to house such a program, or competition among several hospitals may be a barrier to working together.

As noted, all of these programs seek to address the physical as well as psychosocial needs of violently injured youth presenting to the ED; however, the application of these approaches is somewhat different. For example, the Boston program, which is based on the pyschoeducational framework of a counseling orientation, applies a one-on-one approach with youth. Because this program is focused on immediate behavior change, the intervention is conducted prior to discharge. The Chicago, Milwaukee, and Philadelphia HCC and PIRIS programs rely more on a post-discharge intervention, which calls for a greater role for social workers/case managers; however, follow-up care plans are developed prior to discharge for these programs. Finally, the Flint, MI, program took a purely technological approach by implementing a violence prevention intervention on an Internet website.

While outcome data are available for some of these programs, the effectiveness of others is yet to be conclusively demonstrated. However, as noted, with few EDs implementing protocols to identify cases of violently injured youth, these programs represent a first step in that process. Based on this review of existing ED-based intervention and prevention programs, understanding the community's population and forging partnerships with other hospital staff and community-based organizations illustrates a growing recognition that youth violence is more than an acute medical issue—it is also a social issue.

Core Competencies in Violence Prevention for Health Care Professionals

To increase the effectiveness of behavioral health providers and allied health care professionals' efforts to prevent youth violence and its consequence, their skill set should include a set of core competencies (Knox, 2001). A core competency is defined as a discrete area of knowledge, attitude, or skill that a health professional needs to provide effective care to patients, families, and communities.

Implicit in the core competencies are basic principles for effective practice in youth violence prevention, including:

- Youth violence is most effectively addressed as part of a larger continuum of violence;
- Primary prevention interventions should be emphasized; and
- Families, communities, and professionals must be engaged as equal partners in the prevention of violence.

The Commission for the Prevention of Youth Violence (2000) brought together a wide variety of health care and violence prevention experts to determine core competencies for youth violence prevention. Using a social ecological model as a framework, the commission identified core competencies in five categories (for examples of competencies in each category, see Knox 2001):

1) Core knowledge, attitudes, and interaction skills;
2) Competencies with patients and families;
3) Competencies with health care settings;
4) Competencies with communities; and

5) Competencies with policy, societal, and systems change.

The commission report also includes recommendations for educational processes and approaches to promoting training in the core competencies, and provides a summary of health professional training activities taking place at CDC-funded youth violence prevention centers.

Another important resource for health professionals interested in violence prevention and intervention core competencies is a special issue of the *American Journal of Preventive Medicine* (2005, 29[5], Supplement 2). The articles include overviews of the current state of youth violence prevention training in the health professions and approaches for its improvement. Articles also focus on professional training in specific areas such as child maltreatment, youth who witness violence, homicide survivors, and collaboration with schools.

References

American Academy of Child and Adolescent Psychiatry. (2005). Practice parameter for the assessment and treatment of children and adolescents with reactive attachment disorder of infancy and early childhood. *J. of the Amer. Academy of Child and Adolescent Psychiatry.* 44(11): 1206–1219.

American Journal of Preventive Medicine. (2005). Training health care professional in the prevention of youth violence. *Amer. Journal of Preventive Med.* 29(Supplement 2), 5.

American Psychological Association. (1993). *Commission on Violence and Youth: Violence and Youth: Psychology's Response.* Vol. 1. Washington, D.C., American Psychological Association.

Aos, S., Lieb, R., Mayfield, J., Miller, M., and Pennucci, A. (2004). *Benefits and Costs of Prevention and Early Intervention Programs for Youth.* Olympia, WA, Olympia, Washington State Institute for Public Policy.

Aos, S., Lieb, R., Mayfield, J., Miller, M., and Pennucci, A. (2006). *Evidence-Based Adult Corrections Programs: What Works and What Does Not.* Olympia, WA: Olympia Washington State Institute for Public Policy.

Aos, S., Phipps, P., Barnoski, R., and Lieb, R. (2001). *The Comparative Costs and Benefits of Programs to Reduce Crime.* Version 4.0. Olympia, WA: Washington State Institute for Public Policy.

Becker, M. G., Hall, J. S., Ursic, C. M., Jain, S., and Calhoun, D. (2004). Caught in the Crossfire: The effects of a peer-based intervention program for violently injured youth. *J. of Adolescent Health.* 34(3):177–183.

Bernstein E, Goldfrank, L.R., Kellerman, A.L., and Hargarten, S.W. (1994). A public health approach to emergency medicine: Preparing for the twenty-first century. *Acad Emerg Med,* 227–286.

Berthold, K. A., and Hoover, J. R. (2000). Correlates of bullying and victimization among intermediate students in the Midwestern USA. *School Psychology International.* 21:65–78.

Blumstein, A. (2002). Youth, guns and violent crime. *The Future of Children.* 12(2):39–51.

Bonderman, J. (2001). *Working with Victims of Gun Violence* (Bulletin). Washington, D.C., U.S. Department of Justice.

Boney-McCoy, S., and Finkelhor, D. (1995). Psychosocial sequelae of violent victimization in a national youth sample. *J. of Consulting and Clinical Psychology.* 62:726–736.

Bonzar, T. P. (2003). Prevalence of Imprisonment in the U.S. Population: 1974-2001. (No. NCJ 202885): Bureau of Justice Administration.

Braka, A.A., and Kennedy, D. M. (2001). The illicit acquisition of firearms by youth and juveniles. *Journal of Criminal Justice.* 29(5):379–388.

Brewin, C. R., Andrews, B., and Rose, S. (2003). Diagnostic overlap between acute stress disorder and PTSD in victims of violent crime. *Amer. J. of Psychiatry.* 160(4):783–785.

Bryant, R. A., and Harvey, A. G. (2000). *Acute Stress Disorder: A Handbook of Theory, Assessment, and Treatment.* Washington, D.C., American Psychological Association.

Bureau of Justice Statistics. (2004). *Criminal Victimization—2004.* Washington, DC, U.S. Department of Justice.

Butts, J.A., and Snyder, H.N. (2006). Too Soon to Tell: Deciphering Recent Trends In Youth Violence (Issue Brief, November 2006), Chicago, IL, Chapin Hall Center for Children at the University of Chicago.

Carnegie Council on Adolescent Development. (1995). *Great Transitions: Preparing Adolescents for a New Century.* New York: Carnegie Corporation of New York.

Catalano, S. M. (2005). *Criminal Victimization Survey* (Vol. 2006). Washington, D.C., U.S. Department of Justice, Office of Justice Programs, Bureau of Justice Statistics.

Chang, T. L.., Cornwell, E. E., Phillips, J., Baker D., Yonas, M., and Campbell, K. (2003). Community Characteristics and Demographic Information as Determinants for a Hospital-Based Injury Prevention Outreach Program. *Archives of Surgery.* 138:1344–1346.

Chang, T. L., Wright, J.L., Markakis, D., Copeland-Linder, N., and Menvielle, E. (2007), Randomized trial of a case management program for assault-injured youth: Impact on services utilization and risk for re-injury. Unpublished manuscript.

Coie, J.D., and Dodge, K.A. (1998). Aggression and antisocial behavior. In W. Damon and N. Eisenberg (Eds.), *Handbook of Child Psychology: Social, Emotional, and Personality Development.* Vol. 3, Toronto, Wiley: 779–862).

Commission for the Prevention of Youth Violence. (2000). *Youth and Violence: Medicine, Nursing and Public Health: Connecting the Dots to Prevent Violence.* Chicago, IL, American Medical Association.

Cook, P. J., and Ludwig, J. (2000). *Gun Violence: The Real Costs.* New York: Oxford University Press.

Cook, P. J., and Ludwig, J. (2002). The cost of gun violence against children. *The Future of Children.* 12(2):87–99.

Cork, D. (1999). Estimating space-time interaction in city-level homicide data: Crack markets and the diffusion of guns among youth. *J. of Quantitative Criminology.* 15(4):379–406.

Covell, K. (2005). *United Nations Secretary-General's Study on Violence Against Children: North American Regional Consultation.* New York, NY, United Nations Violence Against Children in North America.

Dahlberg, L. L., and Simon, T. R. (2002). Predicting and preventing youth violence: Developmental pathways and risk. In J. R. Lutzker (Ed.), *Preventing Violence: Research and Evidence-Based Intervention Strategies.* Washington, D.C, American Psychological Association.

Daly, R. (2006). Police learn better response to people with mental illness. *Psychiatric News.* 41(5):8.

Davidson, J., and Smith, R. (1990). Traumatic experiences in psychiatric outpatients. *J. of Traumatic Stress Studies.* 3:459–475.

Demmert, H. G. (1979). Crime and Crime Control: What Are the Social Costs? (Technical Report CERDCR-3-79). Center for Econometric Studies of the Justice

System, Hoover Institution, Stanford University.

DuRant, R. H., Kahn, J., Beckford, P. H., and Woods, E. R. (1997). The association of weapon carrying and fighting on school property and other health risk and problem behaviors among high school students. *Archives of Pediatric Med.* 151(4):360–366.

Edwards, V. J., Anda, R. F., Dube, S. R., and Dong, M. (2005). The wide-ranging health consequences of adverse childhood experiences. In K. Kendall-Tackett and S. Giacomoni (Eds.), *Victimization of Children and Youth: Patterns of Abuse, Responses Strategies.* Kingston, NJ: Civic Research Institute.

Ehrlich, P. F., Brown, J. K., and Drongowski, R. (2006). Characterization of the drug-positive adolescent trauma population: should we, do we, and does it make a difference if we test? *J. of Pediatric Surgery.* 41(5):927–930.

Elliott, D. S. (1994). Serious violent offenders: Onset, developmental course, and termination. The American Society of Criminology 1993 presidential address. *Criminology.* 32:1–21.

Elliott, D.S. (1998). *Blueprints for Violence Prevention.* University of Colorado, Center for the Study and Prevention of Violence.

Elliott, D. S., and Tolan, P. H. (1999). Youth violence prevention, intervention, and social policy: An overview. In D. J. Flannery and C. R. Huff (Eds.), *Youth Violence Prevention, Intervention and Social Policy.* Washington, D.C, American Psychiatric Press: 3–46.

Espelage, D. L., and Swearer, S. M. (Eds.). (2004). *Bullying in American Schools: A Social-Ecological Perspective on Prevention and Intervention.* Mahwah, NJ, Erlbaum.

Farrington, D.P. (1998). Individual differences and offending. In M.H. Tonry (Ed.), *The Handbook of Crime and Punishment.* New York, Oxford University Press: 241–268.

Fein, J., Kassman-Adams, N., Gavin, M., Huang, R., Blanchard, D., and Datner, E. M. (2002). Persistence of posttraumatic stress in violently injured youth seen in the emergency department. *Archives of Pediatric and Adolescent Med.* 156:836–840.

Felitti, V., Anda, R., Nordenberg, D., Williamson, D., Spitz, A., Edwards, V. et al. (1998). Relationship of childhood abuse and household dysfunction to many of the leading causes of death in adults. The Adverse Childhood Experiences (ACE) Study. *Amer. J. of Preventive Med.* 14:245–258.

Fingerhut, L.A., and Christoffell, K.K. (2002). Firearm-Related Death and Injury among Children and Adolescents. *The Future of Children.* 12(2):24–37.

Freed, L. H., Webster, D. W., and Longwell, J. (2001). Factors preventing gun acquisition and carrying among incarcerated adolescent males. *Archives of Pediatrics and Adolescent Med.* 155(3):335–341.

Gabarino, J., and Bedard, C. (2001). *Parents Under Siege.* New York, Free Press.

Garbarino, J., Dubrow, N., Kostelny, K., and Pardo, C. (1992). *Children in Danger: Coping with the Consequences of Community Violence.* San Francisco, Jossey-Bass.

Geffner, R. A., Loring, M. T., and Young, C. (2002). *Bullying Behavior: Current Issues, Research and Interventions.* New York, NY, Haworth Maltreatment and Trauma Press.

Gorman-Smith, D., and Tolan, P. (1998). The role of exposure to community violence and developmental problems among inner-city youth. *Development and Psychopathology.* 10:101–116.

Gottfredson, D. C. (2001). *Schools and Delinquency.* New York, Cambridge University Press.

Greene, M. B. (1998). Youth violence in the city: The role of educational interventions. *Health Education Behavior.* 25(2):175–193.

Greenfield, L. A. (1998). *Alcohol and Crime: An Analysis of National Data on the Prevalence of Alcohol Involvement in Crime.* Washington, DC, Bureau of Justice Statistics, Department of Criminal Justice.

Guerra, N. G., and Smith, E. P. (Eds.). (2006). *Preventing Youth Violence in a Multicultural*

Society. Washington, DC, American Psychological Association.

Gunderson, L. (1999). The financial cost of gun violence. *Annals of Internal Med.* 131:483–484.

Hardy, M. S. (2002). Behavior-oriented approaches to reducing youth gun violence. *The Future of Children,* 12(2), 101-117.

Hawker, D. S., and Boulton, M. J. (2000). Twenty year's research on peer victimization and psychosocial maladjustment: A meta-analytic review of cross-sectional studies. *J. of Child Psychology and Psychiatry.* 41:441–455.

Hawkins, J.D., Farrington, D.P., and Catalano, R.P. (1998). Reducing violence through the schools. In D.S. Elliott, B.A. Hamburg et al. (Eds.), *Violence in American Schools: A New Perspective.* New York: Cambridge University Press: 188–216.

Hawkins, J. D., Kosterman, R., Catalano, R. F., Hill, K. G., and Abbott, R. D. (2005). Promoting positive adult functioning through social development intervention in childhood: Long-term effects from the Seattle Social Development Project. *Archives of Pediatrics and Adolescent Med.* 159(1):25–31.

Hemenway, D. (2004). Gun threats against and self-defense gun use by California adolescents. *Arch Pediatr Adolesc Med.* 158:395–400.

Hill, H. M., and Jones, L. P. (1997). Children's and parents' perceptions of children's exposure to violence in urban neighborhoods. *J. of the National Medical Association.* 89:270–276.

Horowitz, K., Weine, S., and Jekel, J. (1995). PTSD symptoms in urban adolescent girls: compounded community trauma. *J. of the Amer. Academy of Child and Adolescent Psychiatry.* 34(10):1353–1361.

Howard, K. A., Flora, J., and Griffin, M. (1999). Violence prevention programs in schools: State of the science and implications for future research. *Applied and Prevention Psychology.* 8:197–215.

llinois Center for Violence Prevention. (1998). *Fact Sheets: Cost of Violence.* Available at: http://www.violence-prevention.com/costofviolence.asp (accessed August 5, 2003).

Jenkins, E. J., and Bell, C.C. (1997). Exposure and response to community violence among children and adolescents. In J. D. Osofsky (Ed.), *Children in a Violent Society.* New York, Guilford Press (9–31).

Kahn, D. J., Kazimi, M. M., and Mulvihill, M. N. (2001). Attitudes of New York City high school students regarding firearm violence. *Pediatrics.* 107(5):1125–1132.

Ketterlinus, R. D. (2002). The Philadelphia HealthCare Collaborative (HCC). Paper presented at the Johns Hopkins Center for Injury Research and Policy 10th Anniversary Celebration of the National Center for Injury Prevention and Control, September 12, 2002.

Kingery, P. M., Pruitt, B. E., and Hurley, R. S. (1992). Violence and illegal drug use among adolescents: evidence from the U.S. National Adolescent Student Health Survey. *International J. of Addictions.* 27(12):1445–1464.

Kivel, P. (1998). *Men's Work: How to Stop the Violence That Tears Our Lives Apart.* Center City, MN, Hazelden Publishing.

Knox, L. (2001). *Youth Violence and the Health Professions: Core Competencies for Effective Practice.* Alhambra, CA, Southern California Center for Youth Violence Prevention.

Koop, C. E., and Lundberg, G. (1992). Violence in America: A public health emergency. *J. of the Amer. Medical Association.* 22:3075–3076.

Lane, M.S., Cunnigham, S., and Ellen, J. (2004). The intentions of adolescents to carry a knife or gun: A study of low-income African—American adolescents. *Journal of Adolescent Health.* 34(1):72–78.

Laub, J. H., and Lauritsen, J. L. (1998). The interdependence of school violence and neighborhood and family conditions. In D. S. Elliott, B. A. Hamburg and K. R. Williams (Eds.), *Violence in Amer. Schools.* Cambridge, England, Cambridge University Press: 127–155).

Leiber, M. J. (2002). Disproportionate minority confinement of youth: An analysis of state and federal efforts to address this issue. *Crime and Delinquency.* 48(91):3–45.

Leiber, M. J., and Mack, K. Y. (2003). The individual and joint effects of race, gender, and family status on juvenile justice decision making. *J. of Research on Crime and Delinquency,* 40(1):34–70.

Lewis, D. O., Mallouh, C., and Webb, V. (1989). Child abuse, delinquency and violent criminality. In Cicchett, D. and Carlson, V, Eds., *Child Maltreatment: Theory and Research on the Causes and Consequences of Child Abuse and Neglect.* Cambridge, Cambridge University Press.

Lipsey M.W. and Derzon, J.H. (1998). Predictors of violent or serious delinquency in adolescence and early adulthood. In Loeber, R. and Farrington, D.P. (Eds.) *Serious and Violent Juvenile Offenders: Risk Factors and Successful Interventions.* Thousand Oaks, CA, Sage Publications: 85–105.

Loeber, R., & Hay, D.F. (1997). Key issues in the development of aggression and violence from childhood to early adulthood. *Annual Review of Psychology.* 48:371–410.

Loeber, R., and Farrington, D. P. (Eds.). (1998). *Serious and Violent Juvenile Offenders: Risk Factors and Successful Interventions.* Thousand Oaks, CA, Sage.

Loeber, R., Wung, P., Keenan, K., Giroux, B., Stouthamer-Loeber, M., Van Kammen, W. B., et al. (1993). Developmental pathways in disruptive child behavior. *Development and Psychopathology.* 5:103–133.

Longjohn, M. M., and Christoffel, K. K. (2004). Are medical societies developing a standard for gun injury prevention? *Injury Prevention.* 10(3):169–173.

Lowry, R., Powell, K. E., Kann, L., DColliins, J. L., and Kolbe, L. J. (1998). Weapon-carrying, physical fighting, and fight-related injury among U.S. adolescents. *Amer. J. of Preventative Med.* 14(2):122–129.

Marcelle, D. R., and Melzer-Lange, M. D. (2001). Project UJIMA: Working together to make things right. *Wisconsin Medical J.* 100(2):22–25.

Maris, R.W., Berman, A.L., and Silverman, M.M. (2000). *Comprehensive Textbook of Suicidology.* New York, NY, Guilford Press.

Mihalic, S., Fagan, A., Irwin, K., Ballard, D., and Elliott, D. (2004). *Blueprints for Violence Prevention. Report for The Office of Juvenile Justice and Delinquency Prevention.* Boulder, CO, Center for the Study and Prevention of Violence, University of Colorado at Boulder.

Moffitt. T.E. (1993). Life-course-persistent and adolescence-limited antisocial behavior: A developmental taxonomy. *Psychological Review.* 100:674–701.

Mones, P. (1991). *When a Child Kills: Abused Children Who Kill their Parents.* New York, Pocket Books.

Myers, W. C., Scott, K., Burgess, A. W., and Burgess, A. G. (1995). Psychopathology, biopsychosocial factors, crime characteristics and classification of 25 homicidal youths. *J. of the Amer. Academy of Child and Adolescent Psychiatry.* 34(11):1483–1489.

National Center for Children Exposed to Violence (NCCEV). (2005). Child Development-Community Policing. Retrieved September 15, 2006, from http://www.nccev.org/initiatives/cdcp/index.html

National Research Council. 2005. *Firearms and Violence: A Critical Review. Committee to Improve Research Information and Data on Firearms.* (Wellford, C.F., Pepper, J,V., and Petrie, C.V., Eds.) Washington, D.C., The National Academies Press.

Office of Juvenile Justice and Delinquency Prevention. (1999). *Promising Strategies to*

Reduce Gun Violence. Washington, D.C., Office of Juvenile Justice and Delinquency Prevention, U.S. Dept. of Justice.

O'Keefe, M. (1995). Predictors of child abuse in maritally violent families. *J. of Interpersonal Violence.* 10(1):3–25.

Olds, D. L., Henderson, C. R., Cole, R., Ecenrode, J., Kitzman, H., and Luckey, D. (1998). Long-term effects of nurse home visitation on children's criminal and anti-social behavior: 15 year follow-up of a randomized controlled trial. *JAMA.* 280:1238–1244.

Olds, D. L., Henderson, C. R. J., Kitzman, H. J., Eckenrode, J. J., Cole, R. E., and Tatelbaum, R. C. (1999). Prenatal and infancy home visitation by nurses: Recent findings. *Future of the Child.* 9(1):190–191.

Olweus, D. (1993). *Bullying at School: What We Know and What We Can Do.* Cambridge, MA, Blackwell Publishers.

Olweus, D., Limber, S. P., and Mihalic, S. (1999). *The Bullying Prevention Program: Blueprints for Violence Prevention,* Vol. 10. Boulder, CO, Center for the Study and Prevention of Violence.

Osofsky, J. D. (1995). The effects of exposure to violence on young children. *Amer. Psychologist.* 50:782–788.

Perry, B. D. (1997). Incubated in terror: Neurodevelopmental factors in the "Cycle of Violence." In E. Osofsky (Ed.), *Children, Youth and Violence: The Search for Solutions* (pp. 124-148). New York, Guilford Press: 124–148.

Perry, B. D. (2001). The neurodevelopmental impact of violence in childhood. In D. Schetky and E. Benedek (Eds.), *Textbook of Child and Adolescent Forensic Psychiatry.* Washington, DC, American Psychiatric Press, Inc.: 221–238.

Pittman, A., Wolfe, D. A., and Wekerle, C. (1998). Prevention during adolescence: The Youth Relationships Project. In Lutzker, J. R. (Ed.) *Handbook of Child Abuse Research and Treatment.* Plenum Publishing Corp.: 341–356.

Pollard, J. A., Hawkins, J. D., and Arthur, M. S. (1999). Risk and protection: Are both necessary to understand diverse behavioral outcomes in adolescence? *Social Work Research.* 23:45–56.

Prescott, J. W. (1996). The origins of human love and violence. *Pre- and Perinatal Psychology J.* 10(3):143–188.

Prescott, J. W. (2002). How culture shapes the developing brain and the future of humanity and what we can do to change it: A brief summary of the research which links brain abnormalities and violence to an absence of nurturing and bonding very early in childhood. *Touch the Future.* Spring: 2–6.

Prescott, L. (1998). *Improving Policy and Practic*e for Adolescent Girls with Co-Occurring Disorders in the Juvenile Justice System. Delmar, NY, The National GAINS Center.

Proctor, B.D., and Dalaker, J. (2003). *Poverty in the United States: 2002.* (Census Population Reports, No. P60-0222). Washington, DC, U.S. Census Bureau.

Pynoos, R. S., Steinberg, A. M., Ornitz, E. M., and Goenjian, A. K. (1997). Issues in the developmental neurobiology of traumatic stress. In Yehuda. R. and A. C. McFarland (Eds.), *Psychobiology of Posttraumatic Stress Disorder.* New York, Academy of Sciences: 176–193.

Reiss Jr., A. J., Miczek, K. A., and Roth, J. A. (Eds.). (1994). *Understanding and Preventing Violence, Vol. 2: Biobehavioral Influences;(Vol. 4: Consequences and Control.* Washington, D.C., National Academy Press.

Resnick, H., and Kilpatrick, D. (1994). Crime-related PTSD: Emphasis on adult general population samples. *PTSD Research Quarterly.* 5:1–7.

Richters, J. E., and Martinez, P. (1993). The NIMH Community Violence Project: I. Children as victims of and witnesses to violence. *Psychiatry.* 56:7–21.

Rosman, E. A., Perry, D. F., and Hepburn, K. S. (2005). T*he Best Beginning: Partnerships Between Primary Health Care and Mental Health and Substance Abuse Services for Young Children and Their Families.* Washington, DC, Georgetown University National Technical Assistance Center for Children's Mental Health.

Sampson, R. J., Morenoff, J. D., and Gannon-Rowley, T. (2002). Assessing "neighborhood effects": Social processes and new directions in research. *Annual Review of Sociology.* 28:443–478.

Sampson, R. J., Radenbush, S. W., and Earls, F. (1997). Neighborhoods and violent crime: A multi-level study of collective efficacy. *Science.* 277:918–924.

Schwarz, E. D., and Kowalski, J. M. (1991). Malignant memories: PTSD in child and adults after a school shooting. *J. of the Academy of Child and Adolescent Psychiatry.* 30(6):936–944.

Sege, R. D., Kharasch, S., and Perron, C. (2002). Pediatric violence-related injuries in Boston: Results of a city-wide emergency department surveillance program. *Archives of Pediatric Adolescent Med.* 156:73–76.

Sheley, J. F., and Wright, J. D. (1998). High school youths, weapons and violence: A national survey. Research in brief. Washington, D.C., National Institute of Justice.

Shemesh, B., Keshavarz, R., Leichtling, N. K., Weinberg, E., Mousavi, A., Sadow, K., et al. (2003). Pediatric emergency department assessment of psychological trauma and posttraumatic stress. *Psychiatric Services.* 54(9):1277–1293.

Shepherd, J. P., Sutherland, I., and Newcombe, R. G. (2006). Relations between alcohol, violence and victimization in adolescence. *J. of Adolescence.* 29(4):539–553.

Sherman, L. W. (2001). Reducing gun violence: What works, what doesn't, what's promising. *Criminology and Criminal Justice.* 1(1):11–25.

Sherman, L. W., Gottfredson, D., MacKenzie, D., Eck, J., Reuter, P., and Bushway, S. (1997). *Preventing Crime: What Works, What Doesn't, What's Promising: A Report to the United States Congress.* Washington, D.C., National Institute of Justice.

Sickmund, M. (2004). *Juveniles in Corrections* (No. NCJ 202885). Washington, DC: Department of Justice, Office of Juvenile Justice and Delinquency Prevention.

Slovack, K., and Singer, M. (2001). Gun violence and exposure among youth. *Violence and Victims.* 16(4):389–400.

Snyder, H.N. and Sickmund, M. (1999). *Juvenile Offenders and Victims: 1999 National Report.* Pittsburgh, National Center for Juvenile Justice.

Spurling, M. C., and Vinson, D. C. (2005). Alcohol-related injuries: Evidence for the prevention paradox. *Annals of Family Med.* 3:47–52.

Stattin, H., and Magnusson, D. (1996). Antisocial development: A holistic approach. *Development and Psychopathology.* 8:617–645.

Stein, B. D., Jaycox, L. H., Kataoka, S. H., Wong, M., TU, W., Elliott, M. N., et al. (2003). A mental health intervention for school children exposed to violence: A randomized controlled trial. *JAMA.* 290(5):603–611.

Straus, M. (1974). Cultural and organizational influences on violence between family members. In Prince, R., and Barried, D. (Eds.), *Configurations: Biological and Cultural Factors in Sexuality and Family Life.* Washington D.C., Health Publishing.

Thorton, T. N., Craft, C. A., Dahlberg, L. L., Lynch, B. S., and Baer, K. (2002). *Best Practices of Youth Violence Prevention: A Sourcebook for Community Action.* Atlanta, GA, Centers for Disease Control and Prevention, National Center for Injury Prevention and Control.

U.S. Department of Health and Human Services. (2001). Mental Health: Culture, Race, and Ethnicity—A Supplement to Mental Health: A Report of the Surgeon General. Washington, DC, U.S. Department of Health and Human Services.

U.S. Department of Health and Human Services. (2001). *Youth Violence: A Report of the Surgeon General.* Rockville, MD, U.S. Department of Health and Human Services, Centers for Disease Control and Prevention, National Center for Injury Prevention and Control; Substance Abuse and Mental Health Services Administration, Center for Mental Health Services; and National Institutes of Health, National Institute of Mental Health.

U.S. Department of Justice. (2005). Drugs and Gangs: Fast Facts. Retrieved October 25, 2006, from http://www.usdoj.gov/ndic/pubs11/13157/index.htm

Vossekuil, B., Fein, B., Reddy, M., Borum, R., and Molzeleski, W. (2002). The Final Report and Findings of the Safe School Initiative: Implications for the Prevention of School Attacks in the United States. Washington, D.C., U.S. Department of Education.

Webster, D. W., and Wilson, M. E. (1994). Gun violence among youth and the pediatrician's role in primary prevention. *Pediatrics,* 94(4), 617-622.

Webster, D.W., Freed, L.H., Frattaroli, S., and Wilson, M.H. (2002). How delinquent youth aquire guns: Initial versus most recent gun acquisitions. *Journal of Urban Health.* 79:60–69.

Wellford, C. F., Pepper, J. V., and Petrie, C. V. (2004). *Firearms and Violence: A Critical Review.* Washington, D.C., National Academies Press.

Wilson-Brewer, R. S., Cohen, L., O'Donnell, 1., and Goodman, I. (1991). *Violence Prevention for Young Adolescents: A Survey of the State of the Art.* Cambridge, MA, ERIC Clearinghouse.

Wyant, B., Thorton, C., Ketterlinus, R. D., Cheney, R., and Wiebe, D. (2006). Approach to Youth Firearm Injuries: Pennsylvania Injury Reporting and Intervention System (PIRIS). Philadelphia, PA, Paper presented at the Annual Meeting of the Pennsylvania Public Health Association.

Yung, B. R., and Hammond, W. R. (1998). Breaking the cycle: A culturally sensitive violence prevention program for African American children and adolescents. In J. R. Lutzker (Ed.), *Handbook of Child Abuse Research and Treatment.* New York, NY, Plenum Publishing Corp.: 319–340

Zara, S., Briss, P.A., and Harris, K.W. (Eds.) (2005). *The Guide to Community Preventive Services. What Works to Promote Health?* Task Force on Community Preventive Services. Cary, NC, Oxford University Press.

Zimring, F.E. (1998). *American Youth Violence.* Cary, NC, Oxford University Press.

Zun, L.S., Downey L., and Rosen, J. (2003). Violence prevention in the ED: Linkage of the ED to a Social Service Agency. *Amer. J. of Emergency Med.* 21:454–457.

Zun L.S., Downey L., and Rosen J. (2004). Violence: Recognition, management and prevention: An emergency department-based program to change attitudes of youth toward violence. *The J. of Emergency Med.* 26(2): 247–251.

Zun, L.S, Downey, L., and Rosen, J. (2006). The effectiveness of an ED-based violence prevention program. *The Amer. J. of Emergency Med.* 24(1):8–13.

NOTE: *Parts of this literature review are adapted from and included in: Ketterlinus, R.D., and Henry, M. (November, 2006).* Community and Youth Violence Prevention: Opportunities for Philadelphia's Behavioral Health System. *Report prepared for Philadelphia Department of Behavioral Health and Mental Retardation Services. Philadelphia, PA: Philadelphia Health Management Corporation.*

Philadelphia HealthCare Collaborative Program Publications and Presentations

Albert Einstein Medical Center (AEMC)

Deitch, K. et al. (2003). Youth violence recidivism among ED patients. *Annals of Emergency Med.* 40(4): S61.

Sorondo, B. et al. (2004) Trend analysis of youth violence in Urban Philadelphia. Accepted for a poster presentation at the 4th Annual NYS Regional SAEM meeting on March 31, 2004.

Lane, P.L., Baez, A., Sorondo, B., and Nituica, C. (2001). Victims of severe violent injuries—Access to care and outcomes. *Annals of Emergency Med.* 38(4): S87. Presented as moderated poster at ACEP Scientific Assembly 2001, Chicago, IL, October 14-16, 2001.

University of Pennsylvania: Children's Hospital of Philadelphia (CHO) and Hospital of the University of Pennsylvania (HUP)

Fein, J.A., Kassam-Adams, N., Vu, T.N., and Datner E.M. (2001). Acute stress disorder symptoms in violently injured youth in the emergency department. *Annals of Emergency Med.* 38: 391–396.

Fein, J.A. and Mollen, C.J. (1999). Iterpersonal violence. *Current Opinion in Pediatrics.* 11:588–593.

Mollen, C.J., Fein, J.A., Vu, T.N., Shofer, F.S., and Datner, E.M. (2003). Gender differences in injuries and event characteristics resulting from youth violence. *Pediatric Emergency Care.* 19: 379–384.

Datner, E.M. and Fein, J.A. (2004). How safe is the "Safety Net" for violently injured youth in the Emergency Department? *Amer. J. of Bioethics.* 4(2): 72–74.

Thomas Jefferson University Hospital (TJUH)

Davis-Moon, L., Corbin, T., Hall, R., Lopez, B.L., and Riviello, R.J. (2003). Injury prevention: intentional injury experiences of women aged 14 to 25 Years (Abstract). *Annals of Emergency Med.* 42:S18.

Lopez, B.L., Davis-Moon, L., Grim, K., Foley, B., Guo, Y., and Christopher, T. (2002). What are the characteristics of young adults who are high risk victims of intentional injury? (Abstract). *Academic Emergency Med.* 9:471.

Davis-Moon, L., Kolecki, P., Christopher, T., Lopez, B. (2001). Injury prevention: Retaliatory violence prevention (Abstract). *J. of the Society for Academic Emergency Med.* 459.

Davis-Moon L, Lopez B, Christopher T, Dutton S. (2000). Community retaliatory violence prevention in young adults (Abstract). *J. of Emergency Nursing.* 333.

Philadelphia Health Management Corporation (PHMC).

Ketterlinus, R. D., Dreisbach, N., Minot, K., Fein, J. A., Corbin, T., Davis-Moon, L., Datner, E. M., and Lindauer, S. (2004). Emergency Department interventions for violently injured youth: Philadelphia Health Care Collaborative. Presented at Philadelphia College of Physicians Annual Meeting, Philadelphia, PA, May, 2004.

Ketterlinus, R.D. (2002) The Philadelphia HealthCare Collaborative (HCC). Presented at the Johns Hopkins Center for Injury Research and Policy 10th Anniversary Celebration of the National Center for Injury Prevention and Control. Baltimore, MD, June 20, 2002.

APPENDIX

Reports Reviewed Regarding Model and Promising Evidence-Based Practices

National Information Sources

Committee on Crossing the Quality Chasm: Adaptation to Mental Health and Addictive Disorders (2006). *Improving the Quality of Health Care for Mental and Substance-Use Conditions: Quality Chasm Series.* Retrieved January 16, 2006, from: http://www.nap.edu/catalog/11470.html

New Freedom Commission on Mental Health, *Achieving the Promise: Transforming Mental Health Care in America. Final Report.* DHHS Pub. No. SMA-03-3832. Rockville, MD: 2003.

Huang, L. et al, (2005). Transforming mental health care for children and their families. *American Psychologist.* Vol. 60, No. 6:615–627.

National Institute for Health Care Management (2005). Children's Mental Health: New Developments in Policy and Programs. Retrieved on January 5, 2006, from: http://www.nihcm.org/childpub.html

U.S. Department of Health and Human Services (2001). *Mental Health: Culture, Race and Ethnicity – A Supplement to Mental Health: A Report of the Surgeon General.* Rockville, MD: U.S. Department of Health and Human Services, Substance Abuse and Mental Health Services Administration, Center for Mental Health Services.

U.S. Department of Health and Human Services (1999). Mental Health: A report of the Surgeon General. Washington, D.C., U.S. Department of Health and Human Services.

Rosman, E.A., Perry, D.F., and Hepurn, K.S. (2005). The best beginning: Partnerships between primary health care and mental health and substance abuse services for young children (0–3) and their families. Washington, D.C., Georgetown University National Technical Assistance Center for Children's Mental Health.

Jennings, A. (2004). T*he Damaging Consequences of Violence and Trauma: Facts, Recommendations and Discussion Points for the Behavioral Health System.* National Technical Assistance Center for State Mental Health Planning, National Association of State Mental Health Program Directors (NASMHPD).

Powell, D, Fixsen, D., and Dunlap, G. (2003). *Pathways to service Utilization: A Synthesis of Evidence Relevant to Young Children with Challenging Behavior.* University of South Florida: Center for Evidence-based Practice.

McLennan et al (2006). Research practice gaps in child mental health. *Journal of the American Academy of Child and Adolescent Psychiatry,* 45(6):658–665.

National Technical Assistance Center for State Mental Health Planning. (2004). Answering the challenge: Responses to the President's New Freedom Commission final report. *Networks,* 8 (3&4): 1–16.

Strode, A. (2003). *A Summary of Best and Promising Mental Health Practices for Select Consumer Populations.* Spokane, WA, The Washington Institute for Mental Illness Research and Training.

Chapter 2

The Violence Intervention Project of The University of Pennsylvania: History and Post-Traumatic Stress Disorder

Elizabeth M. Datner, MD, Joyce Lee-Ibarra, MPH, Nancy Kassam-Adams, PhD, and Joel A. Fein, MD, MPH

Introduction

The Violence Intervention Project was designed and implemented in order to address the needs of youth victims of violence when they presented to the Emergency Departments (EDs) of several West Philadelphia Hospitals. The goal of the project has been to identify psychosocial needs of the youth, and provide referrals to community-based organizations that might fulfill those needs. The project has evolved significantly from phone-based assessments and referrals to ED-based tiered assessments with a subsequent home visit intervention. Many barriers were overcome and lessons were learned throughout the course of this project and a myriad of issues needing exploration, evaluation, and intervention were identified. One particular issue that was elicited was a lack of resources for mental health services. Specifically, the significant impact of violence on acute stress reactions and subsequent development of Post Traumatic Stress Disorder (PTSD) was explored. The literature on PTSD and its impact on victims of violence is discussed.

In one recent year, an estimated 1,021,118 males and 650,361 females were treated in United States EDs for injuries resulting from nonfatal assaults. Approximately 25% of these patients were between the ages of 10 and 20 years (Morbidity and Mortality Weekly Report, 2002). Recent statistics also suggest that more than 75% of children report having been exposed to community violence (Hill and Jones, 1997), and more than 33% of American children and adolescents report being the direct victim of violence (Boney-McCoy and Finkelhor, 1995). Hospital EDs serve on the front lines of this problem, treating young victims and witnesses on a daily basis. The Children's Hospital of Philadelphia (CHOP) ED treats approximately 78,000 children per year and the Hospital of the University of Pennsylvania (HUP) treats approximately 58,000 patients per year. As Level-One Trauma Centers in Southeastern Pennsylvania, these EDs see the most devastating effects of violence among our city's youth. Although physicians and nurses are trained to save lives and handle complex traumas, they are not fully trained to identify and assess one of the major causes of death and severe injury in urban youth: interpersonal violence.

Importantly, the ED is not an optimal place to intervene in the complex cycle of violence—this is best handled in the context of the community and the family. However, throughout the nation there is a broad chasm between the identification of children that are at risk for violence, and the family services that are vital to prevent future injury.

The Violence Intervention Project (VIP) at The University of Pennsylvania is a hospital-based interventional youth violence prevention program created to gain a better understanding of the context in which youth violence occurs, and to reduce the barriers to communication between health care professionals and victims of youth violence. The specific goal of the VIP is to identify and assess violently injured youth, and successfully connect them with existing community-based prevention and treatment services. Although the project has changed dramatically over the past five years, its goal has remained the same since its inception in 1998.

Prior to VIP protocols, emergency care professionals, in our institutions and others, often followed a "treat 'em and street 'em" philosophy—young victims' physical injuries were treated, but the psychosocial issues that caused or resulted from the violent incidents went unexamined. Many patients were discharged without further intervention or serious inquiry regarding the circumstances of and reactions to their injury, and the cycle of violence continued. Through the efforts of the VIP team, the standard of care for violently injured youth at The University of Pennsylvania has been substantially raised, and the groundwork for collaborations with multiple community-based organizations established.

The VIP was made possible with the support of the William Penn Foundation Healthcare Connections grant. We also received several additional contributions that supplemented the further development of the VIP. They included a substantial donation from the Children's Hospital of Philadelphia Women's Committee and the Firearm and Injury Center at Penn.

Project Development and Design

The Initial VIP Model: Identify Patients in the ED and Link Them with Community-Based Organizations

The Violence Intervention Project of the University of Pennsylvania (UPENN) was conceptualized, developed, and implemented in 1998 in response to a request for proposals (RFP) from the William Penn Foundation focused on linking health care providers with Community-Based Organizations (CBOs) around the issue of youth violence. The project was initiated and developed by the current co-directors of the project, Drs. Joel Fein and Elizabeth Datner. The initial development of the project was focused on identifying youth victims of violent injury in the EDs of the Children's Hospital of Philadelphia (CHOP), the Hospital of The University of Pennsylvania (HUP), and Presbyterian Medical Center (PMC), and linking them with CBOs that focused on enhanced resilience and violence prevention. Victims of self-inflicted injury and child abuse were specifically excluded from this project since protocols for evaluation of these situations existed previously.

Identification of youth violence victims was initially the responsibility of existing ED staff, such as clerks, registrars, and physicians. In 2001, the VIP was included as one of the active ED research protocols to benefit from the Academic Associate (AA) Program at UPENN. This is an undergraduate course offered each semester at UPENN. As one component of the course, students become trained research assistants, and work in the EDs for 16 hours a day (8:00 a.m. to midnight), seven days a week with the exception of university calendar holidays. The research assistants receive training from the investigators of each active ED-based study prior to initiation of a research protocol, and are then responsible for reviewing the case of every patient who presents to the ED during the inclusive hours. Any patients identified during these hours are enrolled in the respective protocols.

Assessment was originally conceptualized as occurring in the ED at the time of patient presentation. The initial assessment focused on the immediate risks to the patient and a more detailed assessment was performed over the phone at a later time.

Referral to CBOs occurred through our Intervention Coordinator after she refined the assessment over the telephone with the individual youth. The referral occurred after review with selected CBOs, to determine capacity for the youth.

Phase I (1998–2001)

Design: The VIP responded to the initial RFP as a programmatic initiative with some evaluation. VIP patients were identified based on specific criteria including age (8–24 years), location of residence (eight West Philadelphia zip codes), and having sustained a violent injury. All patients received a basic survey of event and demographic information. For patients residing in four of the eight zip codes, the ED staff contacted a social worker or an on-call "assessment team" (AT) member, depending on the hour. Social workers were available at CHOP until 11:00 p.m., HUP until 5:00 p.m., and rarely at PMC. The social worker or AT member would come to the ED, perform a psychosocial assessment on the patient, and recommend areas for intervention.

The ED assessment occurred at the time of the ED visit, and the patient would be offered either immediate or delayed referrals, or both. Immediate referrals were accomplished through Philadelphia Police, the Philadelphia Anti-Violence/Anti-Drug Network (PAAN), or psychiatric consultation and were geared toward safety promotion. Referrals were arranged over the following weeks through the VIP project manager after further telephone consultation with the injured youth. The information from the assessment team member was relayed to the Intervention Coordinator, who would match the patient with appropriate CBOs in the patient's neighborhood.

The Intervention Coordinator would make contact with the CBOs to determine availability, compatibility, and capacity for the individual patient, and then would give the CBO and the patient appropriate contact information. CBOs included mentoring programs, after-school programs, tutoring programs, mental health services, and recreation programs. It was left to the patient and the CBO to contact each other and to initiate participation. Due to the non- experimental nature of the initial proposal, assignment to control or intervention status was not randomized. However, the two groups of zip code areas were matched for socioeconomic status, race, and age. Patients in both groups were surveyed for outcome measures by telephone six months after the ED visit.

AT members were given special training sessions prior to their employment, to orient them to the ED culture and practices, and to review potential challenges of performing assessments on violently injured youth.

Outcomes and Barriers/Lessons Learned

Enrollment: The project enrolled 519 patients over a 15 1/2-month period, beginning January 16, 1999, and ending April 30, 2000. Seventy-eight youth were enrolled in a two-month pilot period preceding this enrollment period. Initially, the project was conducted at CHOP, HUP and our affiliated hospital, PMC. Of the 519 patients enrolled, only a small percentage were enrolled at PMC. This institution was subsequently dropped from the project.

Various methods of contacting AT members, including a beeper system and answering service, were employed with only minimal success. Even when the AT member was successfully contacted, the patients were often discharged from the ED before the AT member could get to the ED from home. It became clear that the cost of training and labor for the AT was not justified based on the number of assessments performed. This mechanism was subsequently changed to an ED-based assessment model without the need for an on-call staff.

Education of Health Care Workers: The VIP oriented and educated 90 Pediatrics residents, 39 Emergency Medicine residents, and seven Pediatric Emergency Medicine fellows over this two- year period about the project goals and logistics. In addition, each second-year pediatric resident at CHOP received a formal one-hour lecture on violence prevention from one of the faculty affiliated with the VIP. Dozens of nurses, social workers, and support staff were similarly introduced to the project goals and logistics.

Contact with CBOs: After extensive investigation of the CBOs in the West Philadelphia community, it became clear that few CBOs were available to deal with the issues most pressing for the injured youth of the VIP. In addition, the CBOs that were in existence did not have the capacity or the capability of instituting a standard protocol for intake of the VIP patients.

In addition to the lack of capacity of the individual CBOs, it was clear that the telephone-based case management model did not propagate linkages between patients and CBOs. Of the 244 youth who were enrolled in the intervention group, 176 (72.5%) were offered a referral to a community organization. Reasons that a youth may not have received a referral included refusal of referral by youth or parent (N=6, 2.5%), mutual determination (by youth, parent, and project staff) that the youth did not need a referral (N=50, 20.5%), and inability to find an appropriate referral resource (N=1, 0.4%). Of the 176 youth who were referred to a community organization, 38 (21.6%) accessed the referral site.

Improvements to Project Design After First Phase

Focus Intervention for Those Who Need it: Many of our patients (approximately 20%) were determined by themselves, a parent, or the project staff to not need a referral. In conjunction with Dr. Kenneth Ginsburg, our adolescent medicine specialist, we adapted a risk stratification model using risk factors based on the previous work of Drs. Robert Sege and Peter Stringham of the Boston Medical Center. The model was designed to identify "low-risk" patients, allowing us to focus resources on those patients who would benefit the most from the intervention. In addition, most of our community referrals were not appropriate for 8–11-year-olds, and we therefore excluded this age group from the intervention portion of the project.

The risk factors for ongoing violence that were used in the model were school attendance or failure, history of drug use or drug trade, history of fighting or threatening behaviors, weapon carrying, and presence or lack of a caring adult. Patients who did not have any of these risk factors were considered to be low risk for ongoing violent behavior.

Improve Research Design: In addition to the above changes, we developed a more rigorous research design. We eliminated the allocation of patients to an intervention or control group by zip code, and adopted a true randomization procedure for all eligible patients. We also initiated a retrospective surveillance of ED records in order to identify missed patients and developed a telephone enrollment protocol to capture those patients who were missed in the EDs.

Collaborations: A full description of the collaborations with whom the VIP has worked is presented in Appendix 1. We have worked hard to identify and collaborate with UPENN departments or divisions that have expressed an interest in violence prevention interventions. In addition, we have sought out those collaborators that could help facilitate the implementation of this project.

Additionally, we have met with representatives from city organizations and academic institutions that are working to combat the problem of youth violence. These meetings have enlightened us to the workings of important efforts that are occurring in Philadelphia, and have engendered a collaborative mentality among these groups. We have found that by sharing our experiences, both positive and negative, and being open to creative advice and discussion, we were able to gain the support and shared expertise from many of our colleagues from outside agencies and institutions. Their support and expertise has been invaluable to us throughout this project.

Goals for Phase 2

We established the following goals for Phase 2 of the project:

- Establish a mechanism through which physicians, not VIP staff, assess the immediate safety issues of violently injured youth in the ED, thereby building the foundation for the development of a practical ED-based safety protocol.
- Eliminate nonemergent *real-time* ED interventions.
- Provide more information about resources for all violently injured youth seen in the ED.
- Perform risk analysis and stratification to offer appropriate interventions.
- Increase the strength of connection between VIP staff and youth *after* ED discharge.
- Develop a transitional counseling intervention that focuses on building youth strengths and resiliency, thereby increasing the likelihood that youth will attend and benefit from available community resources.

Another major goal for the future of the project was to strengthen the existing connections with community organizations and to build new collaborations. Our success in this area focused on resources specific to West Philadelphia, rather than city-wide organizations. We hoped to solidify connections to school-based programs, criminal justice programs, city-wide social service organizations, and other academic medical centers.

The Improved VIP Model: Transitional Counseling in the Community

Phase 2 (2001–2003): Increased Evaluation and Development of a Transitional Intervention

Design: In Phase 2, the VIP enrolled children and young adults aged 12–24 who presented to the EDs at Children's Hospital or the Hospital of the University of Pennsylvania, and who were victims of intentional violent injury (excluding cases of child abuse). The project focused on boys and girls of all racial and ethnic backgrounds, who reside in ten Philadelphia zip codes. Upon presentation to the ED, the AA identified the youth. The AA was responsible for confirming that the individual met inclusion criteria and did not meet exclusion criteria. The youth were consented to participate in the project, and the AA administered an extensive assessment survey (Appendix 2). This survey includes segments on circumstances of the event, reactions and plans following the event, risk and protective factors, and psychosocial measures for PTSD, emotional expression, anger expression, and depression. The survey also included several "critical risk" questions to assess the need for immediate service referral. The assessment survey addressed specific areas of information described below:

Event circumstances included timing, location, and circumstances leading to the event; who encouraged or discouraged the fight, why and how the fight ended, number, gender, and relationships of others involved in the fight; history of previous fighting with the involved individuals; weapon involvement and most serious weapon to cause an injury; and injuries sustained during the fight. We also classified injuries using the Abbreviated Injury Scale (AIS), an anatomically based system that categorizes injuries by body region on a six-point scale. Injuries classified as AIS 1 are minor injuries, including most abrasions and lacerations; AIS 2 injuries are more severe, including concussions and most extremity fractures.

Risk Factors included smoking cigarettes, smoking marijuana, other illicit drug use, drug sales, fighting behavior, weapon carrying, and school difficulties or failure.

Resiliency Factors included presence of a caring adult, after-school activities, alliance with a religious organization, and hopefulness.

Immediate Safety Factors included perception of safety, retaliation plans for youth, friends, and family.

Emotional Response to the Event included immediate stress reactions (acute stress), depression, anger expression, and coping responses.

The AAs were responsible for notifying ED social workers for all violently injured youth. If there was concern regarding the immediate safety of the youth, the AAs were directed to notify the physician involved in the individual's care. Physicians were also asked to independently perform an Immediate Safety Screen (Appendix 3) on each violently injured patient. This safety screen provided a mechanism to support the physician interaction with the patient around the key indicators of immediate safety. In addition, it served to reinforce the understanding of the physician staff regarding safety issues for the violently injured youth. If there was no need for immediate intervention based on safety concerns, the youth was informed that they would next be contacted by phone (provided consent was given). No further VIP intervention occurred in the ED "real-time." All youth interviewed (regardless of willingness or consent to participate) were given an information packet of available existing Philadelphia youth social service resources put together by VIP staff. If the patient was not identified or enrolled in the ED, VIP staff members attempted to complete this enrollment over the telephone.

After enrollment, VIP staff reviewed the initial assessment interview and categorized the patient's risk status as described above. Moderate and high-risk youth were randomized to intervention or control status. Control status patients were not contacted again until 9- to 12- month follow-up was performed. The VIP assigned a Transitional Counselor (TC) to each intervention status patient. The TCs assisted youth through ongoing face-to-face meetings in progressing through the stages of behavior change necessary to reach and maintain their personal goals. Cases were closed when the patient or parent initiated the closure process, or when the TC and Intervention Coordinator determined that the goals have been met. The VIP Intervention Coordinator worked with each TC to ensure that patients were appropriately assessed, that goals were appropriately chosen, and that the best plans possible were developed to effect positive yet realistic changes in youths' lives. The Intervention Coordinator also served as the primary liaison to the city and community organizations to which patients were referred for additional services.

Outcomes, Barriers, and Lessons Learned

Between September 14, 2001 and April 27, 2003, 565 youth were successfully enrolled using the comprehensive psychosocial assessment tool (see Figure 1). Of these, 290 were enrolled in the ED and 275 were enrolled by telephone. The

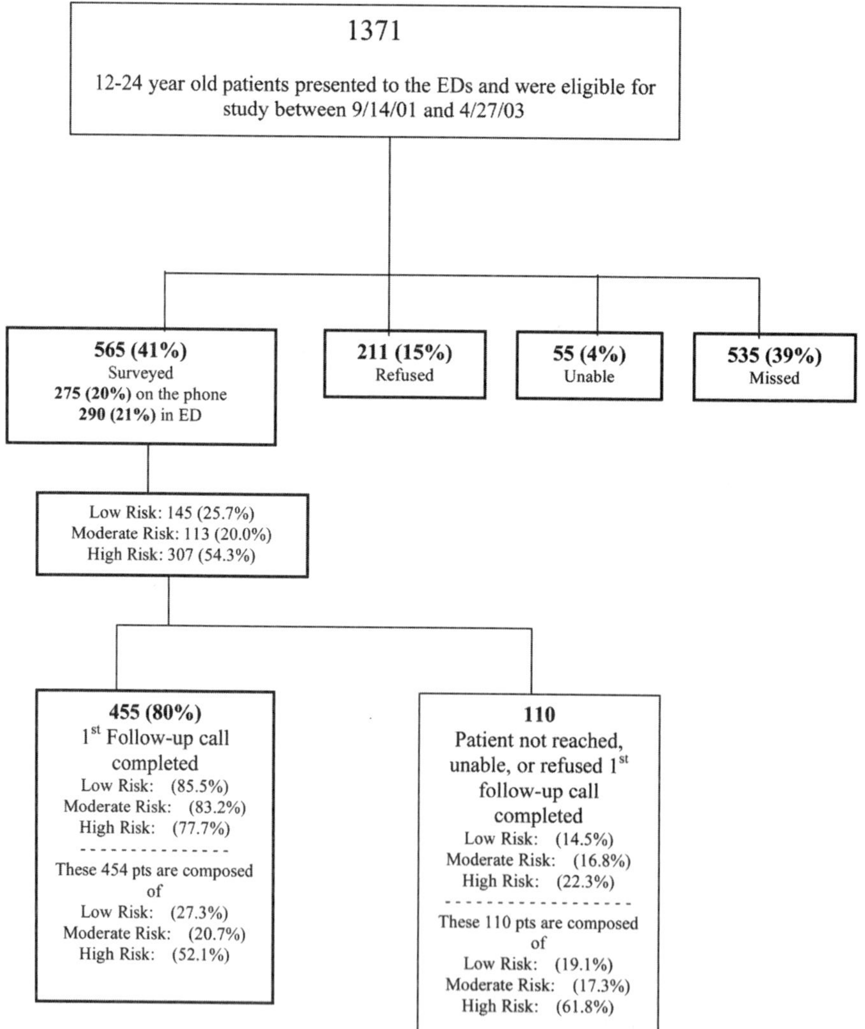

Figure 1. Youth in the Violence Intervention Project: Enrollment Flowchart

VIP also designed and implemented a formal telephone enrollment protocol that could be used for other community-level programs. Of the 565 patients surveyed in the ED, 80.4% completed a follow-up call within weeks of the ED visit, 15.3% were unable to be reached, and 4.2% refused a follow-up call.

Patients who were considered moderate or high risk were eligible for consent into the study. If the patient (or guardian for children less than 18 years old) consented, the patient was randomized to either intervention or control status. Patients who were assigned to the intervention group were contacted by a transitional counselor (TC). The TC maintained contact with the patient by initiating an appointment for a home visit and enrolling them in an evaluation program. The control status patients did not receive any form of intervention or referral after their initial assessment with the exception of a packet of resource information that was given to them in the ED or mailed to their home. Both the intervention and control groups were reassessed nine months after the initial ED visit.

Eighty percent (263 of 330) moderate and high-risk patients consented to a home visit, and 19.7% refused any potential intervention. Of these 263 consented patients, 183 (70%) were assigned to the intervention group and 80 (30%) to the control group. Of those assigned to an intervention, 25 (13.7%) parents refused and 15 (8.2%) patients refused; 67 (36.6%) of the intervention group patients received at least one home visit.

Linkages and Referrals to Community-Based Agencies

VIP faculty and staff have recognized the need to identify and develop ties with community-based agencies possessing the expertise and capacity to provide long-term interventions for our at-risk youth. Our experience during the past three years can guide the VIP in the proper direction in this regard. Through our current intervention, we have a clear understanding of the resources that will assist the youth and families who are enrolled through the ED. These resources include long-term mentoring, mental health services, educational and job opportunities, and family counseling. Unfortunately, the standard route of referrals to these types of organizations is not always successful. There are often waiting lists for mentors and mental health services, and many educational and occupational resources require personalized introductions and follow-through. Many of the available resources have not appealed to the youth participants in a culturally relevant and sensitive manner.

Recognition of Needs of Injured Youth

The VIP made improvements in the rapid early assessment of acute stress symptoms and Posttraumatic Stress Disorder (PTSD) in violently injured youth. The following section of this chapter will address those issues in detail. The VIP also pursued the collaboration within the Children's Hospital of Philadelphia and the University of Pennsylvania regarding PTSD, and plans included future links with the Center for Pediatric Traumatic Stress to develop and test interventions that may alleviate these symptoms in violently injured youth.

Data on Immediate Safety Screening

It has become clear that implementation of an immediate safety screen for violently injured youth will require additional education and training of health care workers. The validity of our existing screen is not yet confirmed, and in fact is not yet routinely used by our colleagues. The reasons for the lack of use of the safety screen are not completely clear, however, lack of time due to other patients and responsibilities and unfamiliarity with the procedure are likely major causes. In general, physicians did not complete assessments without prompting by AAs. Unfortunately, time for physician education was limited given the amount of work that our staff had to do for surveillance, randomization, telephone enrollment, and follow-up telephone calls. We initiated an email reminder campaign to physicians; however, the emails that we sent often went unread or forgotten. Additionally, the safety screen forms were not an automatic part of the ED record (they had to be located by the physician and placed on the chart once completed). It does appear, however, in preliminary review of available data that youth victims of violence are more likely to disclose safety concerns to physicians rather than to research assistants. In the future, efforts will be directed towards incorporating the safety questions into the medical record so that clinicians are persistently reminded of the importance of these issues in the violently injured patients.

Case Studies of Successful Intervention

Case A: N. is a 22-year-old female who presented to the ED due to injuries sustained in a fight at a club. N.'s assessment interview indicated she was high risk due to fight history, arrest history, and marijuana use. N. needed a job referral, and asked for assistance in getting into a trade school. After working with N., her TC was able to help N. find and obtain a job she enjoyed. The TC also assisted N. with the application process to begin trade school in the fall. N. has not engaged in any fights since she began working with her TC, and has stated that talking with the TC has helped her avoid her previous fighting behavior. The TC has also been instrumental in helping N. obtain her driver's license, the lack of which was related to N.'s arrest history.

Case B: B. is a 17-year-old female who presented to the ED with gunshot wounds after being caught in crossfire while walking home. Because of B.'s concern that friends may seek retaliation against the shooter that injured her, she was categorized as moderate risk. After the shooting incident, B. was unable to return to school due to problems with school documentation of her medical records. The TC assigned to B. worked with her to navigate the school administration. With his help, she was ultimately successful in returning to school through the Twilight Program, an accelerated high school program. The TC has also been instrumental in helping B. work through difficulties with her mother, related to the mother's prior drug abuse. B. and the TC have developed a good relationship, and B. has stated that the TC has become a caring adult presence in her life, someone with whom she can discuss important life issues.

Project Impact and Sustainability

The model that we have suggested for the VIP has met with approval by city agencies and collaborating hospitals throughout Philadelphia. The VIP participated in the Healthcare Connection, a collaborative network of four city hospitals with ED-based programs designed to intervene with violently injured youth. There is significant potential to seek funding for our ED-based project through this collaborative. We believe the VIP can serve as a model program for other Philadelphia hospitals, and through our numerous collaborations there is great potential for dissemination of our work. VIP faculty and staff are also members of local and national violence prevention organizations, such as Physicians for Social Responsibility, and city organizations such as the Philadelphia Youth Fatality Review Team. They are also active in nonprofit organizations such as The Philadelphia Anti-Drug Anti-Violence Network (PANN) and the Institute for Safe Families. Collaborations within the University of Pennsylvania include the Graduate School of Education, The Nursing School, and the Departments of Sociology, Criminal Justice, Emergency Medicine, and Trauma. In these partnerships, we hope to make the most of the vast expertise within UPENN.

The Improved VIP: Plans for Phase 3

In the first two phases of the project we made significant progress in addressing the needs of violently injured youth, and in the process also identified three discrete approaches to improve the project. First, we decided that more culturally relevant and sensitive techniques should be infused in the identification and engagement process to decrease the skepticism with which families view ED assessment and psychosocial support organizations. For example, many patients and families perceive the ED to be a part of the larger, insensitive institution and social welfare organizations that have been perceived to not provide resources and support to the community. Second, we felt that we needed to improve our approach to establishing risk-free acceptance of these families into local community-based services by providing information about the families including their strengths and resources. Third, we agreed that our evaluation of these methods and redesigned program required more input from the youth and family participants.

The initial goals of Phase 3 were driven by the need to create improved linkages between the ED and community services. These goals included:

1) Develop project-specific alliances with community-based organizations (CBOs).

2) Transition the intervention portion of the project toward these CBOs using a culturally sensitive "engagement" model.

3) A description of our initial approach to achieving these goals is presented next.

Goal #1: Develop project-specific alliances with community-based organizations

The VIP has recently established ties with several programs geared towards youth and/or family development. For example, we have developed an agreement with Big Brothers/Big Sisters of Southeastern Pennsylvania (BBBS-SEPA) to offer specially chosen mentors to selected VIP patients, ages 12–17. The BBBS mentoring program offers an ideal transition for a number of our patients who could benefit from the consistent presence of an adult mentor in his or her life. We have thus far identified 13 youth for BBBS, and 11 have agreed to participate. The relationship with BBBS-SEPA was initiated through the Healthcare Connection, and forged through a rigorous evaluation of the participating organizations. The first phase of this collaborative effort should result in the establishment of memorandums of understanding between the VIP and other community organizations. Our future plans are to develop additional similar linkages with other community organizations that meet the specific needs of our patients.

Goal #2: "Transition" the intervention portion of project toward community-based services using a streamlined "engagement" model

While some interventions like Big Brothers/Big Sisters (BBBS) have universal appeal and are widely sought by youth and families, other interventions are less appealing to families but may be just as necessary to guide the patient toward a safer, more productive future. Mental health services and substance abuse programs are a few examples of such interventions. To engage our patients and families into these services, we will need to present a culturally relevant approach that is sensitive to the stigma and bias that accompanies these types of interventions.

We plan to be able to integrate our work into that of specific community programs that are poised to receive and assist these at-risk youth and their families. The linkage between the VIP and existing, self-supporting community organizations fosters the sustainability and reproducibility of our project.

Youth Violence Exposure and Post Traumatic Stress Disorder

The issues affecting youth who experience violence are myriad and each deserves its own extensive discussion. However, we were impressed by the significance of the mental health issues that were identified in our VIP population. In addition, we found that the literature on mental health topics as they relate to youth violence was limited in scope. For these reasons, we chose to identify a few areas of potential psychological distress to address within the auspices of the VIP. We will discuss one of these issues, Post Traumatic Stress Disorder (PTSD), in this topic of discussion.

Youth who experience violence are at risk for both ongoing episodes of violence and for a number of significant psychological sequelae. (Sege,

Stringham, Short, and Griffith, 1999; Horowitz, Weine, and Jekel, 1995). Various forms of psychological distress and maladaptive behaviors are commonly seen in youth who experience violence. Children who are exposed to traumatic experiences (such as community violence) have suffered from a variety of psychiatric difficulties including but not limited to depression, suicidal behavior, academic problems, substance abuse, adjustment disorder, and disruptive behavior disorders (Jenkins and Bell, 1997). One such disorder that may result is PTSD (Lynch, 2003).

Until recently, trauma and its impact on children received little scientific examination. However, Acute Stress Disorder (ASD) and PTSD are particular areas of interest at the Children's Hospital of Philadelphia. Significant research has been conducted at our institution to evaluate PTSD in the context of unintentional injuries (Kassam-Adams and Winston, 2004; Winston, et al., 2003; Winston, et al., 2002). In addition, we recognized in the initial phases of the VIP that mental health services were extremely limited and not easily accessible to our patients. This is an area we focused on in an effort to understand the health care resource requirements for our patients. Additionally, we attempted to address issues that could be impacted in an ED setting.

As part of the larger psychosocial assessment of patients enrolled in the VIP, an evaluation of ASD and further subsequent development of PTSD were undertaken. The tool used for evaluation of ASD is available upon request.

This chapter section will focus on PTSD and its links to violent injury. We will review normal psychological responses to trauma and the association between injury and PTSD and risk factors for development of PTSD. We will discuss how we have evaluated the presence of Acute Stress Reactions and subsequent development of PTSD in violently injured youth. In addition, we will identify opportunities in the ED to screen youth and to provide early interventions for secondary prevention of PTSD. We will make recommendations for future study and evaluation in the clinical setting. PTSD treatment will not be discussed.

Most research on post traumatic stress has focused on adult victims of war, natural disasters, and civilian violence. However, growing empirical evidence indicates that injury (both intentional and unintentional) is a primary risk factor for post traumatic stress in children. Most injured children, however, do well, drawing on their own coping skills and the support of their family. Yet, a small percentage of patients develop distressing post traumatic symptoms, including PTSD. Some research also suggests that depression and PTSD have similar symptoms, common causes, and that one diagnosis may cause the other. Alternatively, depression may develop secondary to prolonged PTSD (Shalev, et al., 1998).

Concepts and Definitions: PTSD and the Range of Normal Responses to Trauma

Unwanted and upsetting thoughts or feelings about trauma are common. These reactions appear to be normative: in a recent study more than four-fifths of injured children and their parents reported at least one of these symptoms in the first month post-trauma (Aaron, Zaglul, and Emery, 1999). Certain aspects of these early reactions may even play a role in promoting recovery. However, when these post traumatic stress symptoms persist and impair an individual's functioning, they may constitute a traumatic stress disorder. Acute Stress Disorder (ASD) describes particularly problematic early responses to trauma. Examples of the types of statements a patient with acute stress symptoms might make are shown in Table 1. Posttraumatic Stress Disorder (PTSD) is diagnosed when severe symptoms persist for at least one month. PTSD consists of a constellation of reexperiencing, avoidance, and hyperarousal symptoms following a traumatic experience. By definition, PTSD includes the direct or indirect (witnessing or hearing about) experience of exposure to an extreme traumatic stressor that includes actual or perceived threat of serious harm or death, or harm to the physical integrity of oneself, a family member, or close associate (*DSM-IV, 1994*). The *DSM-IV* (1994) includes violent physical assaults in their examples of traumatic stressors to self, family, or close friends (American Psychiatric Association, 1994). See Table 4 for diagnostic criteria for the diagnosis of ASD and PTSD. Youth who experience just such violence events may be evaluated in emergency departments but never require additional medical care for their wounds and frequently do not have long-term relationships with medical providers, and thus are lost to further medical care. Emergency physicians see children and parents at a key time post-injury, and have a unique opportunity to promote psychological resilience and recovery from injury and to identify individuals in need of further assessment and intervention.

Table 1. Examples of Statements Reflecting Acute Stress Symptoms

Category	Statement
Fear, Helplessness, Horror	"I wanted to make it stop happening, but I couldn't."
Dissociation	"My mind went blank."
	"What was happening seemed unreal to me—like I was in a dream or watching a movie."
Re-experiencing	"Pictures or sounds from what happened keep popping into my mind."
Avoidance	"I am trying not to remember or think about what happened to me."
Arousal	"I feel jumpy."

Legend: *These are examples of statements that would support the consideration of Acute Stress Disorder in given individual.*

Prevalence of PTSD After Pediatric Injury

Significant post traumatic symptoms have been identified in 22% to 50% of children assessed one to three months after an unintentional traumatic injury, and in 12% to 29% of children assessed up to one year after an injury (Daviss, Mooney, Racusin, et al., 2000; DeVries, Kassam-Adams, Cnaan, et al., 1999; Di Gallo, Barton, and Parry-Jones; 1997 Donnelly, Amaya-Jackson, and March, 1999; Fairbank, Schlenger, Saigh, and Davidson, 1995; Fein, Kassam-Adams, Gavin, et al., 2002). PTSD in children and youth from exposure to violence, including witnessing violence in the community, has been well documented, with prevalence rates ranging from 15% to 67% (Fein, Kassam-Adams, Vu, and Datner, 2001; Fitzpatrick and Boldizar,1993; Fletcher, 1996). Acute stress symptoms appear to be common among urban youth seen in an ED for violent injury, with more than 80% reporting some symptoms and about one third reporting significant acute posttraumatic distress (Fein, Kassam-Adams, Vu, and Datner, 2001). A prospective study found that symptoms of acute stress reported by violently injured youth during acute care in the ED correlate with future reporting of post traumatic stress symptoms months after the event (Fein, et al., 2002; Fitzpatrick and Boldizar, 1993).

Risk Factors for PTSD After Injury

The broad empirical literature on posttraumatic stress in adults and children suggests that specific elements are associated with increased risk of PTSD development after any sort of traumatic event. These include history of prior traumatic experience, perceived life threat during the traumatic event; severity of exposure to the trauma; signs of hyperarousal (e.g. elevated heart rate) post-trauma; and (for children) increased parental acute distress (Baren, 2001; Bryant, et al., 2000; Foa, Keane, and Friedman, 2000; Foa, et al., 1999; see Table 2).

In traumatically injured adults, the research literature indicates that prior trauma, female gender, alcohol use, ASD symptoms, and physiological arousal (elevated heart rate in the first week after injury) are associated with increased risk of developing PTSD. (Foy, et al., 1994; Green, et al., 1991; Hembree and Foa, 2000; Horowitz, Kassam-Adams, and Bergstein, 2001). The smaller research literature regarding children's psychological reactions to traumatic injury generally echoes the risk factors found for adults, and also suggests a key role for parents in children's recovery (see Table 3). For children with traumatic injuries, parents' acute stress symptoms have been shown to be highly associ-

Table 2: Elements Associated with Increased Risk of PTSD Development after a Traumatic Event

- History of prior traumatic experience(s)
- Perceived life threat during the traumatic event
- Severity of exposure to the trauma
- Signs of posttraumatic hyperarousal (e.g. elevated heart rate)
- Increased parental acute stress responses

Table 3: Acute Predictors of Child PTSD after Injury

- Female gender
- Prior behavior or attention problems (reported by parent)
- Elevated heart rate at the time of ED triage
- Child's exposure to others injured at the same time
- Separation from parents at the time of injury and ED treatment
- The child was extremely frightened or thought that s/he might die.

Table 4. Diagnostic Criteria for Posttraumatic Stress Disorder (PTSD) and Acute Stress Disorder (ASD)

	ASD	PTSD
	The individual experiences (or witnesses) a traumatic event, and has a subjective response of fear, helplessness, or horror.	Symptoms persist and impair the individual's functioning.
Dissociation	At least 3 symptoms	(not required)
Re-experiencing	"persistent"	At least 1 symptom
Avoidance	"marked"	At least 3 symptoms
Hyperarousal	"marked"	At least 2 symptoms
Duration of symptoms	2 days - 1 month	1 month or more

Adapted from DSM-IV; *American Psychiatric Association, 1994.*

ated with later child PTSD outcomes (DeVries, et al.,1999; Donnelly, Amaya-Jackson, and March, 1999; Norris, et al., 2001).

PTSD Prevention

There are currently no empirically validated interventions for preventing post traumatic stress in injured children. The adult literature on secondary prevention posttrauma provides some ideas in this regard. The cutting edge of current research and practice in early post traumatic intervention is a systematic investigation of which interventions work, for whom, during which time period posttrauma, and in which service delivery context (Saxe, Stoddard, and Sheridan, 1998).

From the inception of the VIP, it was clear that one of the most needed services for our youth were in mental health. The VIP has begun to focus more intently on the availability of and linkage with mental health services for violently injured youth. As the result of our enhanced understanding of ASD/PTSD in the violently injured youth, in combination with the literature

Table 5: Discussion Points for Use with Families and Patients After an Injury

It may be normal for a child to try to deal with what happened by:

- thinking a lot about their injury event
- staying away reminders of what happened.

These reactions may become problems if they last too long or are too extreme. To help your child recover:

- talk openly about the injury event
- answer your child's questions, and gently encourage him or her to talk about it
- older children and teens may benefit from writing down their experiences and feelings
- have your child resume normal activities as much as physically possible.

Ask for help if:

- your child has intense or persisting reactions that get in the way of normal activities
- talking about what happened makes you tense or upset.

If you think that you or your child needs help, please call:______________________

associating violence and mental health problems (depression, anger expression) either causally or secondarily, we have begun to form a stronger link to community health care services. We have also published our experience with measuring ASD and PTSD symptoms in the ED after a violent injury, and the ability of this information to predict the persistence or development of PTSD in these youth (Fein, et al., 2001; Fein, et al., 2002).

Implications for Emergency Physicians/Best Practices

Youth with intentional traumatic injuries who come to the ED for treatment offer us the opportunity to screen and provide early interventions for the secondary prevention of further physical and emotional injury. ED physicians can play a pivotal role in initiating community referrals, as well as promoting resilience and emotional recovery for injured children in their care (Winston, et al., 2003). Table 5 lists possible talking points for discussion with children and family members after a traumatic injury to a child. Clinicians should be aware of the psychological ramifications of even minor injuries in children. Evaluation of these sequelae can begin in the immediate post-injury time period. We are beginning to learn how to identify high-risk individuals, and how to provide effective targeted secondary prevention for injury-related post traumatic stress. Emergency physicians can offer appropriate anticipatory guidance to families to help reduce the persistence and severity of these post traumatic stress reactions. Future directions for research include implementation of ASD screens in EDs with further long-term outcome evaluations regarding development of PTSD, development and implementation of ED-based interventions for individuals who screen positively for ASD, and development of protocols for linkages with mental health professionals for patients at high risk for development of PTSD.

References

Aaron, J., Zaglul, H., and Emery, R.E. (1999). Posttraumatic stress in children following acute physical injury. *J. of Pediatric Psychology.* 24(4): 335–343.

American Psychiatric Association, 1994. *Diagnostic and Statistical Manual of Mental Disorders,* 4th Edition *(DSM-IV)*, Washington, DC: American Psychiatric Association.

Baren, J.M. (2001). Rising to the challenge of family-centered care in emergency medicine. *Academic Emergency Medicine,* 8(12): 1182–1185.

Boney-McCoy, S. and Finkelhor, D. (1995). Psychosocial sequelae of violent victimization in a national youth sample. *J. of Consulting and Clin. Psych.* 63(5): 726–736.

Bryant, R.A., Harvey, A.D., Guthrie, R.M., and Moulds, M.M. (2000) A prospective study of psychophysiological arousal, acute stress disorder, and posttraumatic stress disorder. *Journal of Abnormal Psychology.* 109(2): 341–344.

Daviss, W.B., Mooney, D., Racusin, R., Ford, J. D. Fleischer, A. and McHugo, G. (2000). Predicting posttraumatic stress after hospitalization for pediatric injury. *J. of Amer. Academy of Child Adolescent Psychiatry,* 39(5): 576–583.

DeVries A.P.J., Kassam-Adams N., Cnaan A., Sherman S.E, Gallagher P., and Winston F.K. (1999) Looking beyond the physical injury: Post-traumatic Stress Disorder in children and parents after pediatric traffic injury. *Pediatrics,* 104(6): 1293–1299.

Di Gallo, A., Barton, J., and Parry-Jones, W.L. (1997). Road traffic accidents: Early psychological consequences in children and adolescents. *British J. of Psychiatry.* 170: 358–362.

Donnelly, C.L., Amaya-Jackson, L, and March, J.S. (1999). Psychopharmacology of pediatric posttraumatic stress disorder. *J. of Child and Adolescent Psychopharmacology.* 9: 203–220.

Fairbank, J., Schlenger, W., Saigh, P, and Davidson, J.R.T. (1995). An epidemiologic profile of Post-Traumatic Stress Disorder: Prevalence, comorbidity and risk factors. In M. Friedman, M., Charney, D., and Deutch, A. (eds). *Neurobiological and Clinical Consequences of Stress; From Normal Adaptation to PTSD.* Philadelphia, PA: Lippincott-Raven Publishers: 415–478.

Fein, J., Kassam-Adams, N., Gavin, M., Huang, R., Blanchard, D., and Datner, E.M. (2002). Persistence of posttraumatic stress in violently injured youth seen in the Emergency Department. *Archives of Pediatric Adolescent Med.* 156: 836–840.

Fein, J., Kassam-Adams, N., Vu, T., and Datner, E.M. (2001). Emergency Department evaluation of acute stress disorder symptoms in violently injured youth. *Annals of Emergency Medicine.* 28(4): 391–396.

Fitzpatrick, K., and Boldizar, J. (1993). The prevalence and consequences of exposure to violence among African-American youth. *J. of the Amer. Academy of Child and Adolescent Psychiatry,* 32(2): 424–430.

Fletcher, K. (1996). Childhood Posttraumatic Stress Disorder. In E. Mash and R. Barkley (Eds.). *Child Psychopathology.* New York, NY, Guilford: 241–276.

Foa, E., Keane, T., and Friedman, M. (Eds.) (2000). *Effective Treatments for PTSD: Practice Guidelines from the International Society for Traumatic Stress Studies.* New York, NY: The Guilford Press.

Foa, E.B., Dancu, C.V., Hembree, E.A., Jaycox, L.A., Meadows, E.A., and Street, G.P. (1999). A comparison of exposure therapy, stress inoculation training, and their combination for reducing posttraumatic stress disorder in female assault victims. *J. of Consulting and Clinical Psych.* 67:194 –200.

Foy, D., Madvig, B., Pynoos, R., et al. (1994). Etiologic factors in the development of Posttraumatic Stress Disorder in children and adolescents. *J. of School Psyc.* 34(2):133–145.

Green, B., Korol, M., Grace, M., Vary, M.G., Leonard, A.C., Gleser, G.C., and Smitson-Cohen, S. (1991). Children and disaster: Age, gender, and parental effects on PTSD symptoms. *J. of the American Academy of Child and Adolescent Psychiatry.* 30(6):945–951.

Hembree, E.A., and Foa, E.B. (2000). Posttraumatic stress disorder: psychological factors and psychosocial interventions. *Journal of Clinical Psychiatry.* 61:33–39.

Hill, H.M., and Jones, L.P. (1997). Children's and parents' perceptions of children's exposure to violence in urban neighborhoods. *J. of the National Med. Assn.* 89(4):270–276.

Horowitz, K., Weine, S., and Jekel, J. (1995). PTSD symptoms in urban adolescent girls: compounded community trauma. *J. of the Amer. Academy of Child and Adolescent Psychiatry,* 34(10):1353–1361.

Horowitz, L., Kassam-Adams, N., and Bergstein, J. (2001). Mental health aspects of emergency medical services for children: Summary of a consensus conference. *Journal of Pediatric Psychology.* 26:491–502.

Jenkins, E. J., and Bell, C. C. (1997) Exposure and response to community violence among children and adolescents. In Osofsky, J.D. (Ed.), *Children in a Violent Society.* New York, NY, The Guilford Press: 9–31.

Kassam-Adams N., and Winston, F.K. (2004). Predicting child PTSD: The relationship between acute stress disorder and PTSD in injured children. *J. of the Amer. Academy of Child and Adolescent Psychiatry.* 43(4):403–11.

Lynch, M. (2003). Consequences of children's exposure to community violence. *Child and Family Psychology Rev.* 6(4):265–274.

Morbidity and Mortality Weekly Report, May 31, 2002/51(21):460–3

Norris, F., Byrne, C., Diaz, E, and Kaniasty, K. (2001). *Psychosocial Resources in the Aftermath of Natural and Human-Caused Disasters: A Review of the Empirical Literature, with Implications for Intervention.* White River Junction, Vermont.

Saxe, G.N., Stoddard, F.J., and Sheridan, R.L. (1998). PTSD in children with burns: A longitudinal study. *J. of Burn Care and Rehabilitation.* 19(1, pt. 2): S206.

Sege R., Stringham P., Short S., and Griffith J. (1999). Ten years after: Examination of adolescent screening questions that predict future violence-related injury. *J Adolesc. Health.* 24:395–402.

Shalev, A.Y., Freedman, S., Peri, T., Brandes, D., Sahar, T., Orr, S. P., and Pitman, R. K. (1998). Prospective study of posttraumatic stress disorder and depression following trauma. *Amer. J. of Psychiatry.* 155 (5):630–637.

Winston, F. K., et al. (2003). Screening for risk of persistent posttraumatic stress in injured children and their parents. *JAMA.* 290(5):643–649.

Winston F.K. et al. (2002). Acute stress disorder symptoms in children and their parents after pediatric traffic injury. *Pediatrics.* 109(6):e90.

Suggested Additional Readings on PTSD

Bryant, R.A., et al. (1999). Treating acute stress disorder: An evaluation of cognitive behavior therapy and supportive counseling techniques. *Amer. J. of Psychiatry,* 156(11):1780–1786.

Cella, D., Perry, S, Kulchycky, S, and Goodwin, C. (1988). Stress and coping in relatives of burn patients: A longitudinal study. *Hospital and Community Psychiatry.* 39(2):159–166.

Cohen, J. (1998). Summary of the practice parameters for the assessment and treatment of children and adolescents with posttraumatic stress disorder. *J. of the Amer. Academy of*

Child and Adolescent Psychiatry. 37(9):997–1001.

Levi, R.B., Drotar, D., and Yeates, K.O. (1999). Posttraumatic stress symptoms in children following orthopedic or traumatic injury. *J. of Clinical Child Psych.* 28(2):232–243.

Litz, B., Gray, M., Bryant, R., and Adler, A.B. (2001). Early intervention for trauma: Current status and future directions. *Clinical Psychology: Science and Practice.* 9:112–134.

Marshall, R., et al. (2001). Comorbidity, impairment, and suicidality in subthreshhold PTSD. *Amer. J. of Psychiatry.*158:1467–1473.

Norris, F. (1992). Epidemiology of trauma: Frequency and impact of different potentially traumatic events on different demographic groups. *J. of Consulting and Clinical Psychology.* 60(3):409–418.

Rauch, S., Hembree, E., and Foa, E. (2001). Acute psychosocial preventive interventions for posttraumatic stress disorder. *Advances in Mind-Body Medicine,* 17(3):187–191.

Resnick, H., et al. (2000). Emergency evaluation and intervention with female victims of rape and other violence. *J. of Clinical Psychology,* 56:1317–1333.

Richmond, T. (1997). An explanatory model of variables influencing postinjury disability. *Nursing Research.* 46(5):262–269.

Richmond, T. and Kauder, D. (2000). Predictors of psychological distress following serious injury. *J. of Trauma Stress.* 13:681–692.

Rose, S., Bisson, J., and Wessely, S. (2001). Psychological debriefing for preventing posttraumatic stress disorder (PTSD). *The Cochrane Library.* Oxford, U.K.

Sawyer, M., et al. (1998). Influence of parental and family adjustment on the later psychological adjustment of children treated for cancer. *J. of the Amer. Academy of Child Adolescent Psychiatry.* 37(8):815–822.

Shalev, A., Peri, T., Canetti, L., and Schreiber, S. (1996). Predictors of PTSD in injured trauma survivors: A prospective study. *Amer. J. of Psychiatry,* 153(2):219–225.

Shalev, A., Freedman, S., Peri, T., Glick, N., Brandes, D., Orr, S.P., and Pitman, R.K. (1998). A prospective study of heart rate response following trauma and the subsequent development of Posttraumatic Stress Disorder. *Archives of General Psychiatry.* 55:553–559.

Stallard, P., Velleman, R., and Baldwin, S. (1998). Prospective study of post-traumatic stress disorder in children involved in road traffic accidents. *British Med. J.* 317:1619–1623.

Stallard, P., Velleman, R., and Baldwin, S. (2001). Recovery from post-traumatic stress disorder in children following road traffic accidents: The role of talking and feeling understood. *J. of Community and Applied Social Psych.* 11:37–41.

Yehuda, R., McFarlane, A.C., and Shalev, A.Y. (1998). Predicting the development of posttraumatic stress disorder from the acute response to a traumatic event. *Biological Psychiatry.* 44:1305–1313.

Zatzick, D., et al. (2002). Predicting posttraumatic distress in hospitalized trauma survivors with acute injuries. *Amer. J. of Psychiatry,* 159:941–946.

Appendix 1: Violence Intervention Project Academic Collaborations:

University of Pennsylvania:
Department of Sociology
Psychology Department
Graduate School of Education
Criminal Justice Department

Temple University
Criminal Justice Department

Appendix 2: Violence Intervention Project Long Form

VIOLENCE INTERVENTION PROJECT *Long Form Enrollment*	Patient Name: ______________ (last, first) ☐ CHOP ☐ HUP ED Date: ___/___/___ Patient MRN: ______________ **For VIP USE: Patient ID#_______**
FORM #6 — ONLY COMPLETE THIS PACKET IF CONSENT WAS OBTAINED IN *FORM #4*	

Interviewer Status:

☐1 = **Social Worker**
☐2 = **Academic Associate**
☐3 = **VIP Staff**
☐66 = **Other**: ____________________

Interview Date: _____/_____/_____

Interview Time: _____:_____ (military time)

Interviewer Name: ______________________

Interviewer: Use patient responses to fill out the following fields. **DO NOT** simply copy down the information you obtained and recorded on the *Patient Identification Sheet* (orange form). **This information will be used to verify, confirm, and supplement the information that you obtained from the patient chart and the emergency department computer system.**

Patient Name

Last:______________________ **First:**____________________ **MI:**________

Age: _______ **DOB:** ____/_____/_____ **Gender:** ☐ Male ☐ Female (Ask! Don't assume.)

Address: ______________________________ **Apt # (if applicable):** __________

City:______________________________ **State:** _____ **Zip Code:** __________

Phone #(s): home____________________ cell____________________

pager____________________ work____________________

other____________________ other____________________

Consent for Future Phone Follow-Up

To the parent or guardian (if patient is under age 18):

Would it be OK if someone from our group were to call and check-in on your child once in a while after they have left the emergency department, and possibly ask your child some more questions?

☐ Not Applicable (patient over age of 18)

☐ YES ☐ NO

Name and Relationship of Parent/Guardian Providing/Witholding Consent:
____

To the patient (in all cases):

Would it be OK if someone from our group were to call and check-in on you once in a while after you have left the emergency department, and possibly ask you some more questions?

☐ YES ☐ NO

proceed to the next page…

Violence Intervention Project
ED Assessment: Interview

Part I.

1) Altercation Date: ____/____/____

2) Altercation Time (Military Style): ____:_____

3) Day of Week of Altercation:
□$_1$ = Monday □$_5$ = Friday
□$_2$ = Tuesday □$_6$ = Saturday
□$_3$ = Wednesday □$_7$ = Sunday
□$_4$ = Thursday □$_8$ = Unknown

4) Location of Patient Enrollment:
□$_1$ = Urgent Care/ Walk In
□$_2$ = ED
□$_3$ = Trauma/Resuscitation
□$_4$ = Phone Enrollment

5) □$_{-55}$ **Skipped**

6) □$_{-55}$ **Skipped**

7) How do you describe yourself?

□$_1$ = Black/African American □$_2$ = White/Caucasian □$_3$ = Asian
□$_4$ = Hispanic/Latino □ $_5$ = Multiethnic (please specify)______________________
□$_{66}$ = Other (please specify)______________________

8) □$_{-55}$ **Skipped**

9) □$_{-55}$ **Skipped**

10) □$_{-55}$ **Skipped**

11) Patient Status: □$_1$ **Refused** □$_2$**Missed** □$_3$**Enrolled** □$_4$**Unable** □$_5$**Phone Enrolled**

<u>Directions:</u> At this point, please ask anyone in the room with the patient to leave by saying:
I am a part of a team that is taking care of you. Our goal is to get information to come up with the best plan to help you. We know that it is your <u>mom or dad</u> who can help you the most, but we also know that some things may be hard to talk openly about, in front of your parents. I would like to talk to you alone, to learn about your safety and keeping you safe. I promise to keep our conversation private. If I think that you might be headed for trouble, I will suggest that we work together to figure out the best way to get your parent involved. We will never do this without your permission.

[To the others in the room]: Could I ask you to leave the room for a few minutes while I talk to (patient)?

12) Others in the room at time of interview (Other than patient and Assessment Team Member):

□$_1$ = Parent/Guardian/Caretaker □$_2$ = Police
□$_3$ = No one, interviewed patient alone □$_{66}$ = Other, Please Specify:__________________
□$_{-77}$ = Not applicable (e.g., Phone Enrollment) □$_{-88}$ = Unknown, data unavailable

Version 01/14/03 **2**

Part II. Circumstances

What happened? (#1) *We are worried about you getting hurt again in the future. It is important for my team to understand what happened today, so I am going to ask you some questions about everything that went on. For starters, can you tell me all about what happened?*

(PLEASE use this area to describe what happened with written text, in as much detail as possible. You can use the back of this page if you run out of room.)

1. **What happened?**
   - □$_1$ = Fight, Argument
   - □$_2$ = Assault/Mugging
   - □$_3$ = Injured as a bystander
   - □$_{-88}$ = Unknown
   - □$_{-99}$ = Refused

2. **What caused the event? (CHECK ALL THAT APPLY)**
   - □$_A$ = Romantic Interest/ Relationship
   - □$_B$ = Being Disrespected/Gaining Respect/ Proving One's Self
   - □$_C$ = Conflict over ownership of personal possessions
   - □$_D$ = Teasing/"Making Fun"/Rumors of patient
   - □$_E$ = Teasing/"Making Fun"/Rumors of patient's family
   - □$_F$ = Recurrence of previous fight
   - □$_G$ = Told to fight/ Peer pressure
   - □$_H$ = Jealousy
   - □$_I$ = Boredom
   - □$_J$ = Escalation of play-fighting/ "roughhousing"
   - □$_K$ = Drug Possession
   - □$_L$ = No Reason to Fight
   - □$_{66}$ = Other *(please specify: ________________)*
   - □$_{-88}$ = Unknown
   - □$_{-99}$ = Refused

3. **What caused your most serious injury?**
   - ☐$_1$ = Blunt object (bat, rock, stick, heavy bottle, etc.)
   - ☐$_2$ = Knife/piercing object (includes broken bottles, pens)
   - ☐$_3$ = Gun (Including those used in "pistol whipping")
   - ☐$_4$ = Fists/feet/hands
   - ☐$_5$ = Teeth
   - ☐$_6$ = Mace
   - ☐$_7$ = Razors
   - ☐$_{66}$ = Other *(Please specify)*____________________
   - ☐$_{-88}$ = Unknown
   - ☐$_{-99}$ = Refused

4. **ITEM SKIPPED**
   - ☐$_{-55}$ = Skipped

4a. ITEM SKIPPED
☐ $_{-55}$ = Skipped

4b. ITEM SKIPPED
☐ $_{-55}$ = Skipped

4c. ITEM SKIPPED
☐ $_{-55}$ = Skipped

4d. ITEM SKIPPED
☐$_{-55}$ = Skipped

4e. Did anyone use a weapon at the scene of <u>the event</u>?
- ☐$_1$ = Yes
- ☐$_0$ = No
- ☐$_{-77}$ = Not Applicable
- ☐$_{-88}$ = Unknown
- ☐$_{-99}$ = Refused

4f. If "Yes" to #4e, who used the weapon? (CHECK ALL THAT APPLY)
- ☐$_1$ = Patient
- ☐$_2$ = Primary offender
- ☐$_3$ = Bystander
- ☐$_{66}$ = Other *(Please specify)*________________
- ☐$_{-77}$ = Not Applicable
- ☐$_{-88}$ = Unknown
- ☐$_{-99}$ = Refused

4g. Was the person that used the weapon a male or a female?
- ☐$_1$ = Male
- ☐$_2$ = Female
- ☐$_3$ = Both a male and a female used a weapon
- ☐$_{-77}$ = Not Applicable
- ☐$_{-88}$ = Unknown
- ☐$_{-99}$ = Refused

4h. ITEM SKIPPED
☐$_{-55}$ = Skipped

5. Where did the event happen?

- ☐$_1$ = INSIDE a home or residential setting
- ☐$_2$ = OUTSIDE of a home or residential setting
- ☐$_3$ = INSIDE a school building
- ☐$_4$ = OUTSIDE of a school building (including streets/sidewalks in the vicinity of a school building)
- ☐$_5$ = Streets, including sidewalks (Not specifically in the vicinity of a school building)
- ☐$_6$ = Park, including public playgrounds, recreation centers
- ☐$_7$ = Other public places (businesses, public functions, public transportation)
- ☐$_{66}$ = Other *(Please specify)*____________________________
- ☐$_{-88}$ = Unknown
- ☐$_{-99}$ = Refused

6. Patient reported the following person(s) as physically involved in causing injury: (CHECK ALL THAT APPLY)

- ☐$_A$ = Associate (Acquaintance) / Friend
- ☐$_B$ = (Ex-)Boyfriend/(Ex-)Girlfriend (If patient is older than 14, SEE DIRECTIONS AT BOTTOM OF PAGE!)
- ☐$_C$ = Spouse/Ex-Spouse (If patient is older than 14, SEE DIRECTIONS AT BOTTOM OF PAGE!)
- ☐$_D$ = Parent/Guardian
- ☐$_E$ = Family member (siblings, cousin, etc.)
- ☐$_F$ = Stranger
- ☐$_G$ = Police/ Security Officer/ School Official
- ☐$_{66}$ = Other *(Please specify)*________________
- ☐$_{-88}$ = Unknown
- ☐$_{-99}$ = Refused

FOR VICTIMS OF DATING/DOMESTIC/INTIMATE PARTNER VIOLENCE:

- As of 10/14/02, patients with intentional injuries from dating/domestic violence are EXCLUDED from the Violence Intervention Project.
- If the Patient has indicated (Ex-)Spouse/(Ex-)Boyfriend/(Ex-)Girlfriend caused intentional injury:

AT HUP	AT CHOP
Tell the patient: o **Thank you for answering these questions so far** o **Because you have a special situation that led to you getting hurt, I am going to talk to the team taking care of you to let them know what happened** o **If it's OK with you, I'm going to give you a packet of information that includes phone numbers for places that can help you stay safe in the future**	Tell the patient: o **Thank you for answering these questions so far** o **Because you have a special situation that led to you getting hurt, I am going to talk to the doctor taking care of you to let him/her know what happened** o **If it's OK with you, I'm going to give you a packet of information that includes phone numbers for places that can help you stay safe in the future**
Do NOT continue VIP interview—instead, consider patient for new Domestic Violence Study	Do not continue VIP interview—instead, notify attending physician about possible intimate partner violence
Remember to give gray packet to patient; be sure to point out the "Where to Turn for Help" card	Remember to give gray packet to patient; be sure to point out the "Where to Turn for Help" card

7. ITEM SKIPPED

☐$_{-55}$ = Skipped

8. How many people were actively involved in the event, not just watching?

☐$_{1}$ = Single person and patient
☐$_{2}$ = More than one person and patient
☐$_{3}$ = More than four people
☐$_{-88}$ = Unknown
☐$_{-99}$ = Refused

9. ITEM SKIPPED

☐$_{-55}$ = **Skipped**

10. Was the person (group of people) that hurt you a male or female (boys or girls)?

☐$_{1}$ = Male
☐$_{2}$ = Female
☐$_{3}$ = Group of Girls
☐$_{4}$ = Group of Boys
☐$_{5}$ = Group of Boys & Girls
☐$_{-88}$ = Unknown
☐$_{-99}$ = Refused

11. ITEM SKIPPED

☐$_{-55}$ = Skipped

12. ITEM SKIPPED

☐$_{-55}$ = Skipped

13. ITEM SKIPPED

☐$_{-55}$ = Skipped

14. ITEM SKIPPED

☐$_{-55}$ = Skipped

15. ITEM SKIPPED

☐$_{-55}$ = Skipped

16. ITEM SKIPPED

☐$_{-55}$ = Skipped

17. ITEM SKIPPED

☐$_{-55}$ = Skipped

17(tu). Were you under the influence of drugs or alcohol at the time of the incident?

☐$_{1}$ = Yes
☐$_{0}$ = No
☐$_{-88}$ = Unknown
☐$_{-99}$ = Refused

D17a (tu). If yes, what were you on: (CHECK ALL THAT APPLY)

☐$_{A}$ = Drugs *(Please specify which one(s)):*______________________
☐$_{B}$ = Alcohol
☐$_{66}$= Other *(Please specify)*_________________
☐$_{-88}$ = Unknown
☐$_{-99}$ = Refused

18. ITEM SKIPPED

☐$_{-55}$ = Skipped

19. ITEM SKIPPED

☐$_{-55}$ = Skipped

20. Was a police report filed regarding this incident?

☐$_{1}$ = Yes
☐$_{0}$ = No
☐$_{2}$ = Planning on filing a police report
☐$_{-88}$ = Unknown
☐$_{-99}$ = Refused

21. ITEM SKIPPED

☐$_{-55}$ = Skipped

22(tu). ITEM SKIPPED

☐$_{-55}$ = Skipped

Part III. Reactions & Plans

A. Plans & Urgent Care Assessment: If any of the answers to these questions indicate that urgent care is needed, alert the physician verbally!

We care about helping you to get better now, but we also want to prevent you from getting hurt again in the future. I am going to ask you some questions to see how safe you and others are, now and in the near future. Some of these questions may seem strange because they don't apply to your age or situation. If they don't apply, just say so. If we decide that you are not safe, there are people here who can help you.

22. Do you believe that you will be safe for the next few days?

- □1 = Yes
- **□0 = No ◊ Urgent Care is Needed, Alert Physician**
- □-88 = Unknown
- □-99 = Refused

23. Do you have any plans to hurt someone else now?

- **□1 = Yes ◊ Urgent Care is Needed, Alert Physician**
- □0 = No
- □-88 = Unknown
- □-99 = Refused

24. How do you plan to resolve this situation?

- □1 = No plan
- **□2 = Retaliation ◊ Urgent Care is Needed, Alert Physician**
- □3 = Reconciliation
- □4 = Avoidance
- □5 = File a police report
- □6 = Involve other authority figures
- □-88 = Unknown
- □-99 = Refused

25. Do you think that other people have plans to retaliate?

- **□1 = Yes ◊Urgent Care is Needed, Alert Physician**
- □0 = No
- □-88 = Unknown
- □-99 = Refused

26. Do you have any plans to hurt yourself?

- **□1 = Yes ◊ Urgent Care is Needed, Alert Physician**
- □0 = No
- □-88 = Unknown
- □-99 = Refused

27. When you think about your future, do you feel hopeful?

- □1 = Yes
- □0 = No
- □-88 = Unknown
- □-99 = Refused

28. If you had a problem and needed the help of a caring adult, is there someone you could talk to?

- □1 = Yes **(Who would you talk to?______________________________)**
- □0 = No
- □-88 = Unknown
- □-99 = Refused

Part IV. Assessment of Risk Factors

I have a few questions left to ask you, about your life in general. I am asking these questions because we want to know if you are in danger of getting hurt again in the future. Your answers to these questions will help us to better help you, so please be as honest as you can be. Remember that everything you tell me will be private, unless you tell me that you are going to hurt yourself or someone else.

29. During the school year, are you enrolled in grades K-12?

- □$_1$ = Yes **(If YES, Continue with form)**
- □$_0$ = No **(If NO, SKIP TO #30, PAGE 10)**
- □$_{-88}$ = Unknown
- □$_{-99}$ = Refused

29a. What grade are you in? ______ (Grades K-12)

29b. Is this grade appropriate for patient's age?
*****TO BE FILLED OUT BY VIP STAFF*****

- □$_1$ = Yes
- □$_0$ = No
- □$_{-77}$ = Not applicable
- □$_{-88}$ = Unknown
- □$_{-99}$ = Refused

29c. How often do you miss school (Grades K-12)

- □$_1$ = Never (Always goes to school)
- □$_2$ = Occasionally (May miss one or two days per month)
- □$_3$ = Frequently (Misses 3-9 days per month)
- □$_4$ = Half of the time (Misses about 10 days per month)
- □$_5$ = Almost always (Misses more than half the days)
- □$_{-77}$ = Not applicable
- □$_{-88}$ = Unknown
- □$_{-99}$ = Refused

29d. When you do miss school, what is the most likely reason for your absence (Grades K-12)?

- □$_1$ = Illness
- □$_2$ = Taking care of sibling/relative/child
- □$_3$ = Boredom
- □$_4$ = Problems with schoolwork
- □$_5$ = Fear of violence
- □$_6$ = No appropriate clothing
- □$_7$ = Working to support self
- □$_8$ = Working to support family
- □$_9$ = Suspended
- □$_{-77}$ = Not applicable
- □$_{-88}$ = Unknown
- □$_{-99}$ = Refused

29e. What kind of grades do you get (Grades K-12)? (CHOOSE ONE)

- □$_1$ = Mostly A's
- □$_2$ = Mostly B's
- □$_3$ = Mostly C's
- □$_4$ = Mostly D's
- □$_5$ = Mostly F's
- □$_{-77}$ = Not applicable
- □$_{-88}$ = Unknown
- □$_{-99}$ = Refused

30. In the past two years, have you been held back in school for failing grades K-12?

☐$_1$ = Yes
☐$_0$ = No
☐$_{-77}$ = Not applicable
☐$_{-88}$ = Unknown
☐$_{-99}$ = Refused

31. Other than in the past two years, have you ever been held back for failing grades K-12?

☐$_1$ = Yes◊ Reason for Failure: ______________________
☐$_0$ = No
☐$_{-77}$ = Not applicable
☐$_{-88}$ = Unknown
☐$_{-99}$ = Refused

32. If you are not enrolled in grades K-12, why aren't you enrolled?

☐$_1$ = Failed out
☐$_2$ = Dropped out because of failing performance
☐$_3$ = Dropped out to work, to support self
☐$_4$ = Dropped out to work, to support family
☐$_5$ = Expelled for violence or drugs
☐$_6$ = Graduated
☐$_{66}$ = Other: ______________________
☐$_{-77}$ = Not applicable
☐$_{-88}$ = Unknown
☐$_{-99}$ = Refused

32a. What is the highest grade you completed? ______

33. If patient is older than 14: Do you have a job?

☐$_1$ = Yes
☐$_0$ = No
☐$_{-77}$ = Not applicable
☐$_{-88}$ = Unknown
☐$_{-99}$ = Refused

34. If patient is older than 14: Do you want a job?

☐$_1$ = Yes
☐$_0$ = No
☐$_{-77}$ = Not applicable
☐$_{-88}$ = Unknown
☐$_{-99}$ = Refused

35. What do you do in your free time? ______________________

36. Are you involved in any of the following activities:

36a. After-school programs	☐$_1$ = Yes	☐$_0$ = No
36b. Sports	☐$_1$ = Yes	☐$_0$ = No
36c. Church/Religious organizations	☐$_1$ = Yes	☐$_0$ = No

36d. Other (Please specify): ______________________

The next few questions are a little more difficult to answer, but I want to remind you that anything you tell me will be private.

37. Have you:

	Never	1-2x/life	1-2x/year	1-2x/mo	1-2x/week	Daily	-88 Unknown	-99 Refused
A. Smoked Cigarettes:								
B. Used Alcohol:								
C. Used Marijuana								
D. Used Street Drugs								
E. Sold Drugs								

38. During the past year, were you in a physical fight?

- □$_1$ = Yes **(If YES, Continue with form)**
- □$_0$ = No **(If NO, SKIP TO #40, PAGE 12)**
- □$_{-88}$ = Unknown
- □$_{-99}$ = Refused

39. How many times during the past year were you in a physical fight?

- □$_1$ = Between 1 and 5 times
- □$_2$ = 6 or more times
- □$_{-77}$ = Not Applicable
- □$_{-88}$ = Unknown
- □$_{-99}$ = Refused

39a. In any of those events, was a weapon ever used to hurt or threaten anyone?

- □$_1$ = Yes
- □$_0$ = No
- □$_{-77}$ = Not Applicable
- □$_{-88}$ = Unknown
- □$_{-99}$ = Refused

39b. What type of weapon was involved? (CHECK ALL THAT APPLY)

- □$_1$ = Blunt object (bat, rock, stick, heavy bottle, etc.)
- □$_2$ = Knife/piercing object (includes broken bottles, pens, etc.)
- □$_3$ = Gun (Including those used in "pistol whipping")
- □$_4$ = Razors
- □$_{66}$= Other
- □$_{-77}$ = Not Applicable
- □$_{-88}$ = Unknown
- □$_{-99}$ = Refused

40. Have you ever carried a weapon?

☐$_1$ = Yes **(If YES, Continue with form)**
☐$_0$ = No **(If NO, SKIP AHEAD TO #41, PAGE 14)**
☐$_{-77}$ = Not Applicable
☐$_{-88}$ = Unknown
☐$_{-99}$ = Refused

40a. Have you carried a weapon within the past 6 months? **(formerly 40b)**

☐$_1$ = Yes
☐$_0$ = No
☐$_{-77}$ = Not Applicable
☐$_{-88}$ = Unknown
☐$_{-99}$ = Refused

40b. In the past month, how often did you carry a weapon? **(formerly 40c)**

☐$_1$ = Never
☐$_2$ = Sometimes (Once a week)
☐$_3$ = Often (More than once a week)
☐$_4$ = Almost every day
☐$_{-77}$ = Not Applicable
☐$_{-88}$ = Unknown
☐$_{-99}$ = Refused

40c. What type of weapons have you carried? (CHECK ALL THAT APPLY) **(formerly 40a)**

☐$_A$ = Blunt object (bat, rock, stick, heavy bottle, etc.)
☐$_B$ = Knife/piercing object (includes broken bottles, pens, etc.)
☐$_C$ = Gun **(**IF Patient has carried a GUN, be sure to answer questions #40c1 – 40c7, BELOW)**
☐$_D$ = Razors
☐$_{66}$ = Other
☐$_{-77}$ = Not Applicable
☐$_{-88}$ = Unknown
☐$_{-99}$ = Refused

***The next few questions are about the gun that you have carried. I want to remind you that your answers to these questions will all remain private unless we learn that you or someone else will be injured, and any information that you share with us will NOT be used to get you into any trouble.*

40c1. If you have carried a gun, what type of gun was it?

☐$_1$ = Handgun-Revolver
☐$_2$ = Handgun-Pistol
☐$_3$ = Rifle
☐$_4$ = Shotgun
☐$_{66}$ = Other________________
☐$_{-77}$ = Not Applicable
☐$_{-88}$ = Unknown
☐$_{-99}$ = Refused

40c2. If you have carried a gun, do you know the make & model of the gun? (Indicate below)

____

40c3. If you have carried a gun, have you ever threatened to fire your gun?

☐$_1$ = During this event, but never before
☐$_2$ = During this event, as well as other times prior to this event
☐$_3$ = Once, prior to this event
☐$_4$ = More than once, prior to this event
☐$_5$ = Never threatened to fire gun
☐$_{-77}$ = Not Applicable
☐$_{-88}$ = Unknown
☐$_{-99}$ = Refused

40c4. If you have carried a gun, have you ever fired your gun at another person?

- □$_1$ = During this event, but never before
- □$_2$ = During this event, as well as other times prior to this event
- □$_3$ = Once, prior to this event
- □$_4$ = More than once, prior to this event
- □$_5$ = Never fired gun
- □$_{-77}$ = Not Applicable
- □$_{-88}$ = Unknown
- □$_{-99}$ = Refused

40c5. If you have carried a gun, how did you get your gun?

- □$_1$ = Bought it from a store
- □$_2$ = Bought it on the street
- □$_3$ = Stole it
- □$_4$ = Borrowed it
- □$_{-77}$ = Not Applicable
- □$_{-88}$ = Unknown
- □$_{-99}$ = Refused

40c6. If you have carried a gun, who owns the gun?

- □$_1$ = Patient does
- □$_2$ = Family member
- □$_3$ = Friend or Acquaintance
- □$_4$ = Stranger
- □$_{-77}$ = Not Applicable
- □$_{-88}$ = Unknown
- □$_{-99}$ = Refused

40c7. If you have carried a gun, do you feel safer while carrying a gun?

- □$_1$ = Yes
- □$_0$ = No
- □$_{-77}$ = Not Applicable
- □$_{-88}$ = Unknown
- □$_{-99}$ = Refused

◊ **(CONTINUE FROM HERE IF PATIENT ANSWERED "NO" TO #40)**

41. How often in the past year did you threaten to hurt someone?

- □$_1$ = Never
- □$_2$ = Sometimes (Less than 12 times)
- □$_3$ = Often (More than 12 times)
- □$_4$ = Almost every day
- □$_{-77}$ = Not Applicable
- □$_{-88}$ = Unknown
- □$_{-99}$ = Refused

42. Have you ever had any involvement with the criminal justice system?

- □$_A$ = Placed in a juvenile home◊ # of times:_____ Date of last placement: ____/____/____
- □$_B$ = Arrested◊ # of times:_____ Date of last arrest: ____/____/____
- □$_C$ = Adjudicated (involved in juvenile justice system)◊ # of times:_____ Date of last adjudication:___/____/____
- □$_D$ = Put on probation◊ # of times:_____ Date of last probation: ____/____/____
- □$_{-77}$ = No history of involvement with criminal justice system
- □$_{-88}$ = Unknown
- □$_{-99}$ = Refused

INTERVIEWER, IF ITEM D (PUT ON PROBATION) WAS CHECKED OFF IN QUESTION 42, ASK THE FOLLOWING QUESTION:

42a. When this incident happened, were you still on probation?

- □$_1$ = Yes
- □$_0$ = No
- □$_{-77}$ = Not Applicable
- □$_{-88}$ = Unknown

43. ITEM SKIPPED

- □$_{-55}$ = Skipped

44. ITEM SKIPPED

- □$_{-55}$ = Skipped

45. ITEM SKIPPED

- □$_{-55}$ = Skipped

To Be Completed byVIP Staff:
Total Risk Stratification Score: _____

Part III. Reaction & Plans (continued)

B. Immediate Stress Reaction Checklist (Kassam-Adams, 1999)

Directions: Proceed through the following checklist with the patient, after introducing it with the following statement:

When something bad or scary happens, people have different thoughts or feelings. You've told us a little about what happened to you today/tonight. I'd like to talk more with you about what happened. The first set of items is about what you were thinking and feeling while this was happening. Tell me how true each one is for you.

WHILE IT WAS HAPPENING:	NOT TRUE	SOMEWHAT or SOMETIMES TRUE	VERY or OFTEN TRUE	Unknown -88	Refused -99
1. My mind went blank.	**0**	**1**	**2**	**-88**	**-99**
2. I did things that I didn't even know I was doing.	**0**	**1**	**2**	**-88**	**-99**
3. Things seemed to happen really slowly.	**0**	**1**	**2**	**-88**	**-99**
4. Things seemed to happen really fast	**0**	**1**	**2**	**-88**	**-99**
5. What was happening seemed unreal to me – like I was in a dream or watching a movie.	**0**	**1**	**2**	**-88**	**-99**
6. I felt like I was not there – like I was not part of what was going on.	**0**	**1**	**2**	**-88**	**-99**
7. I felt confused.	**0**	**1**	**2**	**-88**	**-99**
8. I felt numb -- like I didn't have any feelings.	**0**	**1**	**2**	**-88**	**-99**
9. People like my family or friends seemed like strangers.	**0**	**1**	**2**	**-88**	**-99**
10. Everything seemed weird, not normal	**0**	**1**	**2**	**-88**	**-99**
11. At times I was not sure where I was or what time it was.	**0**	**1**	**2**	**-88**	**-99**
12. There were times when I didn't feel any pain even where I was hurt.	**0**	**1**	**2**	**-88**	**-99**
13. I felt really scared.	**0**	**1**	**2**	**-88**	**-99**
14. I wanted to make it stop happening, but I couldn't.	**0**	**1**	**2**	**-88**	**-99**
15. I felt sick because what was happening seemed so horrible.	**0**	**1**	**2**	**-88**	**-99**

These next items are about how you are doing right now. Tell me how true each one is for you.

NOW	NOT TRUE	SOMEWHAT or SOMETIMES TRUE	VERY or OFTEN TRUE	Unknown -88	Refused -99
16. I can't remember some parts of what happened.	**0**	**1**	**2**	**-88**	**-99**
17. I can't stop thinking about what happened.	**0**	**1**	**2**	**-88**	**-99**
18. I don't want to think about what happened.	**0**	**1**	**2**	**-88**	**-99**
19. I feel jumpy.	**0**	**1**	**2**	**-88**	**-99**
20. My feelings are numb -- I feel "cut off" from my emotions.	**0**	**1**	**2**	**-88**	**-99**
21. When I think about what happened, I feel really upset.	**0**	**1**	**2**	**-88**	**-99**
22. I am trying not to remember or think about what happened to me.	**0**	**1**	**2**	**-88**	**-99**
23. I am having a hard time concentrating or paying attention.	**0**	**1**	**2**	**-88**	**-99**
24. I feel spacey or out of touch with the world around me.	**0**	**1**	**2**	**-88**	**-99**
25. Pictures or sounds from what happened keep popping into my mind.	**0**	**1**	**2**	**-88**	**-99**
26. I get upset when something reminds me of what happened.	**0**	**1**	**2**	**-88**	**-99**
27. I feel "hyper" or like I can't stay still.	**0**	**1**	**2**	**-88**	**-99**

Part III. Reaction & Plans

C. Anger Expression & Attitude to Emotional Expression Scales

I am going to read to you a number of statements that young people use to describe themselves when they feel angry or very angry. Listen to each statement carefully and decide if it is hardly ever, or sometimes, or often true for you. There are no right or wrong answers. Remember, choose hardly ever, sometimes, or often to describe how you usually feel or act when you are angry or very angry.

1. I show my temper.	Hardly Ever	Sometimes	Often	Unknown -88	Refused -99
2. I hold my anger in.	Hardly Ever	Sometimes	Often	Unknown -88	Refused -99
3. I do things like slam doors.	Hardly Ever	Sometimes	Often	Unknown -88	Refused -99
4. I hide my anger.	Hardly Ever	Sometimes	Often	Unknown -88	Refused -99
5. I attack whatever it is that makes me angry.	Hardly Ever	Sometimes	Often	Unknown -88	Refused -99
6. I get mad inside but I don't show it.	Hardly Ever	Sometimes	Often	Unknown -88	Refused -99
7. I say mean things.	Hardly Ever	Sometimes	Often	Unknown -88	Refused -99
8. I can stop myself from losing my temper.	Hardly Ever	Sometimes	Often	Unknown -88	Refused -99
9. I lose my temper.	Hardly Ever	Sometimes	Often	Unknown -88	Refused -99
10. I'm afraid to show my anger.	Hardly Ever	Sometimes	Often	Unknown -88	Refused -99

The next few sentences are about sharing feelings with others. Please listen to each question and then decide if you disagree very much, somewhat disagree, have no opinion, somewhat agree, or agree very much with each of the following statements.

1=Disagree very much 2 = Somewhat disagree 3=No opinion 4=Somewhat agree 5=Agree very much
(-88 = Unknown, data unavailable -99 = Refused to Answer)

1. I think you should always keep your feelings under control.	1	2	3	4	5	-88	-99
2. I think you should not burden other people with your feelings.	1	2	3	4	5	-88	-99
3. I think getting emotional is a sign of weakness.	1	2	3	4	5	-88	-99
4. I think other people don't understand your feelings.	1	2	3	4	5	-88	-99

Would you be interested in any of the following programs if they were available at low cost to you? (Check all that apply):

Recreation

- □A = Sports
- □B = Arts/singing & music
- □C = Outdoor activities/summer camp

Youth Development

- □A = Help finding a job
- □B = Big Brother/Big Sister
- □C = Computer Class
- □D = GED Class
- □E = Finding someone to talk to about about my feelings/problems
- □F = Parenting Class/Support Group
- □G = Drug or Alcohol Program

Young people sometimes have different feelings and ideas. I am going to read you 10 different groups of ideas and feelings. I want you to pick one sentence that describes you best for the past two weeks. There is no right or wrong answer. Just pick the sentence that best describes the way you have been recently. Remember, pick out the sentences that describe you best in the PAST TWO WEEKS.

Item 1. ☐Unknown or ☐Refused

- ☐ I am sad once in a while. (0)
- ☐I am sad many times. (1)
- ☐I am sad all time. (2)

Item 2. ☐Unknown or ☐Refused

- ☐Nothing will ever work out for me. (2)
- ☐I am not sure if things will work out for me. (1)
- ☐Things will work out for me O.K. (0)

Item 3. ☐ Unknown or ☐ Refused

- ☐ I do most things O.K. (0)
- ☐I do many things wrong. (1)
- ☐I do everything wrong. (2)

Item 4. ☐Unknown or ☐Refused

- ☐ I hate myself. (2)
- ☐I do not like myself. (1)
- ☐I like myself. (0)

Item 5. ☐Unknown or ☐Refused

- ☐I feel like crying everyday. (2)
- ☐I feel like crying many days. (1)
- ☐I feel like crying once in a while. (0)

Item 6. ☐Unknown or ☐Refused

- ☐Things bother me all the time. (2)
- ☐Things bother me many times. (1)
- ☐Things bother me once in a while. (0)

Item 7. ☐Unknown or ☐Refused

- ☐I look O.K. (0)
- ☐There are some bad things about my looks. (1)
- ☐I look ugly. (2)

Item 8. ☐Unknown or ☐Refused

- ☐I do not feel alone. (0)
- ☐I feel alone many times. (1)
- ☐I feel alone all the time. (2)

Item 9. ☐Unknown or ☐Refused

- ☐I have plenty of friends. (0)
- ☐I have some friends but I wish I had more. (1)
- ☐I do not have any friends. (2)

Item 10. ☐Unknown or ☐Refused

- ☐Nobody really loves me. (2)
- ☐I am not sure if anybody loves me. (1)
- ☐I am sure that somebody loves me. (0)

Total Score: ________

Version 01/14/03

18

Appendix 3: Violence Intervention Project Immediate Safety Screen: Physician Form

Violence Intervention Project: PHYSICIAN FORM

Physicians: Please complete this form for ALL patients ages 12-24 years old with intentional injuries (not suicide/child abuse)

Patient Name (Last, First): ______________________ ED Date: ___/___/___ Hospital: ☐ CHOP ☐ HUP
MRN: ____________________ OR Place Sticker Here

****

Physicians: Please say to patient: "I am going to ask you some questions. Everything you tell me will be kept private unless I know that you or someone else is in serious danger of being hurt. In that case, we will need to tell the appropriate agencies to protect you or that other person."

Question			
1. Do you know who the person is that hurt you?	☐ YES	☐ POSSIBLY	☐ NO
2. Do you want to report this incident to the police? *Check here if incident has already been reported:* ☐	☐ YES		☐ NO
3. Are you concerned about your safety after you leave the hospital today?	☐ YES	☐ POSSIBLY	☐ NO
4a. Do you plan to hurt anyone because of what happened today?	☐ YES	☐ POSSIBLY	☐ NO
4b. Do you think that any of your friends or family members will hurt someone because of what happened today?	☐ YES	☐ POSSIBLY	☐ NO

If "Yes" or "Possibly" to any of these questions, urgent referral is needed:

Check which referral(s) made:
___ Social Work ◊ Social Worker's Name: ____________
___ PAAN* (PAAN Hotline: 215-685-9521)
___ Other: ____________
___ Domestic Violence Agency: 215-386-7777

*PAAN=Philadelphia Anti-Drug/Anti-Violence Network, a 24-hour citywide crisis service to intervene with violent incidents.

Physicians: Please complete the following information:

5. Physician Name: ______________________ Date: ___/___/_____

6. Specialty: ___ Pediatrics ___ Emergency Medicine ___ Internal Medicine ___ Family Medicine ___ Pediatric Emergency Medicine ___ Other: ____________

7. Level of Training: ___ 1st Year ___ 2nd Year ___ 3rd Year ___ 4th Year ___ Fellow ___ Attending

Place this form in patient chart when completed. Thank you!

Chapter 3

Approaching Violently Injured Youth: Making the Most Out of an Emergency Department Encounter

Kenneth R. Ginsburg, MD, MS Ed

Introduction

When victims of violence arrive as trauma stats, doctors and nurses rally quickly to enhance their chances for survival. It seems so clear precisely which steps need to be taken when emergency staff follow well-designed protocols as they react to life-threatening injury. It is far less clear how to prevent such an injury.

Clinicians who see adolescents in an emergency setting are ideally positioned to prevent severe violence-related injury. Young people who present to us with minor injuries related to fighting, or with drug-related concerns, may be more likely to present in the future with other, perhaps more serious, violence-related injuries. We should continue to suture their lacerations, treat their fractures, and apply ice to their contusions—but we should think seriously about how to optimize those precious few moments where we may be able to assess patients for further risk and point them toward healthier futures.

Perhaps because of our inability to comprehensively address the complex factors that increase violence risk, some may question whether doctors and nurses even have a role in prevention. However, emergency staff hold a unique position in society because they see youth at great risk while they are feeling particularly vulnerable. This vulnerability may make them unusually receptive to life-saving messages. Further, emergency staff offer a valued service, are usually highly respected by teenagers, and can make a natural transition from treating injury toward guidance for injury prevention.

Certainly the emergency department (ED) must remain focused on acute care and cannot become a setting for youth to get comprehensive services. Time will always be a precious commodity in the medical setting, and any suggestions to increase clinicians' burden will have to respond adequately to the concerns over limited time and whether or not an investment of time produces any change in outcome. The premise of this chapter is that the ED may be an ideal place for assessment, brief interventions, and referral to appropriate community-based resources.

The research base does not exist to allow for a clear outline of precisely which approaches and interventions will work in the emergency setting to prevent future injury. Therefore, this chapter's aim is to increase the reader's general comfort level in communicating with adolescents, expose the reader to assessment and behavioral change techniques, and help the reader consider how best to set the stage for an appropriate referral. Because the very same vulnerable youth who is receptive to change is also easy to alienate and shame, behavioral interventions with teenagers can backfire. Therefore, considerable attention will be paid in this chapter to "doing no harm."

While this chapter will refer to some theoretical constructs that suggest how to approach youth, much of it will be based on the author's clinical experience working with youth who have existed in a violent world. The interactions used as examples will be drawn from a variety of settings including the primary care setting, the ED, a shelter that serves homeless youth, and directly from interactions on the streets with marginalized teenagers. Ultimately, our youth deserve the rigorous outcome studies that will point us toward the interventions likely to produce the best outcomes.

This chapter is divided into four interrelated sections. The first section will offer an overview on approaching youth and will focus on approaching youth from a strengths-based perspective while avoiding instilling shame. The second section will discuss strategies for assessing youth for current and future risk for violent injury. The third section will offer general approaches for offering behavioral interventions and will give specific examples of brief interventions. The final section will discuss strategies for referral to appropriate community-based resources and further counseling.

Section I: Approaching Youth: Addressing Risk While Building on Strength and Avoiding Shame

When we work with adolescents, our intention is to treat their injury and lower their risk of future injury. However, some of the approaches used to lower their risk may not be the most effective and may even hold the potential of doing harm. The classic approach to "at-risk" youth is to first assess their risk and then to inform them of the dangers their behaviors pose, ideally while giving them the education to help them change their behavior. This approach may work for some highly motivated youth who are prepared to change. However, it may frustrate others because though it successfully motivates them, it leaves them without the tools or resources to change. Further, others may feel offended or judged and could be left alienated from the health care system.

Though many youth sport a brave facade in the ED and even go out of their way to demonstrate that they do not care, it would be a mistake to assume that they are genuinely fearless. In fact, youth injured as a result of violence may be embarrassed or ashamed for a variety of reasons ranging from their antisocial behavioral to their frustration with getting injured rather than clearly winning the fight. At the least, they are feeling vulnerable in an unfamiliar setting, and may fear what will happen to them after they leave the relative safety of a medical setting. While this vulnerability may make them unusually receptive to the opportunity to alter their life direction, it may also make them particularly sensitive to a perceived slight. If the young person experiences shame, then an opportunity for change may be missed and the increased tension and anger may make the youth at greater risk to continue the cycle of violence and retaliation.

Teenagers have offered their view on what characteristics of doctors and nurses they find attractive and which they find offensive (Ginsberg et al., 1995; Ginsberg et al., 1997; Ginsberg et al., 2002a, 2002b). It is clear that they desire clinicians who are honest, respectful, honor their privacy, and do not judge them, while they are offended when they are spoken to in a condescending manner. Certainly, all caregivers strive to be honest and respectful. It is not clear, however, how teenagers interpret an interaction as respectful versus disrespectful, or as enlightening versus condescending. This author believes that youth approached from a strengths-based perspective are less likely to feel offended and more likely to feel respected and valued.

There is a dynamic tension between two different approaches to youth. The risk-based approach assesses for risk and targets issues for which the young person is considered to be at greatest risk. The resiliency or youth-development approach acknowledges risk, but looks instead at how to build protective factors. In the case of a young person who is the victim or perpetrator of violence who presents to the ED, it is clear that their risk is further violence. It would therefore be unwise to ignore that risk. But it would also be unwise to see patients only in the context of one injury because we will miss the opportunity for them to gain the confidence to change. That confidence comes through the recognition that they have existing assets that can be built upon.

Resilience theorists sought to explore why some people from very difficult environmental circumstances rise above their surroundings and thrive. Proponents of the strengths-based approach are not blind to risk, rather they seek to uncover and enhance protective forces in a young person's life. Before I offer examples to illustrate how to integrate the strengths-based approach into clinical care, it may be worthwhile to gain a broader perspective on resiliency, which lies at the core of this clinical style.

Resiliency

Though no standard definition of resilience exists, all theorists describe an individual's capability to respond successfully to adversity. Freiberg describes resilience as "the ability to learn from, and seek out, positive elements of the environment without replicating the disabling elements" (Freiberg, 1993). Howard describes a resilient individual as one who is capable of changing his or her environment to his or her advantage.(Howard, 1996) Wright states, "Resiliency is the ability to successfully overcome the effects of a high risk environment and to develop social competence despite exposure to severe stress" (Wright, 1996).

Resilience is not a fixed attribute, however. One's capacity for resilience changes with circumstances and operates most critically at turning points in one's life (Blechman et al., 1995). It must be stressed that resilience is not synonymous with invulnerability (Franklin, 1995; Blum, 1998). Thus, we must recognize that even resilient youth are subject to the difficult experiences of their environment and may need continued support to foster and strengthen their resiliency at crisis points. This is an important point to consider in the context of the emergency setting—by definition a crisis point.

The classic model for dealing with troubled youth has been the Damage Model, which states that dysfunctional families, communities, or societies cause tremendous harm to their members. This model tends to view young adults from those environments as passive participants in difficult situations that lead to psychopathology. An alternative model, the Challenge Model, acknowledges the problems of these youth but interprets difficulties as challenging opportunities. In this model, youth are made to realize the unique strength they possess in having rebounded from hardships, instead of succumbing to them (Wolin and Wolin, 1997; Wolin, 1995).

The process of guiding youth to recognize their own strengths involves three stages. First, adults must credit youth with the strength and the potential to recover and bounce back from hardship. This honors their power to help themselves, and casts professionals as partners rather than as directors of the change process (Wolin, 1995). Second, youth must acknowledge others' strength. In so doing, they can learn to value each other (Davis et al., 1994). Finally, and perhaps most importantly, youth must be guided to recognize their own innate strengths.

Development in the context of an adverse environment often leads to multiple interrelated risk behaviors. We must recognize associations that predict these behaviors and attempt to ameliorate them, but we miss an opportunity to support change when we focus on risk alone. A fundamental ideological shift needs to occur if we are to prepare youth for a productive adulthood. Though the first steps must continue to assure immediate safety and prevent harm, caring adults must not accept "problem-free" as a full success. Instead, we must communicate through our actions that we expect each adolescent to develop fully into a successful member of our society.

There are important questions that the risk recognition and reduction paradigm does not address, but that the resiliency and youth development paradigms consider of central importance:

- Why do some youth from the same adverse environments thrive?
- How do we see beyond risk behaviors to recognize the strengths youth employ to negotiate a challenging environment?
- How do we support an individual to use those existing strengths to fuel a shift from survival strategies that may be maladaptive to prosocial, adaptive strategies?
- How do we buttress supports external to the individual, such as those from the family, school, church, or neighborhood, to support the young person to transition toward prosocial behaviors?

Protective Factors Fostering Resiliency

The root of resiliency lies in the existence of protective factors within a young adult's environment (Mundy, 1996; Hoge et al., 1996; Guetzloe, 1994; Nettles and Pleck, 1993; Floyd, 1996; Braverman et al., 1994). The personal characteristics that have been shown to be protective include effective problem-solving skills, a happy temperament, a sense of purpose, social competence, and autonomy or an internal locus of control. The literature also emphasizes the role of the family in providing nurturing relationships, faith in overcoming adversity, an expectation that the young adult will help with chores and other responsibilities, and a belief in his/her innate abilities for the future. Finally, the community can establish strong social networks, a nurturing and responsive school, a strong relationship with a teacher or other adult outside the home, and various opportunities for youth to participate in meaningful tasks. In the case of an emergency setting, staff are situated to impart some of the protective messages that ideally come from family members.

The Four Cs of Resiliency Building Programs

Little and Blum describe four basic traits to be promoted in youth as a means to build long-standing resiliency. These four characteristics have come to be known as "the four Cs" and include competence, confidence, connectedness, and character (Blum, 1998).

Competence

Youths' competence correlates directly with their belief that they have control over their environment (Kliewer and Sandler, 1992; McMillan et al, 1992; Sagor, 1996). For example, individuals from at-risk environments who experience an internal locus of control will perform better on exams and achieve better grades than those with an external locus of control (Floyd, 1996; Enger et al., 1994; Gordon, 1996). In order to develop competence, it becomes critical that youth are given opportunities to feel in control.

The focus of the literature on competence building is on providing youth experiences of responsibility, autonomy, and success. Youth must be given opportunities to excel, doing work that challenges them but that they can accomplish (Wolin and Wolin, 1996). Every person has an "island of competence," something at which he or she excels, even if they feel they are drowning in an "ocean of inadequacy" (Brooks, 1994). These islands are potential sources of pride and achievement. ED staff should seek positive attributes in patients and help them to recognize those attributes. Only after this has been achieved can helping adults move on to areas that are less secure and help build overall competence. A young person's ability to cope with life stressors is tightly linked with competence (Smith and Carlson, 1997).

Confidence

Confidence is the subjective belief that one has competence. It is linked with optimistic attitudes and a belief in the value of perseverance. Youth who have not succeeded in classically recognized areas (school, the world of work) might not believe they have the capability to do so. Without this confidence, they may not feel comfortable fully engaging in a process of change.

Related to confidence, one of the protective factors found within the resilient individual is an internal locus of control. That is, one believes that he or she has power over his or her environment. This stands in contrast to an external locus of control, in which a person views him/herself as powerless or passive. Some experts believe that locus of control is the most consistent measure of one's ability to buffer stress (Kliewer and Sandler, 1992; McMillan et al., 1992; Gordon, 1996). By developing an internal locus of control and thus the feeling that one can dictate events, one can drastically reduce the negative impact of events. This becomes an essential step in reducing the effects of risk factors, thereby decreasing the odds of poor outcomes for these youth. An intervention program targeted at youth in high-risk situations can decrease negative outcomes by either altering youths' exposure to risks or by altering the meaning of experiences (Smith and Carlson, 1997). The subjective interpretation of an event will determine its effect on a particular individual.

Connectedness

A critical component in the development of resiliency is the presence of a close bond with at least one other person, adult or peer, who can provide stability and much needed attention to youth (Wright, 1996; Davis et al., 1994; Mundy, 1996; Embry, 1997; Pittman, 1996). The significance of a supportive peer group and mentorship from an adult in the lives of individuals from troubled environments has been emphasized repeatedly (Franklin, 1995; Blum, 1998; Brooks, 1994; Gregory, 1995; Greene, 1993). The most consistent theme in the youth development and resiliency literatures is that guidance and support from a caring adult is pivotal in determining whether a young person can overcome challenges (Blum, 1998; Mundy, 1996; Resnick, 2000). Brooks writes that in order to foster resiliency, every youth needs one supportive relationship with an adult who will help him or her unconditionally. Bowen and Chapman state that efforts to promote adaptation must be directed towards increasing youth's sense of social support, particularly from parents, neighbors, and teachers.

Character

It is worth noting that a young person could be highly competent, overly confident, and deeply connected (e.g., a gang member), and still not be seen as resilient because they cannot thrive in a broader context. Character, therefore, is an important ingredient in assuring success. Character is built "through values that give meaning and direction to youth, such as individual responsibility, honesty, community service, responsible decision-making, and integrity in relationships" (Blum, 1998). Some of these character traits are quite personal, and may be the most difficult to foster. However, Gregory (1995) describes those who turn their lives around as recognizing the personal need to change. He considers such individuals to be motivated by pride and by a desire not to be failures.

One program that has concentrated on character building has been designed to make an individual recognize others' points of view. In this model, conflicts become mutual problems, having optimal solutions that can only be achieved by cooperation between parties, each one considering the other's needs and then formulating a resolution accordingly (Van Slyck, et al., 1996). It may be particularly challenging in an emergency setting, when a young person's thoughts are focused on survival, to get him to see another person's perspective. However, it also may be of particular importance to understand others' perspective if the cycle of violence is to be stopped.

How Do We Develop Protective Factors?

First, we must recognize that resiliency is not something innate, but rather something that can and must be fostered throughout development. Theorists have conceptualized how programs can develop protective factors in youth differently, but each paradigm is instructive.

Wolin and Wolin discuss seven resiliencies (Wolin and Wolin, 1996):

- Relationships—close ties to other people.
- Insight—the ability to recognize the signs of problems in others and to not take blame for one's life circumstances. For example, a young adult whose mother is drug addicted coming to recognize that the problem's origin lies with the mother and not something the individual did to drive the mother to drugs.
- Independence—getting away from one's family and problems, perhaps by taking jobs or becoming involved in after-school activities.
- Initiative—the development of competence to solve one's problems.
- Creativity—taking the difficult and learning to deal with it through art, imagination, or dance.
- Humor.
- Morality—principled behavior and decision-making; sticking up for others.

Karen Pittman of the International Youth Foundation advocates for a resiliency-based model because "problem-free is not fully prepared" (Pittman, 1996). The International Youth Foundation outlines seven community (or program) supports that promote healthy youth development:

1) Stable places.
2) Basic care and services.
3) Healthy relationships with peers and adults.

4) High expectations and standards.
5) Role models, resources, and networks.
6) Challenging experiences and opportunities to participate and contribute.
7) High-quality instruction and training.

Applying a Strengths-Based Approach in a Clinical Setting

An understanding of resiliency may be a first step in shifting from a risk-based approach, in which clinicians may inadvertently communicate low expectations to youth, to a strengths-based approach, in which clinicians communicate they expect the best from youth. Many adolescents have far too many encounters with adults who expect the worst of them. It may be harmful for them to reexperience the shame and disrespect that comes from adults expecting their failure when they come to us for treatment.

When we focus our clinical energies on helping patients overcome worrisome behaviors, we run the danger of only conceptualizing their lives in terms of risk—they are using drugs, affiliated with gangs, etcetera (Figure 1). Then we tell our young patients to "Stop that!" and proceed to give them several rea-

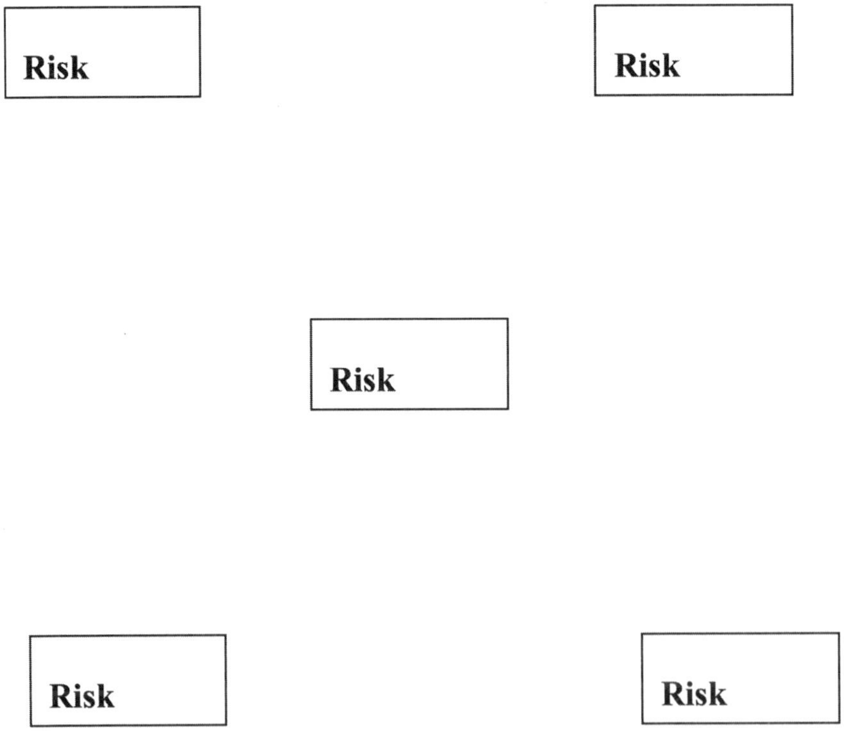

Figure 1. Risk-Based Paradigm

sons why they should change. While a well-intentioned strategy, the problem is that youth rarely alter behaviors merely because someone else points out they are failing. To help our patients develop the resiliency that will help them overcome adversity we need to see their lives differently. We must recognize the context of their lives and listen also for what they are doing right. A person affiliated with gangs understands loyalty, a drug-affected youth may be sensitive, and any patient who has shared negative behaviors with a health professional has the capacity and desire to engage helpful people. Clinicians who recognize these positive points of competency help youth acknowledge their strengths and are better positioned to guide them to build new capabilities based upon these strengths. When a young person builds upon existing competencies a ripple effect may follow that will counteract some of the forces that drive the young person to engage in risk behaviors (Figure 2).

Certainly we should continue to address risk in a manner that comprehensively assesses patients for concerning behaviors, offers them appropriate health care and information to reduce the harm incurred by those behaviors, motivates them to consider changing the behaviors, and offers them needed

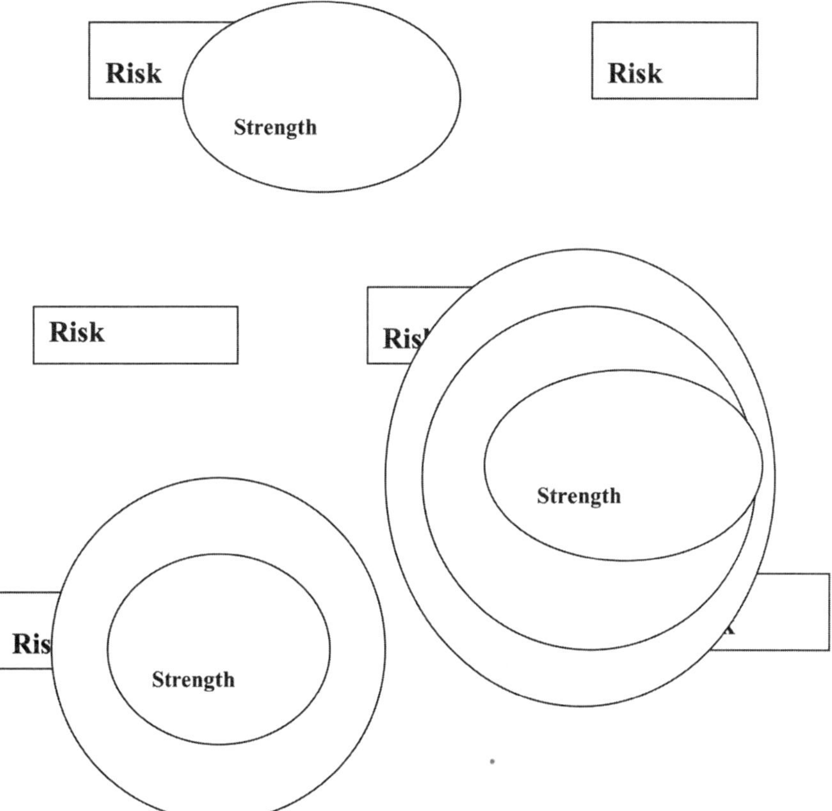

Figure 2. Strength-Based Paradigm

skills and resources to reduce their risks. Proponents of approaching youth by seeking and reinforcing their resiliency are not blind to risk, but they approach risk in the context of the young person's strengths. We believe that a positive approach not only promotes strengths, but also by showing respect lessens the likelihood of alienation and is more likely to engage the young person in reducing risk.

The shift to a strengths-based approach can be incorporated into our daily interactions with youth. Consider how clinicians conceptualize the context of patients' lives. Typically, we obtain a history, listen for risk behaviors, and then respond. When a young person discloses personal behaviors, she takes an emotional risk. Teens usually report their behaviors in a broader context (*"I get in fights because . . ." "when I am really stressed out, I . . ."*). When we focus on the negative, a young person wonders, *"Did that doctor hear who I am or what I've experienced? Why does s/he notice only what I have done wrong?"* We must learn to listen to youth both for the health issues that we may need to address and for what makes the young person special, what makes us really care for him or her. Then, instead of responding only to what she is doing wrong, we put her positive and negative attributes and behaviors in context, and then ask permission to address it. Adults rarely ask a young person permission before they begin sharing their opinion, but when they do the young person is much more likely to be listening. *"I really appreciate your sharing your story with me* (insert what is special about them, what you could see them accomplishing, why you recognize them as strong) . . . pause, deep breath, . . . *"but I'm left feeling worried that (insert problem) may get you injured or get in the way of your succeeding as much as I believe you can. I want to be more than just a guy who addresses (the problem) today, I want to be someone who might help you get to a place where it doesn't happen again and where your future is as good as you deserve. Can we talk about this?"*

I recall a case of a young man engaged in drug dealing who also acknowledged that he had carried and fired a weapon for self-protection. He was an 18-year-old homeless man who silently entered the office with his eyes fixed on the floor. His right to privacy was explained. He was reassured how much I respected, rather than judged, young people who had survived the streets when they were taking steps to improve their situation. His eyes began to leave the floor and he slowly revealed the challenging life he had survived, including the constant dangers of dealing drugs. *"But, at least I was able to eat, and sometimes I didn't have to sleep on the subway."* He spoke of how disturbing it was to have people fear him, and cross the street as he strolled by always assuming the worst of him. With only glimpses of emotion, he described how difficult it was to survive, always running from authorities, vulnerable to street violence, and witnessing drug addicts self-destructing. He spoke of how flashing his gun repeatedly saved his life and that when he had to go as far as to shoot at someone, he always aimed to miss. I listened as he told how he had reached his rock bottom when he watched a stranger nearly die from a drug overdose. He was sickened as "the suits" walked by with no apparent interest. But, he did not allow the stranger to die. Heroically, the young man called 911 and kept her awake until the ambulance arrived. This was the point of intervention. I simply asked, *"How did you—a guy so many feared—manage to maintain your soul and your sense of caring and responsibility when all of 'the suits' were willing to just walk by and let that girl die?"* Guided to recognize his own strength, the young patient cried openly for the first time since he was a boy. Building upon his acknowledged humanity, the shelter staff helped him develop a plan to shift his life direction. Respectful, active and intent listening, rather than teaching or preaching, allows clinicians to see the best in people as young people reveal their strengths. The simple act of recognizing those strengths can catalyze change.

Finally, when we work with youth we must move beyond telling them what behaviors to avoid; we must reinforce for them what to do. Figure 3 simplistically illustrates the importance of healthy coping strategies in the lives of youth. Stress is a driving force toward risky behaviors because some antisocial coping strategies lessen uncomfortable feelings in the short term. However, these same behaviors can be quite destructive in the short term (e.g., violence) or in the long term (e.g., drugs). Virtually all of the behaviors we worry about in adolescents serve as coping strategies (e.g., substance use, sexual activity, violence, self-mutilation, gang affiliation, teen pregnancy, and disordered eating). When we simply respond to these behaviors by saying "Stop that!" we are doomed to fail and are put into direct conflict with the young person. Instead, we must first help an individual to understand that the way they have figured to deal with the circumstances of their lives may be effective, but also is likely to be harmful. Then we guide them to develop prosocial coping strategies that can be used both as immediate and lifelong stress reduction tools and that may even improve the quality of their lives and their communities. This model does not suggest we can prevent experimentation or limit testing, but we certainly can diminish an adolescent's need to rely on easy, but dangerous, coping strategies.

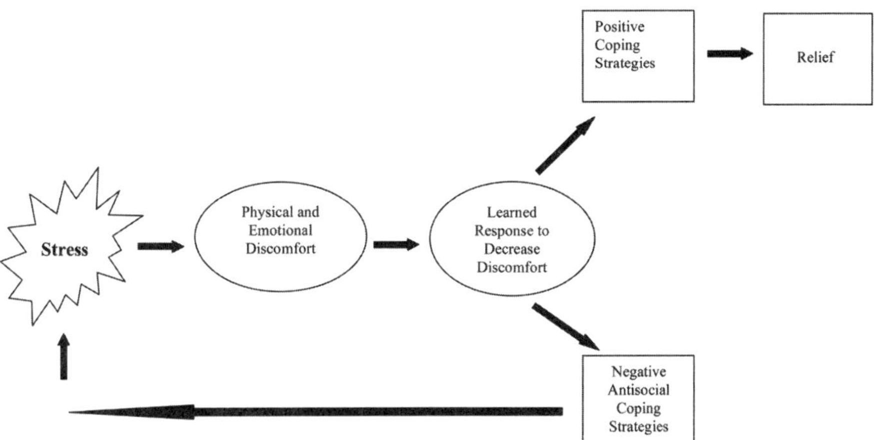

Figure 3. Building Strength Through the Development of Positive Coping Strategies

Coping strategies are generally divided into problem-focused and emotion-focused. Problem-focused strategies attempt to deal with the problem and emotion-focused strategies attempt to deal with the emotional reaction to the problem. For example, a problem-focused response to living in a violent environment would be to learn conflict resolution. An emotion-focused response would be to release fear or anxiety through rage. Generally, adolescents with more problem-focused strategies have fewer adjustment problems (Van Slyck et al., 1996; Wolin and Wolin, 1996).

Regardless of whether the strategy is problem- or emotion-focused, it may be prosocial (positive) or antisocial (negative) in nature. For example, a youth can respond to academic pressure by studying or by smoking marijuana to relax. A youth could respond to feelings of anger or frustration by fighting or through exercise. A young person could respond to a sense of worthlessness by victimizing others to experience power, or by taking responsibility for the well-being of a younger sibling. In all cases the person has successfully coped, but with very different outcomes. Blechman writes that a "competence-oriented worldview...equates mental health with relative success at coping prosocially with the challenges inherent in a chaotic and often hostile social environment." However, she notes that " in many cultures and contexts, antisocial aggression (moving against others) and asocial depression (withdrawing from others) are statistically normal and instrumental methods of coping with and surviving physical and psychological challenges" (Blechman et al, 1995).

It should be our goal to have every young person develop a rich repertoire of positive coping strategies because youth so equipped are prepared to overcome adversity and will achieve a sense of confidence in their ability to handle new situations. Further, effective prosocial coping strategies are essential tools to succeed in the adult world. Support toward developing these strategies is ideally proactive, but must be offered even when stress is acute because it is at these times that youth are tempted to return to destructive, but comfortable, coping strategies.

Section II: Assessment

The medical setting is an important venue to assess youth for potential problems before crises strike. For many youth, a primary care medical setting is the only place where they get to see an adult repeatedly in a confidential setting. Because so many of the readers of this chapter will see adolescents in both a primary and an emergency setting, a comprehensive psychosocial screen will be presented. In the emergency setting, it is unlikely that clinicians will have the time to perform a comprehensive screen; rather they will likely target specific behaviors. In the case of the young person presenting with a violence-related injury, issues around school performance, stress and mental health, and drug use and dealing should be included in the screen as well as the issues more directly associated with safety.

Setting the Stage

No matter the depth of the screen, it is important for the clinician to create a zone of safety that will make it more likely that the adolescent will feel safe disclosing important, but potentially sensitive or personal information.

Creating a Zone of Safety Verbally

The typical adolescent in the health care setting expects to get evaluated and treated—not to be asked to disclose personal information. If the clinician does not "set the stage" and create a safe zone for open communication, the history obtained is likely to be false and the patient is unlikely to be receptive to guidance. In an emergency room setting, the caregiver can make a transitional statement such as *"I know that you came here for me to treat your injury, but I think it is an important part of my job to make sure you avoid future injuries. I'd like to be able to talk to you about this, and that may involve us talking about some subjects that don't seem so obviously related to your injury. First, let me tell you a few things about the way I will ask questions and how I'll deal with the answers to make sure that you feel comfortable talking to me."*

Adolescents will not—and perhaps, should not—disclose personal information without first having a sense of the following questions: 1) Why is the clinician asking personal questions? 2) What will he or she do with the answers; will I be judged or have my business spread around? 3) Is it worth my sharing private information; can this person even do anything to help me? After addressing all of these issues, the limits of confidentiality need to be discussed. Use the word "privacy" instead of "confidentiality" because many adolescents misinterpret the word "confidential" as "confidence." If the limits of privacy are not addressed before obtaining the history, the clinician risks losing the patient's trust if she needs to intervene. Confidentiality is the accepted norm in most states in the adolescent-provider relationship; however, the caregiver is required to intervene if suicidal or homicidal plans or a history of abuse is disclosed. Do not use the standard phrase, *"I will keep your information private unless I am worried you will hurt yourself, hurt someone else, or if an adult is hurting you."* This statement does not even begin to help adolescents understand their rights in the health care setting. For example, adolescents know that doctors think cigarettes "hurt" them, and would therefore assume they cannot disclose smoking. The teenager should be assured that if the interviewer needs to break privacy to save her life or protect her safety, it will first be discussed with the teenager who will be allowed to help strategize how best to deal with her safety issues. Ideally, the parent(s) can be included in this conversation. If they are present, they will understand that this is a strategy to encourage open communication, that there are boundaries to confidentiality in life-threatening situations, and that the clinician will be an advocate of appropriate parental involvement. Once the parents understand the importance of privacy and after they have had the opportunity to offer their concerns, the screen should proceed without parents in the room.

SSHADESS

Strengths, School, Home, Activities, Drugs and other Substances, Emotions, Sexuality, Safety

Strengths

It is nice to begin an interview by allowing the adolescent to have an opportunity to describe himself. A question such as *"How would you describe yourself?"* is sure to be met with *"What do you mean?"* This gives the interviewer the opportunity to say something like *"Well, tell me the best thing about yourself, tell me what you are most proud of."* Some young people will remain at a loss, giving the interviewer a great deal of information about the patient's self-image. In this case, the interviewer can try the followup question , *"Well, how would your best friends describe you?"*

School

School commitment and academic achievement are important individual protective factors. School performance reveals a great deal about overall well-being. Worrisome responses such as *"I don't go to school"* are predictive of other problems. Also ask, *"What would you like to do when you get older?"* The response to this question can be revealing, as youth with no plans may not believe they even have a future, and consequently may put themselves at greater risk.

Home

Most teenagers have challenging relationships with their parents, but it is important to determine when the relationship is reaching crisis proportions. Families in crisis can be helped with family interventions that foster appropriate communication and discipline. It is always important to ask, *"Is your home a safe place for you?"*

Activities

Peer relationships are of exceptional importance to the teenager. Knowing what a patient's friends are doing offers a strong clue into what type of negative pressures the patient is likely to encounter. Further, a youth with "nothing to do" is more likely to fill time with negative behaviors. A relationship with a caring adult also plays a protective role in a youth's life. Research has shown that such adult support is significantly and inversely correlated with violent behavior among urban youth (Salts et al., 1995).

Finally, the constructive use of free time is an important protective factor for youth. Engagement in youth programs, religious communities, and creative activities increases youth access to caring adults, prevents involvement in risky behaviors, and encourages other positive behaviors (CCAD, 1992; Ginsberg et al., 2002).

Drugs/Substance Use

Drug use and drug dealing contribute sharply to violent injuries. If a patient states that he is using drugs, an important followup question is *"Some people use drugs for fun, but most people use drugs to forget about some kind of uncomfortable feeling, like being sad, nervous, or stressed. How about you, why do you use (name of drug)?"* The answer will often give the interviewer an opportunity to offer resources that can address the underlying problem.

Many youth will not acknowledge that they deal drugs even after confidentiality has been assured. It is reasonable to ask, *"Are any of your friends involved in selling drugs?"* If they endorse having friends who deal drugs, the interviewer still has the opportunity to later address the subject of drug dealing without accusing the youth of withholding information.

Emotions/ Depression

Mental health problems in an adolescent can inhibit his or her ability to process information and to gain insight into the causes of behavioral problems. Violently injured youth, because of their victimization, are at greater risk for the development of mental health problems such as depression and Post Traumatic Stress Disorder (PTSD) (McCo and Finkelhor, 1996). Poor mental health has also been associated with an increase in violent behavior (Ellickson et al., 1997).

Suicide, violence turned inward, is the second greatest source of mortality among adolescents (CDC, 2004). While most youth do not seek medical care related to the event, many seek care for routine health concerns in the week or months preceding the attempt (Hawton et al. 1992; Slap et al., 1989; Smith and Crawford, 1986). They may present with a hidden agenda or somatic complaint in a conscious or subconscious help-seeking gesture (Porter et al, 1997; Capelli, et al., 1995; Schneider et al, 1995).

While most adolescents who commit suicide are depressed, some are impulsive. Many depressed youth do not exhibit classic vegetative signs; rather they act out with rage. This is particularly relevant for adolescents presenting to the emergency setting with an injury. For these reasons, all teenagers should be screened for depression and suicidality. If any response is worrisome, a more detailed screen should include past history of suicide attempts by the patient or someone close to them, existence and lethality of a suicide plan, and access to the means to fulfill the plan, particularly access to a firearm. Patients with suicidal intention or strong ideation must be immediately referred to mental health services and held under protective watch until they are thoroughly assessed by a mental health professional.

Many teenagers who present to health care with mental health issues do so discretely. Rather than presenting with a chief complaint of "I am feeling sad/stressed/worried/nervous/suicidal" they present with somatic symptoms, either because they are stress-related symptoms that the adolescent does not yet have the insight to understand, or because they may be reaching out for help.

Sexuality
There are many chief complaints that would present in an emergency setting that would necessitate a full sexual health assessment. However, a full sexual health assessment is beyond the scope of this chapter. One aspect of sexual health that is relevant here is the health of the adolescent's relationship. It is certainly reasonable to ask, *"Does he treat you well?"* A follow-up question of *"Does he get jealous?"* can be helpful at assessing for early stages of domestic violence. Teenagers may not understand the early stages of a controlling relationship, and may actually feel flattered by what they perceive to be innocent jealousy. For this reason, they sometimes report jealousy with a degree of pride, allowing the interviewer an important opportunity for education.

Because sexual minority youth are more likely to be victims of violence and to contemplate suicide, (Garofalo et al, 1999; Allen and Glicken, 1996; Remafedi et al, 1991; Remafedi et al, 1998; Safren and Heimburg, 1999; Savin-Williams, 1994; Hershberger and D'Augelli, 1995) it is vital that the interviewer not assume heterosexuality, and asks about sexuality from a genuinely nonjudgmental stance (Ginsberg et al, 2002).

Safety
The final part of a comprehensive psychosocial assessment for adolescents deals with violence and safety.

Creating a Zone of Safety Using Body Language

Remember that no matter how tough young people appear, they are strangers to the medical setting and are likely to feel intimidated or vulnerable. There is an inherent power dynamic in a medical care setting in which the caregiver holds the power. For a youth who uses toughness and "attitude" as a defensive posture when feeling powerless, this can set the tone for a hostile interaction. Further, remember that many youth are used to being held to very low expectation, and that youth tend to live up to (or down to) adults' expectation of them.

Below are a few general body language rules to follow to convey that you are nonjudgmental, that you expect the best from the patient, and that you are not intimidated—no matter how intimidating the situation.

1) During the interview, sit down close to the patient, not across the room. Standing up conveys you intend to be "in charge" and don't have the time or intent to really listen.
2) Speak with a gentle soft tone. If the patient gets louder and hostile, speak softer in an equal and opposite manner.
3) Watch your body language. Assuming a protective posture sends the message that you are intimidated. Learn to relax your shoulders, and don't cross your legs or keep your hands across your chest.
4) Shake hands warmly. This will do wonders in communicating that you are only there to serve the patient and have no intent of judging. It also communicates that you expect the best and are not intimidated.
5) If you are a man, take special care not to stand chest to chest with a young man, because this will be interpreted as a hostile stance. Either sit or assure that you stand at a slight angle. This is the natural position for two men to stand, but if a teenager is becoming hostile, you may find yourself in a chest-to-chest position. While you will instinctively want to assert your power by standing taller chest to chest, and by speaking louder, you will deescalate the situation by sitting or shifting your legs so you face the patient at a more comfortable angle.

The Comprehensive Psychosocial Assessment

Once in a private setting, the young person should be asked about concerns that were not stated in the parent(s)' presence. The comprehensive psychosocial assessment should follow a few general rules:

1) Proceed from less personal to more intimate topics (SSHADESS is a mnemonic intended to remind interviewers of this rule, detailed on pages 108–109).
2) Questions should initially be focused on friends or the community; for example, *"Are many of the teens in your school getting in fights?"* or *"Is your school safe?"*
3) All questions have to be asked without judgment and the interviewer must not express shock or dismay to the responses. Guidance can be offered later; a quick or judgmental reaction disrupts further disclosure.
4) Be careful not to ask "yes/no" questions for two reasons. First, they limit the depth of the responses. Second, when you ask a sensitive question, patients who do not yet have trust in you become embarrassed to disclose honestly later. Therefore, it is better to leave some items open-ended.
5) The goal is to get the most therapeutic history, not the most thorough

history. Do not push young people further than they are ready to go.

6) Most importantly, and in keeping with the earlier discussion on incorporating a resiliency perspective into the clinical interaction, while listening to responses allow yourself to think beyond risk and consider what you most appreciate or respect about the teen. Even a teenager whose behavior offends you may have been "honest," or could be seen as a "survivor," in a world different from one you relate to. The restatement of the patient's attributes will allow you later to address risk less offensively. *"You know, I enjoyed talking to you, you have really been honest with me"* or *"That's exciting that you want to be a teacher to help kids like you, you are a very caring person . . . but, I have to tell you, I feel worried for you because . . . can we talk about that?"*

The Brief Psychosocial Screen

Because of time constraints, the comprehensive psychosocial screen cannot be incorporated into every clinical encounter. However, we know adolescents in crisis often present to medical care either with somatic symptoms related to stress or with a hidden agenda hoping that a responsible adult will figure out that they are in trouble. In fact, one study revealed that half of youth who completed suicide had seen a clinician in the previous month, and 25% in the previous week (Hawton et al., 1982). As a means to capture youth who are in an unstated acute crisis, a three-part screen can be incorporated into *any* visit. First, *"How is school going?"* Because life's stressors often adversely affect school performance, school success can serve as an important clue as to the adolescent's general well-being. Concerning responses suggest recent changes and include *"I had a bad semester," "not as well as it used to be,"* or *"I'm not going very much."* These responses offer an opportunity for the interviewer to ask, *"What has been going on, why the changes?"* However, some youth do well in school regardless of their other life stressors with school sometimes serving as a respite from other stresses. Therefore, also ask, *"Are you happy?"* or *"How's life going for you?"* followed quickly with *"When you're not happy, how do you handle it? Who do you talk to?"* The unhappy isolated youth is at risk. This adolescent deserves a thorough evaluation for depression.

The Violence Screen

The Acute Injury Setting

It is imperative to know whether the patient being treated for an acute injury is in the midst of a cycle of retaliation. *"What's going to happen now, is this over, or are you going to get even"* or *"Are people still after you?"* When asking these questions avoid use of the words "fear," "afraid," or "worried" as they might force the victim to display a false bravado. If the patient threatens the life of another individual, that information is not protected by confidentiality and ED staff are required to report the threat to the appropriate authorities.

The Acute or Routine Setting

Future Plans

A patient who has no future plans may not even expect to live. The question, *"What are you hoping to do in the future?"* may be met with a blank look or a smirk followed by an answer like *"It's hard out there, I'm living for today."*

Violence Exposure

Patients can be exposed in the home, in school or on the streets. Almost all youth have had repeated violence exposure through the media, but some youth use violent media and video games as a major means of escape and fantasy (Velicer et al., 1998). The patient so used to violence that it is seen as normative, or who sees it as the appropriate way to handle stress or conflict is clearly at risk. A patient disciplined violently may know no other way to raise their own children and will not be prepared to handle disagreement. Use every available opportunity to reinforce with parents that "discipline" means "to teach," not "to punish," and it absolutely does not mean to hurt. Of course patients can also be exposed to violence through their own history of fighting: *"Do you ever get in fights?" "Have you ever been severely injured in a fight?"*

Perception of Safety

Learning whether the patient feels safe can reveal a great deal about their risk and what steps may be taken to lower that risk. *"Do you feel safe at school?" "Are there a lot of fights at your school?" "Do people bring weapons to school?"*

Also, take this opportunity to explore for a history of physical or sexual abuse. *"Do you feel safe at home?" "Is there anyone who hurts you or touches you when you don't want to be touched?"*

Most importantly, learn what they do to make themselves feel safer. Start with an open-ended question such as *"What do you do to keep yourself safe?"* Adolescents often respond in one of two broad manners. The first convinces you they are safe because they describe the safety of their neighborhood or the steps they take to stay out of trouble. Other youth lead with *"Don't worry about me."* These youth are not prepared to divulge their behavior and are not yet comfortable that the interviewer can hear the answer without judgment. When I hear this answer I tend to respond with *"Is someone watching your back, or do you carry something for protection?"* Some youth respond, *"No, I can fight for myself, people have learned not to mess with me."* Others divulge gang affiliation or weapon carrying. Of course, many youth remain silent. If it seems appropriate, ask, *"Do you think a knife or gun would make you safer . . . do you carry one?"* Many youth believe a weapon will protect them and do not even consider that it puts them at much greater risk of death. Though an interviewer is likely to feel uncomfortable learning that a young person carries a weapon, it is important to remember that youths who carry weapons do so believing that their lives has value and deserve to be protected. Their self-protection should be acknowledged before being guided to understand that a weapon makes them more likely to be killed.

Threshold for Fighting

A great deal can be learned about a patient's volatility by exploring what it takes to get him or her to fight. *"What do you usually do when you are really mad or frustrated?" "Do you get in fights?" "Are you able to walk away from fights?" "How do you do that?"*

This is an opportunity to learn a critical marker for conflict avoidance. *"What makes you mad enough to fight?"* Essentially, there are four hierarchical strategies adolescents use to instigate fighting or to escalate a confrontation toward fighting. Different youth reach their personal threshold for fighting at different points. First, a person calls another a name, or insults or disrespects them. If this has not started the fight they move on to insult their mother, family member, or gang member. If the person is still resistant to fighting, the instigator will invade the person's body space, my teens call this *"getting in my face,"* or *"if he steps up to me."* Finally, if the "victim" has not successfully de-escalated the situation, the instigator touches, pushes, or *"puts his hands on me."* In my experience, few adolescents on the street feel able to walk away once they are touched, lest they be labeled a "punk" who can't even stand up for himself, and is therefore deserving of repeated victimization. However, when fights start in institutions with zero tolerance for fighting, potential victims can sometimes say, *"You're not even worth it,"* let off steam verbally, and then be able to walk away with their pride intact saying they don't want to get kicked out of school/the program just because of the instigator.

Section III: Promoting Positive Behaviors

Once the interviewer has set the stage for a trusting relationship and has assessed the patient for psychosocial and violence risk, she is ready to consider how best to engage the patient in a behavioral change process. If one wants to move beyond just giving facts and information to promote change—a style with very limited utility—then one first needs to have an understanding of the stages of behavioral change. With such an understanding, the clinician is able to assess the patient's current stage and is better equipped to consider how to promote the change process by facilitating the patient's movement toward a more advanced stage. Second, the clinician has to have an understanding of how adolescents at different developmental stages process information. Without this basic understanding of cognitive development, well-intentioned messages are often misunderstood and may even generate frustration or anger. Third, the doctor or nurse has to have an understanding of the social context of adolescence. In this context, peer perceptions are of extreme importance. Suggested interventions that do not take into account how a patient's change in behavior will be perceived in adolescent society are doomed to failure.

The Process of Behavioral Change

The Transtheoretical Model of Behavioral Change (TTM) is a helpful tool to conceptualize the process of change in adolescents. The TTM suggests that individuals proceed through a series of stages as they attempt to change aspects of their lives, and it offers important insights into the factors that inhibit or promote positive change at each stage. The TTM (Velicer et al., 1998) has been used to develop assessment tools and interventions for a wide variety of behaviors, including substance abuse (DiClemente and Hughes, 1990), risky sexual behaviors (Evers et al., 1998), and domestic violence (Brown, 1997) across a broad spectrum of populations, varying by gender, socioeconomic status, age and ethnicity. The TTM makes no assumption about how ready individuals are to change. It recognizes that individuals will begin at different stages, and it is designed to allow interventions to be targeted to the specific needs of the individual and his or her current level of readiness for change (Velicer et al., 1998). The TTM offers an effective model for supporting and guiding violently injured youth as they move through the stages of change, away from behaviors that put them at risk for future violence, such as weapon-carrying and fighting, and toward behaviors that are protective, such as family and school connectedness. The TTM predicts that youth will progress through the following stages of change:

1) Precontemplation (youth has no intention of changing or denies need for change);
2) Contemplation (youth is considering change and weighing perceived costs and benefits);
3) Preparation (youth is actively planning to change);
4) Action (youth is making an attempt to change); and
5) Maintenance (youth is solidifying change and resisting relapse).

At the point of initial assessment, a youth may be at any one of these stages of change for a given behavior. An intervention can be most effective if it identifies the stage and appropriately engages an individual's support mechanisms. At the earlier stages, awareness of the causes and consequences of a behavior, or the perception of available alternatives, can influence an individual's progress. Later, the belief that one can change, the acquisition of skills needed to change the behavior, and the level of support from others become crucial. One can assess individuals' progress through these stages not only by tracking behavior, but also by assessing changes in confidence and in relative weighting of the costs and benefits of change.

The coping-stress paradigm is easily incorporated into the TTM because the model considers how decisional balance (the weighting of cost and benefits of proposed behaviors) affects one's progress toward change. If a worrisome behavior (e.g., weapon-carrying) is perceived as a stress reducer or survival tool by the adolescent, then in the young person's decisional balance it is seen as a benefit. It is only when that behavior is replaced with alternative skills or actions that reduce the young person's sense of vulnerability that he may be prepared to reconsider the behavior in terms of its potential serious cost.

Adjusting Counseling Approach Based on Stage of Change

An assessment that includes an area to be addressed as well as a stage of behavioral change allows clinicians to better hone their style of intervention.

During *precontemplation*, the young person is unaware (e.g., patients may be unaware that taking drugs will lower their protective instincts and put them at greater risk in an unsafe neighborhood). At this stage, it is important to guide the adolescent to become aware that a situation needs to be addressed. It makes sense, therefore, to offer facts or information to patients in precontemplation.

During *contemplation*, the young person is beginning to consider change and determining if the change is likely to be worthwhile. An injured adolescent may be jolted into contemplation, wondering what steps need to be taken to assure safety. These steps could be adaptive (e.g., conflict resolution) or maladaptive (e.g., getting a gun). It is critical here that caregivers motivate them to choose the adaptive response. It is equally important that they gain the confidence to believe that if they take positive action, they will succeed in assuring their safety.

During *preparation*, the young person is seriously considering taking action. It is particularly important here that she is equipped with appropriate skills. No matter the level of motivation, the change process will fail without the concrete skills (e.g., staying away from dangerous corners) and negotiation skills (e.g., de-escalating a violent situation) youth need to be able to put their plans into operation.

When an adolescent has decided to take *action*, it is particularly important that negative learned behaviors are replaced with positive ones. At this stage, the adolescent is weighing the risks and benefits of each action. Because many worrisome behaviors serve to reduce stress, it is particularly important that the adolescent has new strategies to deal with stress.

If the patient has already tried out new behaviors and is trying hard to *maintain* those behaviors, it is important that positive reinforcement is forthcoming from parents and peers. Without this reinforcement, the adolescent is likely to relapse in response to negative influence in the form of invitations they will continue to receive from peers who want them to engage in their old habits. It is critical at this stage that parents are supportive of the changes the young person is trying to make, and that they reinforce their belief that he is a good person. If a young person is clear that his parents think he is nothing but trouble, he has nothing to lose when he lives down to their expectations.

Cognitive Development

In order for the clinician to most effectively reach adolescents, she must assess the cognitive level of her patients. Because adolescents are in transition between the concrete thinking of childhood and the abstract thinking of adulthood, a young person's ability to comprehend anticipatory guidance is dependent on the degree to which abstraction is understood. A concrete thinker sees things as they seem to exist, without regard to future consequences and without complex understanding (Piaget, 1997). A concrete thinker views the world and people as "good" or "bad." Therefore, concrete thinkers cannot look beyond actions to determine underlying motivations, and may be easily fooled by seemingly flattering or kind facades. Abstract thinkers can see shades of gray, consider future consequences, and can evaluate underlying motivations (Piaget, 1997). For these reasons, abstract thinking is highly protective. Understanding the degree to which each youth is able to absorb abstract ideas is a critical first step in counseling the adolescent. If a patient is unable to contemplate the future, warnings about long-term consequences of current behaviors are useless. It is vital to remember that up to 15% of individuals never reach the ability to have abstract thought. It is not realistic to conduct formal psychological testing with each clinical encounter. A reasonable rule of thumb is that pre- and early adolescents think largely in concrete terms and that later adolescents have usually acquired abstract thought. However, as long as the caregiver is not condescending, one cannot go wrong by delivering all information in a manner that a concrete thinker could understand.

Children transition toward abstract capabilities through neurological and hormonal maturation as well as through a series of life experiences. With each new experience and its consequences, the adolescent takes a small step toward increasingly abstract thought. Life experience remains the ideal means to acquire knowledge. However, the potential for danger is so great that adults tend to try to rush the process by aggressively informing adolescents of the consequences of their choices. It would be ideal for the caregiver to guide youth verbally through "life experiences" allowing them to make "mistakes" in the safety of a medical setting rather than in the perilous world. However, most adults deliver this kind of information in a lecture format.

Information delivered in a lecture format is poorly understood by concrete thinkers. The lecturer often describes a series of threatened consequences that would follow from a misguided choice. "*Did you know that the choice you are making now is going to lead to consequence A, which will then lead to consequence B, which will lead to consequence C, and so forth . . . until you may die because of this unwise choice!*" The concrete thinker comprehends the anger, the implied threat, and the condescending tone, but simply cannot grasp the abstract connections and is left feeling quite frustrated—and sometimes angry.

Alternatively, these same consequences can be presented with a different cadence, delivered one idea at a time. The key to helping concrete thinkers grasp consequences of current behaviors is to break down abstract concepts into multiple concrete steps. The teenager is guided through each step until they come to an abstract realization, which I call the "cognitive aha" experience. There are three techniques that can be used to achieve a "cognitive aha," but they all have in common that complex ideas are broken into small units, and the adolescent is guided one unit at a time to figure things out independently (Ginsburg and Jablow, 2002).

The first technique is called "the choreographed conversation." As in musical choreography, every step should be planned, but should appear to flow smoothly and spontaneously. The caregiver maps out the direction that she believes the conversation needs to flow. However, instead of delivering the message in one bolus—lecture style—she puts out one idea at a time. With the counselor using probing questions followed by appropriate silence, the teenager is guided to slowly come to their own realization of the consequences of their current path.

The second technique is the role-play. This gives the teenager the opportunity to practice a scenario in the safety of a medical setting, while being exposed to some of the responses to their actions that might occur in the real world. Adolescents sometimes envision the rosiest of scenarios (I will fight, he will lose), without thinking through the other alternatives. When doing role-plays follow three rules: 1) Do not inform patients that you are about to do a role-play, they may get embarrassed and disengage. Instead, walk into them. *"Yeah, you said that he was just going to give up, but suppose he said . . ."* 2) Do not act aggressively; rather, stay calm and act out situations in slow motion. This enables the teenager to think things through rather than responding emotionally/aggressively; and 3) Use short, universally understood phrases and let the patient do most of the talking. If you use too much of your own language, recalling your own youth, you will be turned off. If you attempt teen language, you will look foolish. In either scenario, the teenager will say, *"It's not like that,"* or *"That's corny."* Both phrases are polite ways of suggesting you are an idiot.

The third technique is the decision tree. It is essentially a choreographed conversation written out on paper. The patient describes her plan as well as the perceived outcome if she follows the plan. The counselor guides the patient to consider alternative outcomes as she writes out each choice and its associated consequences. The ultimate product is a diagram representing a series of choices, each leading to an often unintended outcome. One nice thing about a decision tree is that a patient is able to take it home and continue to contemplate what might be her best choices.

Taking Social Context into Account When Devising a Safety Plan

Adults often suggest that teenagers should change their behavior in order to reach a higher level of success or safety. Even when the teenager is in full agreement that the proposed change is beneficial, he still has to worry about how his change in behavior will be received by his peer community. Adult-proposed interventions that do not take into account how peers will respond are likely to fail. Major suggestions for changes in behavior should be accompanied by a plan to "save face" or maintain pride. For example, leaving town will be interpreted as cowardice, and improving school behavior may be seen as giving in to parents or teachers. A first step is for the counselor to ask the patient, *"How do you think this will play with your friends, will they back you?"* Then, each proposed change should be matched with a face-saving maneuver. These maneuvers include shifting the blame to parents or disciplinarians—*"My mother said if I get suspended one more time I will . . ."* or *"Principal Smith says that if cut class one more time he will expel me, that would kill my mother, you know she has high blood pressure."* In the case of a young person who needs to leave town quickly for her own safety, make sure she has a place to escape to and a good excuse for going other than fleeing violence (e.g., *"I had to go down to take care of my grandmother, she's real sick"*).

Examples of Brief Interventions

The SSHADESS screen (see pages 108–109) offers a glimpse into those behavioral areas that pose the greatest risk to the patient, as well as those areas where the patient possesses the greatest strengths to build upon. Through a combination of discussion, decision trees, and role-plays adjusted to match the patient's cognitive level, the clinician can offer information to the patient and can help them to develop the skills needed to resist pressures and retain control over their own behaviors.

Following are a few examples of how you might proceed based upon the responses you obtained in the psychosocial screen. Some of the examples have been previously published. (Ginsburg, 1998; Ginsburg, 1997; Ginsburg, 1997; Ginsburg, 1999) Certainly, any patient may merit several counseling points, but be cautious not to overwhelm the patient in the ED setting. Also, remember that any guidance offered in the ED will be far more effective and potentially long-lasting if combined with appropriate referrals and parental involvement.

Prior to any intervention, consider who is the person in the adolescent's life that he or she most wants to please (e.g., their grandmother), or for whom they serve as a role model (e.g., their seven-year-old brother). When you are equipped with this knowledge, you will be much better prepared to bring out the best in the adolescent. They will be heartened by the reminder that their better behavior is very important to someone.

...if the patient is beginning to become involved in the drug trade ...

Many adolescents get involved in the drug trade at an early age, first serving as lookouts for police, then serving as "runners." Pre- and early adolescents are chosen for these positions because they are less likely to be caught, and if caught are less likely to be prosecuted. Because most of these young adolescents are concrete thinkers, they do not grasp the complex motivations behind the drug dealers' desire for them to help out. They are eager to be seen as mature, and are often thrilled that they have been chosen for such an honored position. Further, they are charmed by the dealers' kindness toward them, and are eager to get the presents and money associated with their new jobs. They are missing the abstract understanding that they are being exploited.

I use the following choreographed conversation to bring them to awareness that the dealer has an underlying motivation. I put out the questions, one at a time, and wait as the young person comes to a new, hopefully protective, awareness.

- *So, is the guy you are working for nice to you? The answer will most certainly be "yes."*
- *Why do you think he is being nice to you? The answer is usually, "Because he thinks I am cool and can handle things."*
- *What usually happens to drug dealers? Even young children from high drug trade areas are able to quickly respond that they die or go to jail.*
- *Hmm. So, if you are running drugs, and bullets go flying, who gets hurt? If there is an arrest, who gets picked up?*
- *What happens to the dealer? The patient often comes to awareness that he will get away.*
- *Hmm. So, why are the dealers so kind to you? At this point most young adolescents get that they are being exploited.*
- *Right. You would be the one getting shot and being sent away to Juvie. No wonder he is so nice to you. You are saving his life.*

. . . if a very young patient is beginning to become involved in drug use . . .

Dealers may give drugs away for free or at seriously discounted rates in order to assure that a new generation of users is created. Of course, young adolescents do not understand the underlying motivation. The choreographed conversation follows:

- *So, how do dealers get young kids to try drugs?* Most young adolescents know the system.
- *So, when a drug dealer offers you drugs, would they be nice or mean?* Very young adolescents and children may assume they will be mean, because drug dealers are "bad."
- *So, I actually think they would be very nice to you, like you said, even give them to you for free. Why do you think they would do that?* Most pre-adolescents will answer, *"because they like me."*
- *So, hmm. Does your mom or dad use coupons in a store?*
- *So, why do you think a storeowner offers your mom coupons?* Most pre-adolescents will answer, *"because the owner likes her."*
- *So, suppose you see a cereal you really like and your mom has a coupon for it, will you ask her to get it?*
- *So, suppose you like it as much as you thought you would? Would you want your mom to keep buying it?*
- *So, suppose she ran out of coupons, would you still want her to get the cereal?*
- *So, hmm. So, why do you think the storeowner gave your mom coupons in the first place?*
- *So, I see. So, why do drug dealers give away drugs for free?*

. . . if the patient is in the middle of a cycle of retaliation . . .

The most important intervention may be to guide the patient to get out of town until tensions subside. Expect a great deal of resistance, with the adolescent telling you that would be "punking out." They are worried about their social context. But, if your patient's life is in danger, it is clearly the best advice. Work with the patient and family to "create" a viable out-of-town crisis that emergently needs the patient's attention (e.g., a sick relative). Don't tell anyone but his parents that it is fabricated, make the story as consistent as possible. Though the patient's best long-term chance may be to break from the delinquent peer group, this may be highly challenging and even dangerous if not handled carefully.

An adolescent about to engage in a retributive violent act wants an immediate emotional release, but may be unaware of the peril because of the inability to grasp future consequences. A style of producing a "cognitive aha" regarding future consequences is the decision tree. The clinician discusses the teenager's fantasies and draws a map toward the future, with each junction described by the teenager in response to an open-ended question such as "Well, what would happen if the knife were taken from your hand, and instead you were stabbed in the back?". At each junction, the provider inquires whether the fantasy is realistic and suggests other possible outcomes. Using a diagram accompanied by slow-motion role-play, the provider can demonstrate potential outcomes of retribution including death, maiming, and life in jail. The patient can be taken through the length of his jail time, including the sadness inflicted on his family, the loss of his education, and the prevention of his fatherhood. Upon release from jail, discuss his elder years in which he is poor and alone because of missed opportunities of parenthood and education. Ultimately, the one day when he will feel badly for not getting even seems minimal when compared to a life outcome that is more to his liking (see Figure 4).

This decision tree was used with a 14-year-old female, who presented to me with a scleral hemorrhage in a school-based clinic. She became mad enough to fight when a girl insulted her mother. When I asked her what was going to happen next, she responded *"I'm going to kill her, that's why I brought this knife* (which she had in her pocket) *to school."* I asked how that would make her feel. She responded, *"Good!"* When asked how long she would feel good she responded, *"All day!"* She needed a technique that would allow her to contemplate future consequences, and that took into account how her actions would affect her mother since she was getting into this fight to protect her mother's honor. We slowly acted out the role-play with different scenarios (having the knife reversed on her, etc.) and wrote down each possible outcome. It convinced her to engage in a process of conflict resolution.

... if the patient seems vulnerable to violence escalation ...

You have asked the youth what makes him/her mad enough to fight. If the answer is:

1) "*If someone calls me a name,*" recognize that this child is very high risk, and may have an impulse disorder.
   - Try to get her to realize that the person is calling her names not

because she believes it, but because she is trying to get her angry.

- How could you win in this situation? What could make it worse?
- Talk about the strength of walking away.
- Teach how deep, slow breathing is calming. Teach how it allows people to think things through wisely instead of jumping into situations.

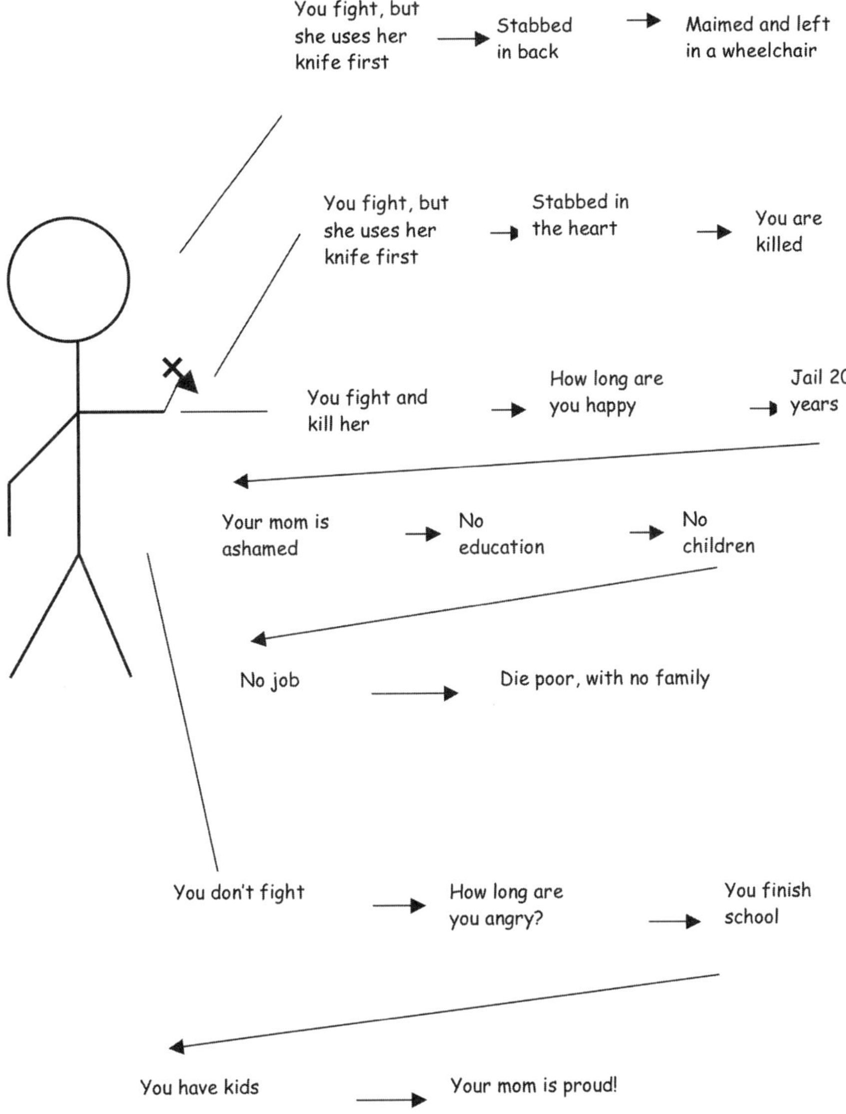

Figure 4. A Life-Saving Decision Tree

2) "*If someone calls my mother a name*"
- Does the person know your mother?
- How could you win? How could you make this worse?
- Could you use a sense of humor to help out in this situation?
- Suppose you defend your mom's honor, but get hurt, have you helped her? How will she feel if you get killed just because someone called her a name?

3) "*If someone gets in my face steps up to me*" [invades body space].
- Don't let yourself be cornered.
- You can keep a leg in front of you, standing at an angle, to help protect your space. This position will still allow you to lunge if you have to, but nobody can get in your face.
- Ask whether giving street respect "My fault" or "My bad, excuse me" might de-escalate the situation.
- Turn/sit down/avoid the chest to chest in your face posture that escalates tension.

4) *Only if someone hits me.* Recognize that this is a teen with a high threshold. Respond with: Great, I am so glad you try to avoid fights But, I want you to understand a few things to make sure you can stay safe:
- Carrying a weapon makes you less safe. Fighting clean (using fists only) means the fight will probably stay that way. Pulling out a weapon begins the cycle of retaliation.
- Try not to be around when fights happen—that gets you into the cycle of escalation and retaliation just for being a bystander.
- If you are in a fight, try to break even, if you win big; they may keep coming after you. If you can break even, the anger may be used up.

Provide scenarios for the child and try to have her come up with non-violent ways to deal with a problem. Be concrete in your advice:
- Avoid fights by hanging out with other kids.
- Don't let someone force you into a fight—think about what you want, not what the other kid wants.
- You and your friends should talk about and practice what you'd do if someone tried to fight you or pulled a knife.

...if the patient is considering obtaining a weapon to enhance their sense of safety ...

Tell the patient how pleased you are that he values his life, but tell him that you believe if he carries a gun, he may be more likely to die than to live. Ask him if he will give you permission to try to show him why. Tell him that you do not live in his world and it is up to him to decide if what you say makes sense. The following "cognitive aha" role-play must be done calmly and in slow motion so that the patient remains thoughtful, does not feel threatened, and does not react viscerally.

- I'll swing back at you/I'll hit you/I'll pistol whip you/I'll knock you out.

If he says this, say, *Exactly! I'm going to get hurt, but I'm going to live.*

- I'm going to shoot you.

If he says this, respond, *Will you really shoot me if we've played this clean* (meaning no weapons) *up to now?*

Most youth will say, *No—I'd probably still fight clean.*

Some youth will say, *You don't know what you're talking about. Where I come from, if you swing at someone, you're dead.*

If he makes the latter statement, he is probably correct, you must trust him. Respond by saying, *You know your neighborhood better than I do. We need to keep thinking about how to keep you alive.*

Assuming he said the fight would stay clean, proceed to the following step. Ask:

- *What if we're in each other's face and a conflict is about to happen, and I do this* . . . (Reach for something at your right hip. The patient will know that means you are reaching for a gun.)

In virtually all cases, he will say, *I would shoot you first.*

Respond, *Exactly. You should. Do you see that carrying a weapon here made me much more likely to be killed? Even if I had a reputation for packing a weapon, do you see that you might have killed me up front, because you wouldn't even have taken the chance?*

Youth will generally have acquired the protective abstraction. But this new understanding may be so inconsistent with the way they have been thinking that they may repeat the scenario verbally for their other fears, such as being mugged or being the victim of a drive-by shooting. In the case of a mugging, you can clearly demonstrate that a criminal needs to kill the victim who has a weapon, but not the unarmed victim. In the case of a drive-by shooting, the presence of a weapon is not protective.

. . . if they know what the right behaviors are, but feel that they will not be able to escape danger, if their friends are involved . . .

Teenagers often have the desire to avoid risk behaviors but simply cannot escape their social context where worrisome behaviors are expected from them. It is an important learned skill to replace risky activities and behaviors with safer ones. Learn what your patient does with his friends—both the positive and the negative. For example, if he either plays basketball or smokes marijuana when there is nothing else to do, teach him to always carry a basketball. This allows him to maintain his friendships while avoiding negative behaviors. As obvious as this skill seems to adults, it is new to younger teenagers. However, if it comes down to a major conflict with friends, often the teenager cannot avoid the situation. It is developmentally difficult for a youth to say to his friends, "I disagree with your behavior." However, it is downright normal to say, "My mother's a b.... " For this reason, teenagers should be prepared to shift the blame to their parents. The adolescent should create a code word with his parents. If the parent receives a call in which the teen uses the code, it signals the parent to demand that the teen returns home immediately. "What do you mean you're calling now, you were supposed to be home hours ago!" They should express their anger loudly and aggressively so witnesses hear their rage through the phone. Then, the youth can blame their parents for having to leave while the teenager retains control over his actions without losing esteem among his friends. If the teen is not able to extricate himself, he secretly calls for his parents to help by being rude over the phone. "You're lucky I even called. I'll be home when I feel like it!" In response, parents then demand to know exactly where he is, tell him he will lose all privileges if he moves, and arrange for him to be picked up *immediately.*

... if you are at a loss ... or the teenager states "How can you know what it's like for me"...

Frequently, teenagers reject our guidance or we are at a loss to suggest strategies for survival in an adolescent world so different than the one we grew up in. Patients are often not subtle when you don't understand their lives. I often hear *"You just don't get it."* When I hear that, I realize that I just don't get it. This is a signal that the best I can do now is to listen. If nothing else, listening is a sincere sign of respect, and active listening helps people to develop their own solutions. When I have reached this point, I simply state, *"I know you're in trouble, but I don't know the right thing to say. It is up to you to figure out how to stay alive. I do know that there are two possible roads you're headed down, one is to make and follow your dreams and the other might be death or bringing down your community."* At this point I draw a simple diagram, its starting point is the present. It has two endpoints represented by open boxes. I fill one box with the teenager's dreams for his future, which I know from his history. The other box is filled with something foreboding, depending on what he said (e.g., death or death and destruction). I draw a ladder toward both endpoints and tell the teenager that there are paths in both directions. His assignment is to figure out what are the steps that will take him in the alternative directions. Usually, the teenager has no difficulty figuring out what behaviors move him toward the worrisome outcome. All I ask at the first visit is for him to imagine what would be a good first step in the positive direction. In a primary care setting, this may be the beginning of a relationship in which I guide him to take one step at a time. In an ED setting it may be enough to just reinforce that the patient does have some control over his future. If the teenager realizes this, he can be referred to a trusting adult, a parent or professional, who can help him formulate these next important steps. I have found that even the toughest, most hopeless of street youth are moved if they can be brought to awareness that they do have some control over their future.

See Figure 5 for a depiction of a ladder diagram used with a 14-year-old girl trapped in a gang run by her 16-year-old cousin. She wanted to become an architect when she got older so she could build buildings for the children in

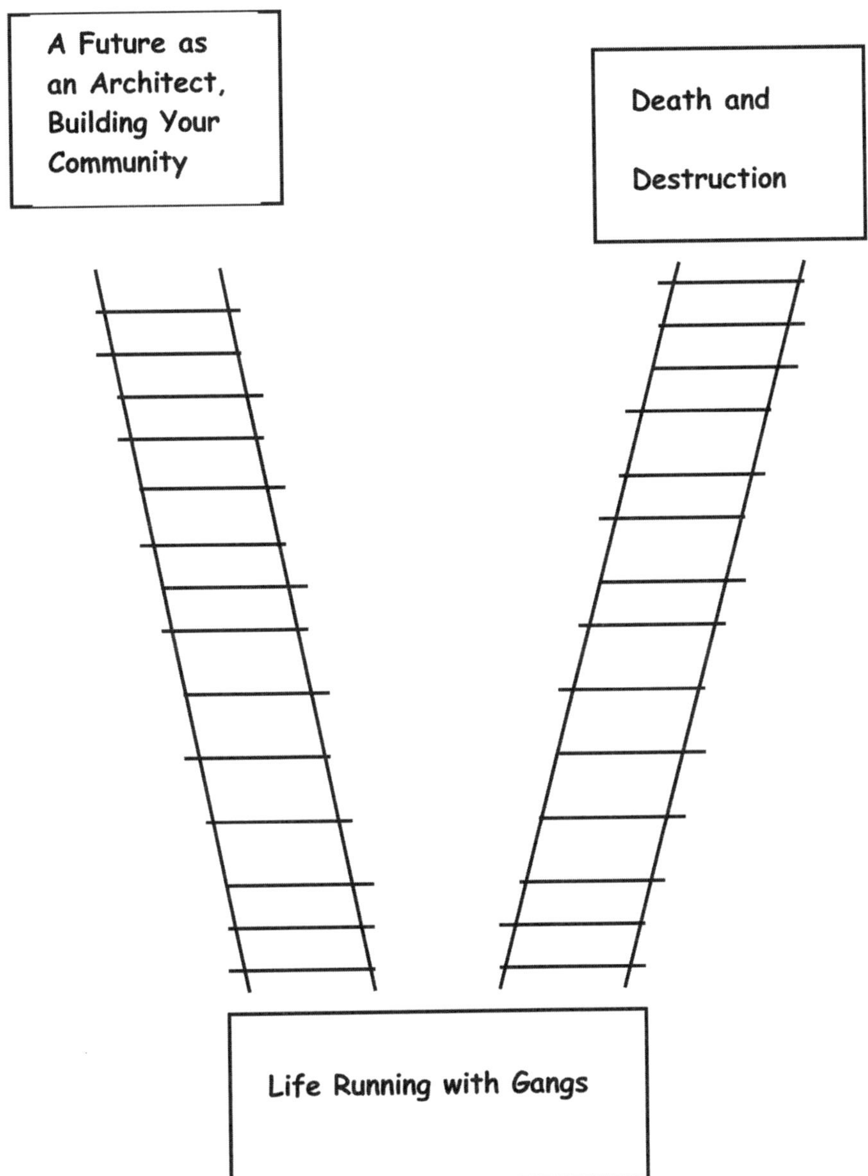

Figure 5. Locus of Control: We All Make Choices

her community to keep them off the streets. She appreciated all of my ideas, but told me that I just didn't get how hard it would be to break from her cousin's gang—*"That's family!"* We could not even get her to the first step on the positive path on her first visit. After a week, she returned ashamed that she could still not think of one right step. When I reinforced to her that just returning was a positive step, she realized that she had some control over her life. She immediately began brainstorming other techniques she could use to break with the gang. She engaged her mother in a conspiracy. When she was in the most trouble, she would call her mother who would demand she come home. This worked because of how much respect her cousin had for her mother. Eventually they moved less than a mile away, but that short distance freed the girl from the gang territory.

. . . if it is clear that the teenager's behavior is a reaction to stress, or if they are so stressed now that they can't even think clearly and are likely to react rashly . . .

There are many alternative positive coping strategies to instill in youth to prevent their need to turn to dangerous strategies. Most of these strategies are beyond the scope of this chapter. However, it is worth knowing how to deal with patients who are very angry or afraid. When a patient is filled with rage, catecholamines are surging through their body and their only thoughts are related to fight or flight. Therefore, he is unlikely to come up with rational protective decisions. I work with patients to help them determine if their primary feeling is "fear" or "rage." If they can acknowledge fear, I guide them to run it out (or play it out through sports). Sometimes, I even have a patient run in place before I try to counsel them. If they acknowledge rage, then I suggest that they mimic fighting by shadow punching, using a punching bag, hitting pillows, or by lifting weights (mimicking getting someone off of one's chest). This basic skill of "listening to your body" uses up acute stress hormones and can allow patients to maintain their ability to think clearly through crises. A routine exercise regimen is central to stress reduction plans I develop with patients to deal with long-term ongoing crises.

Section IV: Referral to Appropriate Community-Based Resources

Youth who have existed in a dangerous world cannot just be told to avoid violence—or be referred passively to counseling or to existing programming. Rather, they must be nurtured through the transition process—until they believe that positive actions will ensure their safety and enhance their likelihood of success. For this reason our colleagues in the ED who make those referrals are vitally important to our ability to make the ED a place where we can do more than treat acute injuries.

It is important for the caregiver to understand how some youth interpret advice that they seek counseling or an intervention program. They hear, "I think you are crazy," or "I think you have failed." Caregivers in the ED have the opportunity to explain that seeking help is a sign of strength. *"A weak man says that life is terrible, but it just doesn't matter. A strong man says, 'this isn't fair and I deserve better'. The only way I'll be able to take care of my family is if I live and I know how to take care of myself."* Next, a clinician can disabuse the adolescent from the notion that a counselor is going to try to fix their problems for them. First, if an adolescent approaches counseling with the expectation that the counselor will magically solve her problems, she will be deeply disappointed. Second, she will feel weak for having to go to someone to solve her problems. *"I want to make sure you understand what counselors can do. They don't fix your life or solve your problems for you. Good counselors figure out what your greatest strengths are and then help you to figure out how to use those strengths to best deal with your problems."*

Youth may reject the option of going to a special program either because they perceive the program is for kids who are somehow different from them, or because they think they won't succeed in the program. Young people should be reassured that among the most important positive influences in their lives can be other young people who have been through similar circumstances and have decided to improve themselves and strive for a positive future. The adolescent should be reassured that they won't be judged in such a program, and that instead they will be mentored by people eager for them to succeed. Remember to close your encounter with why you are so eager for them to succeed. Demonstrate your sincerity when you make that statement by reflecting their strengths back to them and recounting why you believe they can reach their dreams.

Final Thoughts

This book deals with the most feared risk behavior—youth violence. The answer is clear to many: punishment, deterrence, and sequestration away from "the rest of us." Based on my experience, I respectfully, but emphatically, disagree. I believe the answer is in guiding youth to believe that they have an authentic stake in the future.

Violence is produced through the complex interaction of multiple factors. I do not suggest that the problem can be solved through brief ED-based interactions. Contributing issues such as family breakdown, economic disparities, and the ever-present supply of weapons will not be altered by exchanges of words. Our young patients are discharged from our emergency departments into a culture that fosters and reinforces health-threatening behaviors. Many return to families living in poverty and inadequate educational institutions. We understand these contexts, but must not allow frustration and the fear of futility to prevent us from doing the small part that we can do well.

Caregivers cannot independently change the lives of our youth. But, if we make ourselves consistently available to them, we can position ourselves to make a difference. If we become familiar with community resources available to adolescents in crisis, then our role as assessors can be invaluable. For those youth not in crisis, we can serve as adults who offer respectful guidance and who teach effective strategies to maintain healthy behaviors and avoid crises. A first step is in connecting with them in every opportunity that becomes available.

Finally, as professionals who save lives, we have earned the right to be advocates for youth. As their advocates, and as members of respected professions, we can use our "bully pulpit'" to call for programs and policies committed to the healthy development of productive youth who are given the opportunity to grow in the context of strong families, vibrant communities, and a superb educational system that prepares all of its students for future leadership. Until adolescents are held to high expectations, they will not thrive. And, until each adolescent is connected with caring adults, offered genuine opportunity, and prepared with positive, adaptive means to address life's stressors, we will have to get used to those trauma stats.

References

Allen, L.B. and Glicken, A.D. (1996). Depression and suicide in gay and lesbian adolescents. *Physician Assistant.* 1996; 20: 44–60.

Blechman, E.A., Prinz, R.J., and Dumas, J.E. (1995). Coping, competence, and aggression prevention: Part 1. Development model. *Applied and Preventive Psychology.* 4:211–232.

Blum, R.W. (1998). Healthy youth development as a model for youth health promotion: A review. *J. of Adolescent Health.* 22:368–375.

Bowen, G.L. and Chapman, M.V. (1996). Poverty, neighborhood danger, social support, and the individual adaptation among at-risk youth in urban areas. *J. of Family Issues.* 17(5):641–666.

Braverman, M. T., Meyers, J.M., and Bloomberg, L. (1994). How youth programs can promote resilience. *California Agriculture.* 48(7):30–35.

Brooks, R.B. (1994). Children at risk: Fostering resilience and hope. *American J. of Orthopsychiatry.* 64(4):545–553.

Brown, J. (1997). Working toward freedom from violence: The process of change in battered women. *Violence Against Women;* 3(1):5–26.

Capelli, M., et al. (1995). Identifying depressed and suicidal adolescents in a teen health clinic. *J. Adolesc Health.* 16: 64–70.

Carnegie Council on Adolescent Development. (1992). A Matter of Time: Risk and Opportunity in the Nonschool Hours. Recommendations for Strengthening Community Programs for Youth. Washington, D.C.: Carnegie Council on Adolescent Development.

Center for Disease Control. National Center for Health Statistics. (2004). *Health, United States, 2004 with Chartbook on Trends in the Health of Americans.* Hyattsville, MD.

Davis, R.B., Wolfe, H., Orenstein, A., Bergamo, P., Buetens, K., Fraster, B., Hogan, J., MacLean, A., and Ryan, M. (1994). Intervening with high risk youth: A program model. *Adolescence.* 29(116):763–774.

Dekovic, M. (1999). Risk and protective factors in the development of problem behavior during adolescence. *J. of Youth and Adolescence.* 28:667–685.

DiClemente, C. and Hughes, S. (1990). Stages of change profiles in outpatient alcoholism treatment. *J. of Substance Abuse;* 2:217–235.

Ellickson, P., Saner, H., and MgGuigan, K. (1997). Profiles of violent youth: substance use and other concurrent problems. *AJPH.* 87:985–991.

Embry, D.D. (1997). Does your school have a peaceful environment? Using an audit to create a climate for change and resiliency. *Intervention in School and Clinic.* 32(4):217–222.

Enger, J.M., Howerton, D.L., and Cobbs, C.R. (1994). Internal/external locus of control, self-esteem, and parental verbal interaction of at-risk Black male adolescents. *J. of Social Psychology.* 134(3):269–274.

Evers, K., Harlow, L.L., Redding, C.A., and Laforge, R.G. (1998). Longitudinal changes in stage of change for condom use in women. *Amer. J. Health Promotion;*13:19–25.

Fields, L. and R.J. Prinz. (1997). Coping and adjustment during childhood and adolescence. *Clinical Psychology Review.* 17(8):937–976.

Floyd, C. (1996). Achieving despite the odds: A study of resilience among a group of African American high school seniors. *J. of Negro Education.* 65:181–189.

Franklin, W. (1995). *Risk and Resilience in African-American Adolescents: The Role of Protective and Compensatory Factors.* School of Education. Palo Alto, CA, Stanford University:127.

Freiberg, H.J. (1993). A school that fosters resilience in inner-city youth. *J. of Negro Education.* 62(3):364–376.

Garofalo, R., Wolf, C., Wissow, L.S., et al. (1999). Sexual orientation and risk of suicide attempts among a representative sample of youth. *Archives of Pediatric Adolescent Medicine.* 153: 487–93.

Ginsburg, K.R. (1997). Guiding Adolescents away from violence. *Contemporary Pediatrics.* Vol. 14, No. 11: 101–111.

Ginsburg, K.R. (1997). Teen violence prevention: How to make a brief encounter make a difference. *The Physician and Sports Medicine.* Vol. 25, No. 3: 69–83.

Ginsburg, K.R. (1998). Youth violence: If we are not active in prevention efforts, who will be? *Archives of Pediatric and Adolescent Med.* 152: 527– 530.

Ginsburg, K.R. (1999). Teen violence: Turning the tide. *Emergency Medicine.* 70–91.

Ginsburg, K.R., Alexander, P.A., Hunt, J., Sullivan, M,, Zhao, H., and Cnaan, A. (2002) Enhancing their likelihood for a positive future: The perspective of inner- city youth. *Pediatrics.* 109:1136–1143.

Ginsburg, K.R., Alexander, P.A., Hunt, J., Sullivan, M., and Cnaan A. (2002) Enhancing their likelihood for a positive future: Focus groups reveal the voice of inner-city youth. *Pediatrics.* 109 (6). Available at: http://www.pediatrics.org/cgi/content/full/109/6/e95. (Abstract) *Pediatrics.* 109: 1165.

Ginsburg, K.R., Forke, C.M., Cnaan, A., et al. (2002). Important health provider characteristics: The perspective of urban ninth graders. *J. of Developmental and Behavioral Pediatrics.* 23(4): 237–43.

Ginsburg, K.R., Menapace, A.S., and Slap, G.B. (1997). Factors affecting the decision to seek health care: The voice of adolescents. *Pediatrics.* 100(6): 922–30.

Ginsburg, K.R., Slap, G.B., Cnaan, A., et al. (1995). Adolescents' perceptions of factors affecting their decisions to seek health care. *JAMA.* 273(24): 1913–8.

Ginsburg, K.R., Winn, R.J., Rudy, B.J., et al. (2002). How to reach sexual minority youth in the health care setting: The teens offer guidance. *J. of Adolescent Health.* 31(5): 407–16.

Ginsburg, K.R., with Jablow, M. (2001). *"But, I'm Almost Thirteen!!: An Action Plan for Raising a Responsible Adolescent."* New York: Contemporary Books, McGraw-Hill Publications.

Gordon, K.A. (1996). Resilient Hispanic youths' self-concept and motivational patterns. *Hispanic J. of Behavioral Sciences.* 18(1):63–73.

Greene, M.B. (1993). Chronic exposure to violence and poverty: Interventions that work for youth. *Crime and Delinquency.* 39(1):106–124.

Gregory, L.W. (1995). The turnaround process: Factors influencing the school success of urban youth. *J. of Adolescent Research.* 10(1):136– 154.

Guetzloe, E. (1994). Risk, resilience, and protection. *J. of Emotional and Behavioral Problems.* Summer:2–5.

Hawton, K., O'Grady, J., and Osborn, M. (1982). Adolescents who take overdoses: their characteristics, problems, and contacts with helping agencies. *Brit J Psychiatry.* 140: 118–123.

Hershberger, S.L. and D'Augelli, A.R. (1995). The impact of victimization on the mental health and suicidality of lesbian, gay and bisexual youths. *Developmental Psychology. 31*: 65–74.

Hoge, R. D., Andrews, D.A., and Leshied, A.W. (1996). An investigation of risk and protective factors in a sample of youthful offenders. *J. of Child Psychology and Psychiatry.* 37:419–424.

Howard, D.E. (1996). Searching for resilience among African-American youth exposed to community violence: Theoretical issues. *J. of Adolescent Health.* 18:254–262.

Kliewer, W. and Sandler, I.N. (1992). Locus of control and self-esteem as moderators of stressor-symptom relations in children and adolescents. *J. of Abnormal Child Psychology.* 20:393–413.

McCo, S.B. and Finkelhor, D. (1996). Is youth victimization related to trauma symptoms and depression after controlling for prior symptoms and family relationships? A longitudinal, prospective study. *J. Consult Clinical Psych.* 64:1406–1416.

McMillan, J. H. et al. (1992). *A Qualitative Study of Resilient At-Risk Students. A Review of the Literature.* Richmond, VA, Metropolitan Educational Research Consortium: 1–25.

Mundy, J. (1996). Tipping the scales from risk to resiliency. *P and R*: March: 78–86.

Nettles, S.M. and Pleck, J.H. (1993). *Risk, Resilience, and Development: The Multiple Ecologies of Black Adolescents.* Baltimore, MD, Center for Research on Effective Schooling for Disadvantaged Students: 1–24.

Piaget, J. (1997). *The Essential Piaget* (Gruber, H.E. and Voneche, J.J. Eds). New York, Basic Books.

Pittman, K. and Irby, M. (1996). Preventing Problems or Promoting Development: Competing Priorities or Inseparable Goals? Baltimore, MD: International Youth Foundation, 1996.

Porter, S.C., Fein, J.A., and Ginsburg, K.R. (1997) Depression screening in adolescents with somatic complaints presenting to the emergency department. *Annals of Emergency Medicine.* 29(1) : 141–145.

Remafedi, G, French, S., Story, M., et al. (1998). The relationship between suicide risk and sexual orientation: Results of a population-based study. *American J. of Public Health. 88*: 57–60.

Remafedi, G., Farrow, J.A., and Deisher, R.W. (1991). Risk factors for attempted suicide in gay and bisexual youth. *Pediatrics. 87*: 869–75.

Resnick, M.D. (2000). Protective factors, resiliency and healthy youth development. *Adolescent Medicine State of the Art Reviews.* 11(1): 157–65.

Rich, M. (2003). Boy, mediated: effects of entertainment media on adolescent male health. *Adolescent Medicine State of the Art Reviews.* 14 (3): 691–715.

Safren, S.A. and Heimburg, R.G. (1999) Depression, hopelessness, suididality, and related factors in sexual minority and heterosexual adolescents. *J. of Consulting and Clinical Psychology. 67*: 859–866.

Sagor, R. (1996). Building resiliency in students. *Educational Leadership* 54(1): 38–43

Salts, et al., (1995). Predictive variables of violent behavior in adolescent males. *Youth and Society*. 26;377–399.

Savin-Williams, R.C. (1994). Verbal and physical abuse as stressors in the lives of lesbian, gay male and bisexual youths: Associations with school problems, running away, substance abuse, prostitution, and suicide. *J. of Consulting and Clinical Psychology*. *62*: 261–69.

Schneider, M.B., Friedman, S.B., and Fisher, M. (1995). Stated and unstated reasons for visiting a high school nurse's office. *J. Adolesc Health*. 16: 35–40.

Sege, R., Stringham, P., Short, S., and Griffith, J. (1999). Ten years after: Examination of adolescent screening questions that predict future violence-related injury. *J. of Adolescent Health*. 24:395–402.

Slap, G.B., Vorters, D.F., and Chaudhuri, S. (1989). Risk factors for attempted suicide during adolescence. *Pediatrics*. 84: 762–771.

Smith, C. and Carlson, B.E. (1997). Stress, coping, and resilience in children and youth. *Social Service Review*. June: 231–256.

Smith, K. and Crawford, S. (1986). Suicide behavior among "normal" high school students. *Suicide and Life Threatening Behavior*. 16:313–325.

Van Slyck, M., Stern, M., and Zak-Place, J. (1996). Promoting optimal adolescent development through conflict resolution education, training, and practice: An innovative approach for counseling psychologists. *The Counseling Psychologist*. 24: 433–461.

Velicer, W.F., Prochaska, J.O., Fava, J.L., Norman, G.J. and Redding, C.A. (1998). Smoking cessation and stress management: Applications of the Transtheoretical Model of behavior change. *Homeostasis*, 38, 216–233.

Wolin, S. (1995). Resilience among youth growing up in substance-abusing families. *Pediatric Clinics of North America*. 42(2): 415–429.

Wolin, S. and Wolin, S.J. (1996). Beating the odds. Understanding children. *Learning*. 25(1): 66–68.

Wolin, S. and Wolin, S.J. (1997). Shifting paradigms: taking a paradoxical approach. resiliency in action magazine. Project Resiliency. Available at: http://www.projectresilience.com/article15.htm. [2000, January 24].

Wright, N. D. (1996). *From Risk to Resiliency: The Role of Law-Related Education*. Calabass, CA, Center for Civic Education: 1–14.

Chapter 4

Faith-Based Approach to Care of Violent Youth in the Emergency Department

Theodore J. Corbin, MD, FACEP, Millicent West, MS, Linda Davis-Moon, MSN, CRNP, APRN, BC, Theodore A. Christopher, MD, FACEP, and John Rich, MD, MPH

Introduction

Youth violence is one of the most pressing public health issues in the United States. Philadelphia, the sixth most populated American city, experienced an epidemic of adolescent violence in the last decade. A distressing 300 homicide deaths occurred among Philadelphians' 18-25 year-old youths from 2006 to 2007. Statistics of nonfatal injury from violence also soared as Philadelphia's emergency departments (EDs) treated a constant stream of young patients with devastating injuries. Even more upsetting, many of these patients returned within weeks because of repeat injuries and/or death.

Concern for youth violence naturally arose in Philadelphia. To ameliorate this public health issue, the William Penn Foundation funded the *Violence Prevention Initiative* (VPI) at Thomas Jefferson University Hospital (TJUH) in November of 1997. The grant provided an opportunity for Philadelphia emergency departments to cooperate with each other and create a network of services to at-risk youth. These services consisted of employment, education, and personal counseling.

The VPI was founded on the belief that ED physician and nurse interventions are not sufficient to prevent the high level of youth violence in Philadelphia. Because ED medical providers are busied by the pace of incoming patients, their time to address the many issues these young victims face is severely limited. A second challenge many medical providers experience is overcoming the culture difference between patient and physician or nurse. While most of the young victims of intentional violence (VIV) are African American or Latino, the vast majority of ED providers are white. Philadelphia's VIV regularly come from impoverished homes in destitute neighborhoods; medical providers typically have a middle-class background and are part of a distinctively different social class. Despite their dedication to health care delivery and best intentions, medical providers are challenged by these definite differences to connect with these young patients.

Chaplains are a vital part of the TJUH ED staff. They are a constant presence to assist in healing, caring, and reassurance to patients experiencing difficult times. At times there has been a tendency to see VIV as somehow culpable for their own injuries; however, the VPI believes that a model based upon religion would not only provide spiritual healing and comfort but also remove the propensity to "blame the victim." This is important for patient compliance because the young VIV are often frightened, angry, and confused when they enter the dynamic setting of an ED.

The VPI recognizes what others state in medical literature. Researchers have published evidence indicating young VIV frequently view their experiences as having some deeper spiritual meaning. They regard their injuries as a "wake-up call" or a "message from God," that somehow they need to change their lives (Rich and Sullivan, 2001). Therefore, there is a window of opportunity for an intervention based upon spirituality and faith.

While the medical and public health literature has reports of health-related partnerships with faith-based organizations and faith-based interventions, few have focused on such interventions in the context of victims of violence in the ED. Connor and colleagues have elaborated on the importance of spiritual beliefs in healing trauma related symptoms in survivors of violence (Connor, Davidson, et al., 2003). Similarly, Kataoka and colleagues developed a faith-based community research partnership to develop a trauma intervention for youth in an inner-city Latino community in Los Angeles (Kataoka, Fuentes, et al., 2006). Pastoral crisis intervention models have also been applied to community disaster response, crisis intervention, and emergency mental health (Everly, 2000). However, not much has been reported in the context of the emergency department.

The Jefferson Community Violence Prevention Program (JCVPP) was part of the VPI. It was formally designed as a multidisciplinary collaboration (among physicians, nurses, social workers, and chaplains) that provided support and a referral service to VIV. Attempts were made to identify young VIV in the ED and facilitate their referral to community-based resources that address the causes of violence. This notion emerged from realizing that an ED staff has limited control to connect a patient with community resources after he or she leaves the hospital. A second goal was to understand the different lives of these patients with regard to the social factors that put them at risk for violence. During the three-year program, 831 young victims of intentional violence were enrolled in the program and 357 were referred for follow-up.

Program Design

TJU Hospital ED nurses and physicians identified VIV between the ages of 14 and 24 for participation in the program. The physician or nurse then placed a call to the TJUH Department of Pastoral Care and Education, where chaplaincy service is provided 24 hours a day, seven days a week. TJUH chaplains were particularly well versed in violence prevention because of special training they received independent from seminary school.

Once the patient was medically stabilized, the chaplain performed a bedside assessment (involving a 56-question survey) of the injured youth and provided empathic comfort to the patient and family. Participation in the JCVPP was voluntary and patients consented to receive services under the program. The assessment tool was a 56-question survey developed by the Philadelphia HealthCare Collaborative, a panel of experts with experience in urban youth violence from the fields of emergency medicine, pediatrics, sociology, and psychiatry. The survey includes items related to socioeconomic status, employment history, school enrollment and performance, drug and alcohol use, history of intentional injury or violence, and other factors potentially related to violence. The evaluation results are shown in Table 1. Most notable are the number of young people who knew their perpetrator and who felt unsafe after discharge. In addition, a substantial number of victims had easy access to firearms.

The assessment's purpose was twofold: to determine if the youth was at risk of becoming a repeat victim or future perpetrator, and to decide how the ED staff could best help the patient after leaving the hospital. Patients were designated high, medium or low risk, according to their chances of adverse outcomes (Felitti, Anda, et al., 1998). The referral to community resources was prioritized for those who were at highest risk.

In the beginning of the program, chaplain work was not finished in the ED. They went out into the community as hospital liaisons to follow up with discharged patients. Unfortunately, it soon became apparent that the chaplains faced significant obstacles in connecting with the VIV. Working in Philadelphia's

Table 1. Characteristics of Injured Youth—Jefferson Community Violence Prevention Program

Gender	
Female	184 (42%)
Male	252 (58%)
Race	
African-American	266 (61%)
Caucasian	120 (28%)
Latino	12 (3%)
Other	38 (9%)
Unemployed	344 (79%)
Currently involved in school or community program	181 (42%)
Knew perpetrator	185 (42%)
Lived with perpetrator	25 (6%)
Had specific plans for retaliation	30 (7%)
Concerned about personal safety after discharge	112 (26%)
Involved in violence within 12 months	102 (24%)
Could easily obtain firearm	76 (17%)

inner city requires knowledge of the neighborhoods and the people living there. While the chaplains were respected for their spiritual work, they lacked the understanding of the streets necessary to keep them safe. Based upon this, the JCVPP decided the chaplains would be most effective by only visiting the patient in the ED. To follow up with the patients in their neighborhoods, outreach workers from Philadelphia Anti-Violence/Anti-Drug Network (PAAN) were hired as hospital liaisons.

Patients identified as "high risk" were treated with special concern. After discharge from the ED, the chaplain made an appropriate referral to the PAAN worker assigned to the patient's neighborhood. The chaplain then shared the assessment's results with the PAAN worker to identify the patient's greatest needs. The PAAN worker then arranged a meeting with the patient and/or family to match the VIV with the community-based program or organization that best attended to the patient's needs.

Originally, written referrals were given to all VIV, regardless of their level of risk, so they could utilize community resources for help. Regrettably, tabulated statistics show that follow-ups were least successful when moderate and high-risk young VIV were given written referrals to go at their own discretion. To alleviate this problem, Community Transitional Mentors were hired and incorporated into the program. Big Brothers/Big Sisters provided these mentors, and were used in conjunction with the PAAN workers.

In the third year, TJUH expanded the program to include the Methodist Hospital, another hospital in Philadelphia. With the assistance of the Methodist Hospital Foundation Grant, Methodist Hospital could also provide pastoral care and support for young VIV. The program at Methodist Hospital mirrors the one at TJUH because it utilizes ED staff to identify young VIV so that the pastoral care staff could perform an assessment of the youth.

Program Challenges

Several challenges threatened the JCVPP's effectiveness. Problems began at ground level when the interviewing physician or nurse failed to notify a chaplain of a VIV. Because of constant turnover, new staff members sometimes did not know about the program. Some medical providers claimed not to have the time necessary to identify VIV in the busy ED. Consequently, the program coordinator made a constant effort to improve VIV identification. Prompts that reminded ED staff of the JCVPP took different forms: lectures to residents and attending physicians, in-services for nurses, and written reminders to all ED staff. This highlighted the need for constant training of ED staff to make the appropriate identification and referral.

Early in the project the JCVPP staff recognized that its success depended on a strong Director of the Partnership. Unfortunately, there was a delay in finding this director, which caused the program's late start-up. This interfered with the time needed to establish clear communication with ED staff regarding desired outcomes and their roles in making referrals. Once the Director was hired, the project was smoothly constructed and implemented.

The results of the chaplain-administered, 56-item risk-assessment test indicated two things: concrete demographics of young and recurrent VIV, and a formal evaluation of the needs of VIV. With a functioning database, the ED staff identified patients returning to the ED with similar injuries of violence to see how positively they were affected by the JCVPP. PAAN workers reported their successes and failures in their ED follow-ups with discharged VIV. Both these reports from the VIV and PAAN workers were incorporated into a central data system. The data were analyzed so factors important in predicting who responded to the intervention became evident.

Program Outcomes

The JCVPP achieved success with its goal to identify young VIV and refer them to community resources. One year after the start of the program, 307 had been enrolled in the program and 64 (21%) were referred for follow-up. Since the start of the program, 831 VIV were enrolled in the program and 357 (43%) were referred for follow-up. Because referrals to community resources were dependent on correctly identifying VIV, the JCVPP's effectiveness soared with increased ED staff awareness of VIV. The goal to increase the percentage of accurate VIV assessments was met to prevent recurrent violence or perpetration. A third goal was to construct an interdisciplinary team within the ED to provide seamless service to young VIV. Diverse employment was the optimal approach to this challenge: physicians, nurses, social workers, chaplains, and PAAN workers collectively and synergistically achieved the intended outcome. The broad goal of building rapport between the ED and surrounding community was best achieved through the PAAN workers. This workforce specifically understood the home area and needs of most young VIV, thereby increasing the project's efficacy.

Prominent risk factors associated with young VIV were African American male, median age 21 years, unemployed, prior violence-related behavior, and involved in drug activity. Most of the injuries suffered by females were the result of domestic violence. Male injury ranged from random violence to violence perpetrated by peers and known assailants. In a JCVPP pilot study, female VIV demonstrated an alarmingly high percentage of prior violent incidents and unemployment. Another JCVPP study revealed that VIV of all ages often have prior violent incidents, unemployment, and access to a gun. This confirms the need to continually investigate this area to aid in prevention and intervention.

Faith Based Approach in the Emergency Department

Jefferson's Community Violence Prevention Program is unique in that it employs faith-based staff as a core component of ED staff. The JCVPP does not view medicine as just a science because optimal health care attends to more than the physical body. For this reason, the JCVPP is unique because it utilizes chaplains to spiritually and emotionally support young VIV. After extensive review of the latest medical literature, the JCVPP realized that little has been written related the topic of faith-based follow-up to VIV. Landry explains the roles and activities of a chaplain within a level-one trauma hospital, seeing the chaplain as part of an interdisciplinary team and providing a "ministry of presence" to the family (Landry, 1996).

The Barnes-Jewish Hospital, a level-one trauma center in St. Louis, Missouri, is the only other hospital using pastoral care services for VIV in the ED. Their methodology involves five stages: rapport, reflection, realization, reorientation, and reintegration (Landry, 1996). Chaplains build rapport with VIV so the patients feel comfortable and safe to talk openly. The chaplains' intent is to help VIV see the need to destruct their current lifestyles and create better ones through processes of reflection and realization. The chaplains facilitate a reorientation of VIV into their communities through social service agencies (such as Big Brothers/Big Sisters). Finally, the patients are reintegrated into faith-based communities, where they will not be judged by their past lifestyles.

At Jefferson, chaplains are constantly present in the hospital (24 hours a day, seven days a week) and are automatically paged to visit VIV between the ages of 14 and 25. Their primary responsibility is to provide them with bedside spiritual and emotional support. Also, they had the opportunity to enroll the patient into the JCVPP. Their non-threatening presence enhanced their abilities to connect with these young people. This is important because they were often intimidated in the vigorous ED environment.

For these reasons, TJUH's Violence Prevention Initiative embraced a faith-based approach to help young victims of violence seen in the ED. Pastoral care and follow-up referral services were provided to young patients with the goals of improving personal lives and preventing a return to violence. Religion is known to have profound effects in African American and Latino communities; studies have documented the powerful role played by the Black Church. An example that expresses this is in the changing emphasis of African American church leaders from the Civil Rights Movement to civic engagement in aiding communities and individuals. While many are not members of a church, young VIV often express a strong foundation of spirituality and religion in their lives. Their faiths become evident in the setting of tragedy (like violent injury) as a way to comprehend and understand. During their stay in the ED, VIV and their families are visited by chaplains. Thus, a patient–chaplain understanding develops that allows VIV to feel comfortable expressing themselves.

Lessons Learned

TJUH is dedicated to excellence in patient care. The JCVPP expressed this commitment because its mission was to treat the total person. Physical, spiritual, and emotional comfort has an integral role in the healing process of patients and their families. Many VIV entered the ED with unexpressed emotions: fear, anger, bitterness, resentment, helplessness, and it is not uncommon for VIV to seek vengeance against their attackers. The JCVPP upheld the notion that chaplain interference with this aggressive behavior could convince the VIV to peacefully handle these conflicts. In this way, the chaplain catalyzed the JCVPP's goal to reduce episodes of repeat and retaliatory violence.

Because the JCVPP pioneered a faith-based approach to VIV in the ED, the process to achieve its goals did not follow an established and pre-existing path. The approach needed to be flexible and open-minded to adjust to the unexpected. It should come as no surprise that the methods changed at many steps along the way. Each change was a step closer to efficacy and the possibility to achieve the anticipated goals. The first roadblock encountered occurred when the chaplains were sent into the VIV community for ED follow-ups. Because of their lack of "street smarts" and experience in dangerous neighborhoods, the chaplains' efficiency to communicate well with discharged VIV was severely impeded. The JCVPP adjusted its methods and necessitated phone calls to follow the discharged VIV. This also proved ineffective (and therefore worthy of change) because many patients were difficult to reach by phone. It was finally decided that chaplains would be most useful by visiting VIV in the ED. PAAN workers, who knew the culture and neighborhoods of the VIV, were hired as community contacts to follow up with discharged patients. They proved to be the most efficient liaison group. Although not at first, Community Transitional Mentors from Big Brothers/Big Sisters were later incorporated into the program to be used in conjunction with the PAAN workers. Their role was to assure that patients made a successful transition from the hospital to community support services.

Summary and Recommendations

The JCVPP's main goal was to lower the number of VIV in Philadelphia through follow-up service to discharged patients. Chaplains provided understanding and compassion to VIV in a daunting ED; their concern and work outside the hospital was a TJUH effort to reduce the incidences of repeat injury and retaliatory violence. By reporting both successful and ineffective findings, the JCVPP hopes other violence prevention initiatives can use our experience to construct the most effective programs for the future.

The JCVPP identified three key points in the process of VIV health care. Several lessons were learned in the process of providing health care to VIV patients. For example, the volume of injured patients often overwhelmed busy health providers in the ED. This stress decreased both their ability to distinguish high-risk VIV and time to administer the 56-question survey. Chaplains helped the medical staff because they needed only to be made aware of a VIV; the chaplain could then give the assessment for VIV prevention. When the survey was completed, the chaplain then reviewed its findings with the medical and administrative directors to formulate the appropriate intervention.

Using chaplains in the ED had implications besides giving VIV prevention assessments: they sometimes connected with the patient and family on a spiritual level. The JCVPP recognized the inherent value of every person and placed a special importance to avoid blaming the victim at his/her time of greatest vulnerability. By incorporating pastoral care into the interdisciplinary team, the JCVPP believed that it has improved the care of young VIV. The chaplain also provided a certain harmony that many VIV could identify with which health care providers, in many instances, could not provide. The ethnicity difference between provider and patient created a lack of trust on the part of the patient. This evidence leads to much of the literature on health care disparities (Smedley, 2003). Chaplains provided a nonjudgmental presence that allowed the patients to express themselves.

Another lesson learned related to the community. The JCVPP recognized that a medical care system could not provide the full range of services needed for VIV. Discharged patients returned to a community challenged by poverty, crime, and violence. By employing PAAN workers as community liaisons, the JCVPP was able to utilize the capacity of the community itself to address the needs of young VIV. This community collaboration strengthened TJUH's relationship with many parts of Philadelphia and paved the way for future cooperation and collaboration.

For the future, the TJUH looks to establish an Intentional Injury Center. The center's purpose would be to continue the interdisciplinary approach to lowering the VIV number in Philadelphia. Program administrators of the JCVPP are currently seeking funding for such a center.

Recommendations for Best Practices, Research, and Implementation of Faith-Based Activities

The JCVPP holds several implications for future research and implementation of faith-based intervention activities. Synergy in sundry employment is the best discovery of the project. The most effective practice for addressing the needs of young VIV is hiring an interdisciplinary team, consisting of specialized workers, to cover the spectrum of care for VIV. This includes primary medical care providers, social workers, pastoral care staff, and community workers. All workers should be regulated by continuous feedback of positive and negative outcomes emanating from the project. Community outreach workers are key in the navigation of VIV to resources in the community. Investment in their growth is important to work for the community and within the community in collaboration with academic medical centers. Other health care institutions should look to incorporate their unique resources into the care of VIV.

Future research collaborations between health care institutions and divinity schools would be beneficial in constructing effective models of synchronous pastoral and medical care. In particular, future programs similar to the JCVPP would benefit from specialized pastoral training that impact young people entrenched in an urban context of violence. Furthermore, rigorous ethnographic research is necessary to understand how the remnants of trauma affect young VIV in their home communities.

References

Connor, K. M., J. R. T. Davidson, et al. (2003). Spirituality, resilience, and anger in survivors of violent trauma: A community survey. *J. of Traumatic Stress*. 16(5):487–94.

Everly, G. S., Jr. (2000). The role of pastoral crisis intervention in disasters, terrorism, violence, and other community crises. *International J. of Emergency Mental Hlth.* 2(3):139–42.

Felitti, V., R. Anda, et al. (1998). The relationship of adult health status to childhood abuse and household dysfunction. *Amer. J, of Preventive Med.* 4(4):245–258.

Kataoka, S. H., S. Fuentes, et al. (2006). A community participatory research partnership: The development of a faith-based intervention for children exposed to violence. *Ethnicity and Disease.* 16(1 Suppl 1):89–97.

Landry, V. (1996). Pastoral care in a trauma center. *J. of Religion and Health,* 35:211–214.

Rich, J. A. and L. M. Sullivan (2001). Correlates of violent assault among young male primary care patients. *J. of Health Care for the Poor and Underserved,* 12(1):103–12.

Smedley, B.D., Stith, A.Y., and Nelson, A.R. (eds.) (2003). *Unequal Treatment: Confronting Racial and Ethnic Disparities in Health Care.* Washington, D.C., National Academy Press.

Chapter 5

Project Ujima: Working Together to Make Things Right

Marlene D. Melzer-Lange, MD, Michael R. McCart, MS, Lori F. Phelps, MS, Wendi Heuermann, MPA, and W. Hobart Davies, PhD

Introduction

Ujima is a Swahili word meaning "collective responsibility" or "working together to make things right." Project Ujima is a unique hospital- and community-based program providing integrated violence intervention and prevention services for youth assault victims and their families. Goals of the program include 1) to reduce the physical and psychosocial consequences of the violence injury, 2) to reduce the chances of violent re-injury, and 3) to reduce the risk of the victim becoming a violent offender. In this chapter, we will present the background for program development, a description of the program components, including the medical and psychosocial services, and a case example, which illustrates the program's multidisciplinary intervention approach. We will also discuss outcome data, lessons learned, and future directions for the program.

Background of Program Development

In 1994, there was a significant increase in youth firearm violence in Milwaukee as well as in the United States (Centers for Disease Control, 1994; Fingerhut, 1993). C. Everett Koop, former Surgeon General of the United States, called this surge of violence "a public health emergency" (Koop and Lundberg, 1992, p. 3075). At the time, the leading cause of death for adolescent males living in urban areas was homicide (National Center for Health Statistics, 1998), and youth gang violence had been increasing since the early 1980s (U.S. Department of Justice, 2001). In 1994, nurses and physicians at Children's Hospital of Wisconsin (CHW) treated over 180 children between the ages of five and eighteen years for firearm injuries. Complicating the problem, many assault victims required medical follow-up for their injuries, yet health professionals were providing inadequate instructions at the time of the Emergency Department (ED) visit (Melzer-Lange, Lye, and Calhoun, 1998). At the same time, experts were recommending a comprehensive approach to the care of interpersonal victims of violence in the medical setting (Dolins and Christoffel, 1994; Walsh-Kelly and Strait, 1998). Later, other investigators would examine post traumatic stress in children exposed to violence (McCart, Davies, Harris, Wincek, Calhoun, and Melzer-Lange, in press; McClosskey and Walken, 1999), and violent injuries became one of the national priorities for injury control (National Committee for Injury Prevention and Control, 1989).

One particular case served as a catalyst to begin planning for Project Ujima. A 16-year-old male presented to the ED at CHW with a fatal gunshot wound to the chest. A review of this patient's medical record revealed that in 1988, when he was nine years old, he was treated in the ED for an "accidental" injury. In 1990, he had been treated in the ED for multiple contusions and abrasions resulting from an assault. At 13 years of age, he was treated for multiple stab wounds. Again in early 1994, he was treated for a firearm injury to the leg. By the end of that same year, he was dead from another firearm injury (Wincek, personal communication).

Through the efforts of a multidisciplinary group organized by the CHW trauma and injury prevention nurse, planning for Project Ujima ensued. Nurses, physicians, and social workers joined with community partners including youth development specialists, youth advocacy workers, law enforcement personnel, mental health professionals, and family advocates. Key partner agencies included CHW, the Medical College of Wisconsin, the Milwaukee Youth Opportunities Collaborative, Family Services of Milwaukee, the Milwaukee Health Department, and the Social Development Commission.

This group worked toward a model similar to Wraparound services (Grundle, 2002) to assist youth victims of violence and their families. The initial entry point for services was designed to be at the time of the youth's care in the CHW ED. Services were then designed to provide aftercare in the youth's community setting; care was taken to ensure that these services were family-centered, culturally competent, and developmentally appropriate, as well as periodically evaluated. Initial financial support was provided by each of the partners in the form of in-kind services. Subsequent funding for a more developed program was provided by the Children's Hospital Foundation, Targeted-Issues funding from Emergency Medical Services for Children, the Allstate Foundation, and Victims of Crime Assistance through the U. S. Department of Justice.

Theoretical Framework

Project Ujima is built around the complementary theoretical frameworks of the Public Health Model (Haddon, 1980; Hammond and Yung, 1993) and Developmental Psychopathology (Cicchetti and Toth, 1997a). The Public Health Model begins with the youth assault and attempts to work backwards to identify all of the potentially remediable factors associated with the assaulted youth and his/her environment, the perpetrator and his/her environment, access and use of the weapon (if applicable), and the community as a whole. In utilizing the Haddon (1980) matrix as it applies to youth violence, the victim (host), perpetrator (vector), firearm (agent), social environment, and physical environment can be viewed pre-event, during the event, and following the event. For example, pre-event strategies for the host include anticipatory guidance around violence, whereas strategies immediately after the event would include medical and psychological services. Post-event strategies for the victim could include physical rehabilitation, medical follow-up, and psychological services. In the case of the social environment, pre-event strategies include job opportunities and adult-supervised activities for youth. Event strategies include school crisis intervention. After the event, social environmental strategies include reintroduction to school, peer activities, and family support.

Developmental psychopathology is an approach to understanding maladaptive and adaptive behaviors and processes over developmental time (Lewis, 2000). Embedded in ecological context, it recognizes the transactional influence of the different systems that impact development, from the cellular level up to the level of the individual and outward to the neighborhood and society as a whole (Cicchetti and Toth, 1997b). Developmental psychopathology attends to processes related to the establishment and maintenance of both positive and negative behavior patterns, and especially factors associated with movement into and out of the maladaptive range. This approach also recognizes the influence of cultural context in influencing behavior and development (Coll, Akerman, and Cicchetti, 2000).

Both of these models are in keeping with the multisystemic nature of Project Ujima. Solutions to the problems of injury and re-injury are seen as most likely to be obtained through interventions aimed at simultaneously or sequentially addressing numerous risk factors or groups of risk factors. Primary activities are focused on the youth and families who are participating in the project, but we also collaborate with others attempting to alter the overall level of violence in the city and the overall risk picture for the city's youth. Some interventions are directed specifically at reducing the risk of re-injury (e.g., assisting families in moving to new neighborhoods, grappling with the influence of family members who are urging retaliation), but more often our interventions are aimed at improving the overall well-being and functioning of the youth and family, which is assumed to change the risk nexus for re-injury and psychosocial morbidity.

Program Components and Participants

Description of Program

Project Ujima builds on the strengths of multiple community agencies to address the physical, mental, and emotional needs of youth violence victims and their families to 1) alleviate violence-related grief and trauma-related symptoms, 2) promote a return to normal functioning following the injury, and 3) reduce the risk of repeat violent injuries. Project services, in keeping with the developmental psychopathology framework, address individual, family, and neighborhood issues. At the individual level, Project Ujima provides medical follow-up and referrals for treating physical wounds, as well as mental health education and treatment addressing the effects of violence and the trauma response. At the family level, Project Ujima assists victims and their families in stabilizing their lives after the victimization through crisis intervention services that address educational, mental, and physical health, as well as basic human needs. Project Ujima also serves as a legal advocate in helping victims and their families navigate the criminal justice system, facilitating the pursuit of Crime Victim Compensation benefits, and providing victims and families with a measure of safety and security.

Identification of Clients

The majority of youth served by Project Ujima are referred from the CHW ED. Criteria for offering services include 1) patient is a victim of an intentional, interpersonal injury such as a non-weapon assault, firearm injury, or stabbing 2) patient is between 7 and 18 years of age; and 3) patient is not the victim of child abuse or a suicide attempt. By training the triage nurses and registration staff regarding Project Ujima criteria, we have been able to obtain staff support for Project Ujima, which has led to timely and appropriate referrals.

Following admission of a youth assault victim to the ED, staff page the CHW Social Worker as well as the Project Ujima Community Liaison and Volunteer Peer Liaison during daytime and evening shifts. During the overnight shift, the patient is referred to the Project Ujima telephone hotline, and the Community Liaison then contacts the family at home after discharge or during an inpatient hospitalization. During the ED visit, the Social Worker conducts a psychosocial assessment and provides information about potential resources (e.g., insurance). The Community Liaison offers support to the family and describes Project Ujima services. The Liaison also may clarify medical procedures, in conjunction with the ED nurses and physicians, provide support related to the fear and pain that the youth may be experiencing, facilitate communication between the family and law enforcement personnel, and introduce strategies to reduce youth or family retaliation for the violent event. Finally, Liaisons offer ongoing Project Ujima services and seek consent from the injured youth's parent or guardian for further participation in Project Ujima.

In addition to referrals from the CHW ED, Project Ujima receives referrals from outside sources including community and school health clinics, local public safety organizations, court and child welfare systems, and social service agencies. The program also serves clients referred by their primary physician, family members, other hospital emergency departments, other Project Ujima clients, and Child Protective Services where there is concern that the child may have witnessed violence personally. In these cases, initial information is collected by telephone, and a home visit is scheduled.

Types and Nature of Services

Project Ujima provides a variety of services to aid youth victimized by interpersonal violence and their families, the aim of which is to help break the cycle of violence. Since services are collaborative and community-based, Project Ujima relies on a system of linkages throughout Milwaukee County that serve to ensure optimal physical, mental, and emotional well-being of youth and families. Services also emphasize in-home delivery of health assessments, therapy for post traumatic stress symptomatology, and positive coping skills as a means to address needs in a nonthreatening manner.

Project Ujima services can be categorized into the following components:

1) Social Services—The focus of Social Services is on-call response and support to victims and their families at the time of the injury. Services include immediate referral response and follow-up, crisis intervention at the ED, outreach resource and support, peer visitation and support in the ED, and intervention to meet basic needs and to address safety and legal advocacy.

2) Mental Health Services—The focus of Mental Health Services is to assist victims and families in developing positive coping actions and to provide counseling, psycho-education, and support from other victims. Services include Post Traumatic Stress Disorder (PTSD) screening and education, home and center-based victim/family counseling, group treatment, monthly parent/youth support groups, clinical mental health screening, and referral to intensive psychological or psychiatric services.

3) In-Home Nurse Services—The focus of In-Home Nurse Services is to address the physical needs of the victim to ensure good medical outcomes. Services include in-home medical follow-up, assessment of health risks and interventions, referral to appropriate medical providers, and assistance with medical insurance.

4) Outreach Services—The focus of Outreach Services is to help victims continue the recovery process, combat negative coping actions such as social isolation, and promote resiliency factors including problem-solving skills and social competence. Services include summer camps, skill-building classes, victim retreats, and expressive arts programs.

5) Victim Advocacy—The focus of Victim Advocacy is to represent the victims' interests and to empower victims to advocate for themselves. Services include crime victim advocacy in court, schools, and the community, and assisting victims to address their personal safety, medical care, and educational needs.

Project Ujima Clients

Project Ujima annually targets approximately 240 youth who present to the CHW ED with assault-related injuries. Approximately one-third of the injuries are firearm-related, with the remainder due to physical assaults. Historically, nearly 70 percent of youth participating are African American, and nearly 70 percent are male (Marcelle and Melzer-Lange, 2001). Almost half of participating youth live in six neighboring zip codes in areas with the highest poverty rates in Milwaukee. Approximately 60% of the youth are insured through public insurance, 20% have commercial insurance, and 20% are uninsured.

Delivery of Services

Project Ujima offers a culturally sensitive and holistic approach to addressing the health care needs of youth and families exposed to interpersonal violence. The methodology to achieve the Project Ujima goals is based on a unique blend of research and practice guidelines from the American Academy of Pediatrics (1996) for treating violently injured youth, as well as "Lessons Learned" during our seven years of operation. Because no single strategy can accommodate the needs of all youth and families, Project Ujima offers a wide array of physical and mental health services to children and families exposed to violence. Achieving program goals and objectives requires a collaborative effort, including a commitment from youth victims who volunteer to participate in Project Ujima for at least one year.

One of our "Lessons Learned" is that youth are more likely to join Project Ujima if they are introduced to the program while they are still in the CHW ED. Therefore Community Liaisons and Volunteer Peer Liaisons strive to meet families in the ED and to immediately begin to build a trusting relationship. While youth are being treated for their wounds in the ED, Community Liaisons, Peer Liaisons, and an Emergency Room Social Worker begin to address the broader problems associated with interpersonal youth violence. The initial response to the youth victim who presents to the ED is primarily focused on providing comfort and assurance. As a relationship is built with the youth, risk factors and strengths are identified. The underlying goal of the Project Ujima intervention team is to provide the victim with tools to achieve recovery and gain a commitment to engage in more comprehensive victim services through the in-home visit. Community Liaisons help injured youth to recognize their immediate reactions of fear, helplessness, or rage, and to understand the consequences of acting upon feelings of anger through retaliation. Working together with Volunteer Peer Liaisons, the Community Liaisons evaluate factors evident in the youth or family that are known to be associated with violent victimization and begin addressing those needs before discharge from the ED. Volunteer Peer Liaisons and Community Liaisons also educate victims about common reactions and feelings that may surface over the next few days following victimization and discuss strategies to deal with these reactions.

Before discharge from the ED, the Community Liaison schedules a follow-up home visit with injured youth and their families. This follow-up visit focuses on reducing the emotional impacts of violence and facilitating youths' natural strengths. While Community Liaisons and Volunteer Peer Liaisons address the youth victims' needs, an Emergency Room Social Worker focuses primarily on the family. The Social Worker completes a comprehensive youth and family social history and shares relevant information with the rest of the Project Ujima team. Equally important, Project Ujima staff discuss crime victim compensation criteria with youth and families, and provide brochures regarding the Wisconsin Crime Victim Compensation Program. For eligible youth and families, Community Liaisons facilitate the client's application process. The Community Liaison and the Social Worker also assist in helping the victim and the family better understand their legal rights with respect to prosecution of the perpetrator, and are able to facilitate communication with the police regarding the incident.

Subsequent to treatment in the hospital and within four weeks of the violent incident, a care team, including Community Liaison, Licensed Nurse, and Therapist, conducts a follow-up home visit. During a home visit, the team administers surveys to assess youth risk-taking behaviors, exposure to violence, and post traumatic symptomatology. The health care team also provides appropriate crisis counseling, enrolls youth and their families in health education programming, and provides referrals to other social services that contribute to health and well-being. For example, Community Liaisons facilitate linkages to food pantries, housing and job placement services, and prenatal or parenting classes. They also re-establish ties to schools as indicated.

Weekly multidisciplinary case review meetings are held to review treatment options, goals, and progress. Meeting participants include Community Liaisons, Youth Support Specialist, Program Manager, Medical Director, Trauma Advanced Practice Nurse, Mental Health Therapists, Ujima Nurse, and CHW Social Worker. Collectively, these efforts lead to long-term health outcomes that reduce the risk of reinjury, delinquency, and premature death of youth experiencing interpersonal violence.

Youth and Family Development Program

Outreach services are developed and implemented to assist youth and their families in the recovery process. Youth services include individual and group counseling to help combat maladaptive coping strategies such as social isolation and anger, often resulting in increased school truancy. Positive activities that promote resiliency related to social competence, problem-solving skills, autonomy, and sense of purpose also are offered. A victim assistance curriculum is available that explores topics such as the impact of violence and victimization on individuals, families, and communities; the influence of peers, family, and culture on attitudes and beliefs about violence; and the development of safety strategies, communication, and support skills. Through role-playing and modeling, youth examine their experiences, learn to identify their choices, and practice new skills that can be transferred to real life situations. Structured group activities that include focused group discussions and skill-building sessions are provided to promote positive peer relationships. These activities provide youth with the chance to identify problems and create solutions, to explore topics in depth, and to learn how to channel distress through other outlets such as artistic activities, physical games, or relaxing activities.

Project Ujima also organizes activities for youth that provide exposure to new environments and opportunities to learn new skills in an effort to improve self-esteem. Activities include an annual rafting/camping trip; camps focusing on entrepreneurial efforts, computer skills, and arts creation/performance; and public speaking opportunities. One example is Girls Express, an expressive arts program for teenage girls. The program is funded by a grant from the United Way and is a collaborative effort between Project Ujima and a local dance company. Girls in the program work with local artists (e.g., dancers, actors, sculptors) to explore their concerns associated with exposure to community violence, living in violent neighborhoods, and being females. Under the guidance of the artists, the girls craft a performance that includes dances, songs, and skits, demonstrating their struggles and ways they strive to overcome them. During weekly rehearsals, the girls experience the rigors of artistic training and expression, with the end goal of performing at local venues (e.g., schools, community centers, festivals). Both the training and performances provide opportunities to gain self-esteem and to express potentially traumatic experiences in a cathartic manner. A program is also available for young men to help them address issues of anger and to help them cope with the violence in their lives. Mentored by adult males, the young men bond through sharing personal experiences and feelings about issues they face and participate in recreational activities. Providing transportation to and from group sessions, along with nutritious and appealing snacks and meals, has been found to be important for the success of all youth programming.

Project Ujima also sponsors family-focused activities to provide families with positive activities and opportunities to interact with other families in the program. In addition to monthly Family Nights, which include a meal, presentations for parents, and fun activities for youth, Project Ujima sponsors a summer picnic, Thanksgiving and Christmas celebrations, and other group activities such as sporting events, theatrical plays, and museum events.

Psychosocial Support

Psychosocial support services are provided to family members participating in Project Ujima to address their mental health needs. Results from interviews with 35 African-American families, whose children received ED treatment for assault-related injuries and whose families were eligible for participation in Project Ujima, guided the development of these services.

During the interviews, the youth reported experiencing high levels of distress (McCart, Davies, Phelps, Heuermann, and Melzer-Lange, 2004). The highest percentage of youth reported experiencing difficulties with anger and aggressive behavior. The most commonly reported forms of aggression included physical fights, verbal arguments, and hitting objects. A setting analysis revealed that these aggressive behavior problems most frequently occurred at home and at school. Other difficulties reported by the youth included internalizing symptoms, such as anxiety and depression, peer relationship difficulties, parent/family conflict, PTSD symptoms, academic concerns, physical health concerns, and concerns about neighborhood safety.

The mothers of the assaulted youth also reported experiencing high levels of distress, which were unrelated to various aspects of their child's assault (e.g., severity of the injury, time since the assault) but were directly related to maternal level of violence exposure (Phelps, Davies, McCart, Klein-Tasman, Melzer-Lange, and Heuermann, 2004). Most notable were the avoidant tendencies and emotional blunting associated with PTSD (American Psychiatric Association, 2000). The most common concerns described by mothers involved family safety, maternal mental health, and youth externalizing behavior since the assault. Specifically, mothers described chronic worry and difficulty sleeping related to living in violent neighborhoods. They also described frustration with their child's externalizing behaviors, which often were present prior to the assault but were exacerbated by it, and preexisting academic difficulties. Mental health services offered through Project Ujima are based on a phase-oriented intervention protocol, which starts with stabilization, progresses through assessment, and ends with implementation of a treatment plan individualized for each family's needs.

Stabilization

The first phase of the intervention, stabilization, begins at the initial home visit conducted two weeks post-injury. During this visit, families are introduced to Ujima staff (e.g., caseworker, nurse, therapist), learn about youth and family programming, and receive medical follow-up attention (if needed) by the nurse. The therapist's primary goal during this visit is to conduct a brief screening interview with the youth and parent to explore whether the youth or parent are experiencing Acute Stress Disorder or any other trauma-related symptoms. Emerging research suggests that providing mental health services in response to these acute trauma symptoms, before an individual has had time to process the trauma, can actually lead to worse psychosocial outcomes (Van Emmerik, Kamphuis, Hulsbosch, and Emmelkamp, 2002). Therefore, Project Ujima therapists limit their immediate interventions to brief education with the family on common responses to traumatic injury and healthy strategies family members can use to cope with their distress. An example of what the therapists might say during the education phase of the screening interview is included below.

Traumatic events such as your injury can be distressing. It is natural for people who experience these events to have different types of reactions. Some reactions include shock, worry, sleep difficulties, school difficulties, appetite changes, feeling irritable or angry, or feeling jumpy. Sometimes people say they just don't feel like themselves after a traumatic event. Other times people say that they are doing just fine and were not really affected by the event.

The therapist then asks the youth and his/her caretaker if the youth has experienced any of these (or other) reactions since the injury. If the youth reports experiencing trauma-related distress, the therapist explores the methods the youth is using to cope with that distress and recommends the strategies described below.

Most people find it helpful to talk about what happened with family and friends once they feel comfortable. Sometimes youth want to talk about what happened, but it's hard for parents to listen. If that's the case, youth can talk with other family members or friends, and that can help them work through what happened. It is also important to take care of your basic needs following a trauma. This includes trying to get enough sleep, eating well, exercising, drinking enough water and juice, and avoiding alcohol and caffeine. Keeping to your daily routines and activities can also be helpful. For many people, these coping strategies will lead to a reduction in symptoms over time.

Parental reaction to the youth's assault also is explored. Research indicates that there are elevated rates of posttraumatic stress symptomatology among parents of youth diagnosed with serious illnesses (e.g., Landolt et al., 2002; Kazak et al., 2004). In addition, parental support is important to the recovery of a child following a traumatic experience, such as exposure to community violence (see Garbarino, Dubrow, Kostelny, and Pardo, 1992). Therefore, common parental responses to youth trauma are normalized (e.g., worry, guilt, fear) and the importance of support during recovery from the injury (for both the parent and youth) is emphasized.

The therapist's next steps depend primarily on the information gathered during this initial home visit. For the youth or parent who report trauma symptoms during the screening interview, another home visit is scheduled about four weeks following the assault to assess post-injury adaptation. If symptoms continue to persist at the time of this subsequent visit, the youth or parent is referred for follow-up assessment and intervention services. The goal here is to suspend the delivery of more intensive mental health support until after the youth or parent has had sufficient time to stabilize after the acute event.

If the youth or parent does not report trauma-related distress, but he or she is experiencing other, nontrauma-related concerns (e.g., depression, externalizing problems, academic difficulties), a referral for a more thorough psychological assessment can occur immediately. For these cases, the timing of the assessment and intervention is less of a concern and these services may occur within a few days or weeks of the initial home visit.

Assessment

Youth and parents referred for a psychological evaluation complete a standard assessment battery. The purpose of the evaluation is to gather additional information about the nature of the concerns. This information is used to aid in case conceptualization and treatment planning.

The standard youth assessment battery includes self- and parent-report rating scales, a semi-structured interview, and a brief measure of intelligence. This battery was designed to cover the broad range of psychiatric symptoms and contextual concerns commonly experienced by youth exposed to community violence (McCart, et al., 2004). The assessment measures included in this standard battery are listed in Table 1.

Other assessment measures/techniques may be added to this battery if the therapist wishes to gather additional information about the youth's psychological concerns. As an example, for youth displaying externalizing behavior problems at school, the therapist may conduct an observation of the youth in the classroom and the youth's teacher may be asked to complete a teacher-report measure. Furthermore, Project Ujima youth experiencing academic difficulties are frequently referred to the UWM Psychology Clinic for a more comprehensive psycho-educational evaluation to assess for the presence of Attention Deficit/Hyperactivity Disorder and/or a specific learning disability.

The standard parent assessment battery includes self-report rating scales and a semi-structured interview. It was designed to provide information relevant to both parental and youth functioning, and was based on research exploring the concerns of low-income African-American mothers whose children had been assaulted in the community (Phelps et al., 2004). The assessment measures included in this battery are listed in Table 2.

As with the youth battery, additional measures can be added to the parent battery in order to gather further information about parental functioning. One example is the use of self-report inventories assessing mood states (e.g., depression, anxiety or anger). Once the initial assessment of youth and/or parents is complete, the therapist develops a conceptualization of the case and assists the family in choosing an appropriate intervention. In the next section, we describe some of the interventions commonly used with the youth and parents participating in Project Ujima.

Table 1. Standard Youth Assessment Battery

Assessment Name	**Assessment Type**	**Domain(s) Assessed**
Screen for Adolescent Violence Exposure (SAVE; Hastings and Kelly, 1997)	Self-report	Historical violence exposure
Trauma Symptom Checklist for Children	Self-report	Post-traumatic (TSCC; Briere, 1996) stress and related trauma-symptoms
Behavior Assessment System for Children (BASC; Reynolds and Kamphaus, 1998)	Self- and parent-report versions	Internalizing symptoms, externalizing behaviors, adaptive ' functioning, school maladjustment, and personal/family adjustment
Schedule for Affective Disorders And Schizophrenia for School Aged Children (K-SADS; Kaufman, Birmaher, Ryan, 1996)	Semi-structured Interview	PTSD section and any other symptom clinical elevations on domains showing Brent, Rao, and the TSCC and BASCs
Kaufman Brief Intelligence Test (K-BIT; Kaufman and Kaufman, 1990)	Objective measure	Intellectual functioning

Table 2. Standard Parent Assessment Battery

Assessment Name	Assessment Type	Domain(s) Assessed
Screen for Adolescent Violence Exposure (SAVE; Hastings and Kelly, 1997)	Self-report	Historical violence exposure
Trauma Symptom Inventory (TSI; Briere, 1995)	Self-report	Post-traumatic stress and related trauma symptoms
Structured Clinical Interview for DSM-IV-TR (SCID; First, Gibbon, Spitzer, and Williams)	Semi-structured interview	PTSD section and any other symptom domains showing clinical elevations on the TSI

Intervention

Intervention services for the Project Ujima youth may include any or all of the following: group therapy, individual therapy, school advocacy, or community referral. Youth who are displaying aggressive behavior problems (representing a majority of the Project Ujima participants) are invited to participate in our group-based Strengthening Youth and Families Program (described later). PTSD and other internalizing problems are typically addressed using an in-home individual therapy approach. For the youth who are experiencing academic difficulties, the results from the psycho-educational evaluations are commonly used to advocate for more appropriate school or classroom placements. Youth experiencing serious psychiatric concerns such as psychosis, chronic substance abuse, or suicidal ideation are typically referred to more intensive psychiatric services in the community.

Intervention services for Project Ujima parents are aimed at addressing assault-related concerns and/or other mental health concerns exacerbated by the assault. Service formats include individual, couples, family, or group therapy. Therapy has targeted posttraumatic stress symptomatology (associated with the youth's assault or with a prior traumatic incident experienced by the parent), difficulty adjusting to ramifications of the assault (e.g., remaining in the neighborhood where the assault occurred, frustration with school and legal responses), and parent training to address youth externalizing behaviors. Therapy also has addressed preexisting concerns that may impact recovery from the youth's assault, including long-standing parent–child communication difficulties, emotional dysregulation, and symptoms associated with mood disorders.

In order to bolster social support among families, and to provide education regarding how to effectively address some of the most common concerns described by parents, Project Ujima also organizes monthly family nights. Dinner, transportation, and childcare are provided, along with informative presentations from local service providers that discuss topics such as teenage sexual behavior, housing advocacy, and stress management.

Strengthening Youth and Families Program

Urban youth exposed to, or victimized by, violence often respond by becoming more aggressive (Yung and Hammond, 1995). In fact, our research with the young men and women participating in Project Ujima revealed that over 75% were experiencing difficulties with anger and aggressive behavior following their injury (McCart, et al., 2004). These high rates of aggression place violently injured youth at a higher risk for violent injury recidivism (DuRant, Cadenhead, Pendergrast, Slavens, and Linder, 1994; Fitzpatrick, 1997). In fact, studies have shown that urban youth are much more likely to become victims of expressive violence, such as aggression directed toward family and friends, compared to random acts associated with violent crime (Griffith and Bell, 1989). Given the evidence that being a victim of violence is a significant predictor for becoming a victim in the future (Thomas, Leite, and Duncan, 1998), assaulted youth presenting to the ED represent an important at-risk population for secondary prevention.

In this section, we describe our Strengthening Youth and Families (SYF) Program as an example of a secondary prevention technique that can be used to target aggressive behavior problems among assaulted youth. This program combines elements of cognitive-behavior therapy and behavioral parent-training to reduce violence and aggression among African-American adolescent males (ages 14–17 years). This population of youth was chosen as the target for the SYF program because African-American adolescent males represent a majority of the youth participating in Project Ujima and because these youth are more likely than any other ethnic or gender group in the U.S. to experience violent crime (Hennes, 1998). In the paragraphs that follow, we briefly review the content of the intervention and discuss some strategies used to promote participant engagement.

Cognitive-behavior therapy and behavioral parent-training have each received substantial empirical support as effective violence prevention techniques (Thornton, Craft, Dahlberg, Lynch, and Baer, 2002). The success of these intervention programs can be attributed, at least in part, to their focus on two well-documented risk factors for youth violence, namely, impaired social-cognitive skills and maladaptive parenting practices. Regarding social-cognitive skills, studies have shown that aggressive youth tend to hold hostile attributional biases, they make errors in their interpretation of social cues, and they have stronger expectations that aggression will lead to positive outcomes (Crick and Dodge, 1994; de Castro, Veerman, Koops, Bosch, and Monshouwer, 2002; Lochman and Dodge, 1994). Cognitive-behavioral interventions target these cognitive skill deficiencies by training youth to attend more effectively to social cues, to generate multiple interpretations for others' behavior, and to engage in nonviolent problem-solving strategies. Youth also learn about the short- and long-term consequences of aggressive behavior and learn how to manage their negative affect. Regarding maladaptive parenting, there is an abundance of research showing that parenting styles characterized by coercive parent-child interchanges, inconsistent discipline, and poor parental monitoring place youth at risk for the development of aggression and other behavior problems (Compton, Snyder, Schrepferman, Bank, and Shortt, 2003; Patterson, 2002; Tolan and Loeber, 1993). Behavioral parent-training programs address these maladaptive parenting practices by training parents to use effective behavioral management techniques. Parents learn how to avoid coercive interchanges by positively reinforcing youths' prosocial behavior and by consistently implementing developmentally appropriate consequences for youths' aggression and defiance.

Our SYF program combines cognitive-behavior therapy and behavioral parent-training into one intervention package because studies have shown this multi-modal approach to be more effective than either intervention alone (Kazdin, Siegel, and Bass, 1992; Thornton et al., 2002). The cognitive-behavior therapy component of SYF is modeled after the Positive Adolescent Choices Training (PACT) program developed by Yung and Hammond (1995). PACT is a group-based intervention that includes components of social problem-solving skills training, anger management training, and education about violence.

The behavioral parent-training component of SYF is drawn from the intervention developed by Barkley, Edwards, and Robin (1999) for working with defiant youth. This intervention teaches parents about the causes of youth aggression and reviews principles of effective behavior management. The PACT and parent-training interventions use a social skills training approach to replace maladaptive parent and adolescent behaviors with ones that generate less hostility and lead to safer results. Parents and youth learn these new behaviors by participating in a series of intervention exercises such as didactic instruction, facilitator modeling, role-play practice, in-session feedback, and weekly homework.

All of the African-American male adolescents in Project Ujima who are referred to the UWM Psychology Clinic with aggressive behavior problems are invited to participate in the SYF program. The young men participate in 12 weekly PACT group sessions while their parents participate in 6 individual and home-based parent-training sessions conducted biweekly.

Promoting Engagement

Researchers have discussed a number of critical strategies for promoting the success and engagement of families in mental health interventions (Kazdin, Holland, and Crowley, 1997; Tolan and Gorman-Smith, 1997; Webster-Stratton and Herbert, 1994; Yung and Hammond, 1995). First, researchers have suggested that interventions should seek to build supportive and rewarding relationships for the participants. We chose a group treatment approach for the PACT intervention to provide the youth with opportunities to develop positive friendships with other Project Ujima youth. Another obvious benefit of the group-based intervention approach is that it provides the youth with in vivo opportunities for interpersonal learning and development of social skills (Lochman, Whidby, and Fitzgerald, 2000). To circumvent the potential problems associated with aggregating all aggressive youth in a group setting (Dishion and Andrews, 1995), we regularly invite Project Ujima youth who do not have aggressive behavior problems and who can serve as prosocial models for the other group members (Feldman, Caplinger, and Wodarski, 1983). It should be noted that although we made attempts to conduct the parent-training intervention in a group setting, our efforts were largely unsuccessful because the chronic stressors experienced by these parents made it difficult for them to consistently attend the group meetings. Therefore, the decision was made to provide the parent-training sessions during scheduled home visits.

Second, research and clinical work suggests that interventions with minority youth and families are more effective when they possess cultural relevance. Therefore, in the PACT program, ethnically similar role models are used as group facilitators and role-plays are designed to accurately reflect the conflict situations that African-American youth experience in their everyday lives (Yung and Hammond, 1995). In the parent-training intervention, therapists and parents work together in a nonhierarchical, collaborative relationship. This collaborative style is demonstrated through open communication and encouragement of alternative viewpoints. Therapists are acutely sensitive to the environmental stressors and cultural values of parents, and they adapt the concepts and skills to best meet the needs of the family.

Third, researchers have shown that interventions result in lower levels of attrition if they are held in easily accessible locations. Therefore, all PACT group meetings are held at a local community center close to the participants' homes. Project Ujima is used to providing transportation for its families and vans are available to transport the young men to and from the center.

A fourth critical component is the availability of tangible benefits for participating in treatment. The parents receive a financial stipend following completion of the parent-training intervention. The young men's attendance during the group meetings is rewarded with well-balanced meals and with opportunities to earn free time to play basketball.

Fifth, studies have shown that interventions with urban populations are most effective when additional services are in place to address a family's social concerns (e.g., unemployment, education, access to food and other resources). As participants in Project Ujima, all families are assigned a Community Liaison who regularly help to address the family's social needs.

The SYF program is currently being evaluated in a federally funded study from the Centers for Disease Control and Prevention (CDC). Researchers are using a randomized clinical trial to compare the families participating in SYF with a wait-list control group. A variety of empirically validated assessment measures are being administered to program participants at baseline, post-intervention, and at a three-month follow-up time point to examine the effects of the program on participants' aggressive behavior.

Case Example

Project Ujima was paged in March 2001 as a result of a stabbing to a 16-year-old African-American female. This patient was a high school student in the 11th grade attending school on a regular basis. She was stabbed above her left eye and received over 40 stitches to her forehead. The patient was in an altercation with a female in her neighborhood who had assaulted the patient's younger sister earlier that morning. Following the incident, the patient was transported to CHW ED via ambulance.

After talking with a Community Liaison in the ED about Project Ujima and the services available to her and other family members, the patient agreed to participate and her mother signed a consent form. At the initial home visit, the Ujima Nurse assessed her wounds and reviewed the plans for her wound check and suture removal at the medical center. In addition, the Mental Health Therapist completed an assessment of the patient and her mother and developed a treatment plan. The Community Liaison provided additional support, encouraged the family to participate in Project Ujima activities, and ascertained that she would return to school in a timely manner.

The patient, her sister, and other immediate family members have participated in and benefited from many services/activities offered through Project Ujima. The family received tickets for local sporting events and participated in Project Ujima family activities. Project Ujima also provided funding for the patient's mother to enroll in an early child care licensing class, which enabled her to earn a certification in child care. Within 30 days of completing the course, the patient's mother found employment at a day care facility, thus reducing some of the financial strain experienced by the family.

The patient and her sister have actively participated in the program's monthly youth development meetings. In addition they shared their experiences and spoke out against community violence during a "Teaming Up on Gangs" Conference, and participated in a two-day youth retreat, where they were interviewed by a local television team. The patient's Community Liaison has assisted her in finding employment, spoke with her regularly about her future aspirations of becoming a neonatal nurse, and assisted her in meeting academic goals to insure her graduation from high school.

The patient has grown and matured tremendously since her injury and participation in Project Ujima programs. In the past, peers had played a significant role in her decision-making, usually resulting in negative consequences. The patient has chosen to make wiser choices and no longer "hangs around" the same group of peers. She tries harder to set a more positive example for her younger siblings, has maintained a job for over 7 months, and has helped her mother financially during a time that she was unemployed.

Outcomes

Re-injury Rates

One of the major concerns with victims of interpersonal violence is the chance of re-injury. Investigators have found that re-injury rates may be as high as 35% among adult victims of violence (Becker, Hall, Ursic, Jain, and Calhoun, 2004; Hausman, Spivak, Roeber, and Prothrow-Stith, 1989; Morrissey, Byrd, and Deitch, 1991; Poole et al., 1993). Therefore, we examined the re-injury rate of patients participating in Project Ujima. During the first years of the program (1995–2000), we found that youth participating in Project Ujima for at least two months following their injury had a repeat injury rate of 2%, as measured by presentation with a violent injury to the CHW ED during the year following their initial injury. Rates of repeat violent injuries for those youth electing not to participate in Project Ujima were not measured during the early years of the program. In 2000, Emergency Medical Services for Children (EMSC) provided funding to examine Project Ujima outcomes, including cost-effectiveness. Between June 2000 and December 2003, we enrolled 32 clients who gave informed consent to perform the evaluation and who also consented to be enrolled in Project Ujima. The control group consisted of 85 violently injured youth during the same time period who refused Project Ujima services. None of the youth receiving program services sustained a repeat violent injury requiring an ED visit, while eight non-program youth suffered injuries requiring ED attention.

Costs

Costs for program services associated with direct care, administrative oversight, and mental health services were calculated for the youth who participated in the EMSC evaluation. (Indirect costs associated with loss of parental wages, decreased school attendance, and other ancillary costs were not included in this analysis.) The average program cost for each youth-family unit was $2,419 for the duration of Project Ujima involvement, while their hospital charges, not including physician fees, was $5,910 per youth. For the 85 youth who did not receive Ujima services, the average initial hospital charges were $2,545. These youth also had additional hospital charges of $1,447 per patient for the eight repeat injury visits. On average, clients receiving Project Ujima services received 37 hours of service during their enrollment period. Location of services included the hospital, clinics, patient's home, patient's school, community churches, the youth detention center, a health education center, and public libraries.

Utilizing a base cost-effectiveness analysis model, with Project Ujima costs of $2,419 per patient and a cost of hospital visits of $1,466 per recidivism episode, a success rate of 100% for Project Ujima patients and 90.6% for patients not receiving Project Ujima services, we found that Project Ujima is a cost-effective strategy at a "willingness to pay" threshold of the inpatient recidivism cost of $1,466. This means that even if society was willing to simply pay $1,466 (money spent per recidivism episode which is already being spent indirectly by society), Project Ujima is a cost-effective societal program.

Community

Since 1998, homicide rates have been decreasing in Milwaukee. (Skiba, 1998, p. 1). In addition, numbers of firearm victims presenting to the CHW ED have been declining. Although many factors may account for this decline, it has occurred while Project Ujima has been providing services in Milwaukee.

Psychosocial Outcomes

Since outcome data are considered critical for evaluating the overall effectiveness of psychosocial interventions, Project Ujima collects clinical- and service-level outcomes among youth receiving a variety of services. In order to assess global clinical outcomes among youth participating in psychotherapy, therapists complete the Target Symptom Rating (TSR; Barber, et al., 2002) each month. The TSR is a 13-item measure of common psychiatric problems displayed by youth ages 4 to 21, and contains two subscales labeled Emotional Problems (consisting of five items labeled depression, anxiety, psychosomatic problems, suicidality, and psychotic symptom) and Behavioral Problems (consisting of eight items labeled family conflict, peer relationship problems, school difficulties, self-destructive/dangerous behaviors, aggression, substance abuse, runaway/out-of-control/legal problems, and impulsivity). Therapists rate the extent of each problem using a 5-point scale ranging from 1 (no problem) to 5 (severe problem). The TSR has been shown to have good internal consistency on the Emotional Problems (median alpha = .70) and Behavioral Problems (median alpha = .76) subscales (Barber, Neese, Coyne, Fultz, and Fonagy, 2002). The subscales have also been shown to correlate in expected directions with the Internalizing and Externalizing scales of the Child Behavior Checklist (CBCL; Achenbach, 1991) and the Child and Adolescent Functional Assessment Scale (CAFAS; Hodges, 1998). Furthermore, the TSR is sensitive to change in brief and extended treatment, demonstrating its usefulness as an outcome measure in applied settings (Barber, et al., 2002). One limitation of the TSR is that it was developed using a predominantly (86%) white standardization sample, raising questions about its utility with minority populations. Nevertheless, we decided to use the TSR with our predominantly African-American clients because as of yet there are no global outcome measures for African-American youth, and because the domains assessed by the TSR closely match the presenting concerns of the youth participating in Project Ujima.

The following TSR data come from a sample of 14 youth receiving individual psychotherapy between the months of January and August 2004. Paired-sample t-tests were used to compare the Emotional Problems and Behavioral Problems scale scores at baseline with the ratings made either at termination (for the 10 cases who had completed therapy) or in August (for the 4 cases whose therapy was ongoing). Results revealed a significant reduction on the Behavioral Problems scale over time (baseline $M = 2.0$, $SD = .69$ versus termination $M = 1.7$, $SD = .56$, $t\ (13) = 2.67$, $p < .05$), although there was a nonsignificant effect on the Emotional Problems scale (baseline $M = 1.4$, $SD = .31$ versus termination $M = 1.4$, $SD = .44$, $t\ (13) = .22$, ns).

The clinical impact of treatment was examined by exploring the percentage of youth experiencing moderate to severe distress (i.e., a rating of 3 or higher on each item of the TSR) at baseline compared to the percentage experiencing this level of distress at termination or in August. As shown in Table 3, there was a reduction in the percentage of youth experiencing distress on eight of the thirteen TSR scales. The magnitude of the reduction was larger on the

Table 3. Percentage of Youth Experiencing Moderate to Severe Problems on Each TSR Item

Scale/Item Name	Baseline August Rating	Termination Change	Percentage
Behavior Problems Scale			
Family Conflict	57%	21%	-36%
Peer Relationship Problems	36%	21%	-15%
School Difficulties	43%	21%	-22%
Self-Destructive Behavior	14%	14%	0%
Aggression	43%	14%	-29%
Substance Abuse	7%	14%	+7%
Runaway/Legal Problems	36%	21%	-15%
Impulsivity	29%	7%	-22%
Emotional Problems Scale			
Depression	29%	14%	-15%
Anxiety	21%	14%	-7%
Psychosomatic Problems	7%	7%	0%
Suicidality	0%	7%	+7%
Psychotic Symptoms	0%	0%	0%

items comprising the Behavioral Problems Scale compared to the Emotional Problems Scale. There are several potential explanations for these findings. First, given the high-risk nature of the behavioral disturbances frequently exhibited by the Ujima youth, these behaviors are typically targeted more intensely in treatment. Second, when compared to behavioral problems, emotional problems tend to be more covert, potentially leading to an underestimation on the ratings of emotional distress at baseline.

Service-level outcomes for youth receiving psycho-educational assessments through Project Ujima also are monitored, as parents in the program commonly report concerns with academic performance. Between August 2002 and September 2004, 15 youth received comprehensive assessments examining cognitive, achievement, and behavioral functioning related to academic difficulties (e.g., poor grades, failing classes, behavioral problems interfering with schoolwork). During the same time, Project Ujima therapists worked directly with the schools of 12 youth to facilitate appropriate classroom placements and strategies for teachers, based on each youth's unique pattern of academic strengths and weaknesses as revealed by the testing results. Insuring that youth are receiving appropriate educational service is especially helpful to families in Project Ujima, given the inverse relationship between school participation and other factors related to the risk of exposure to community violence (e.g., association with deviant peers).

Lessons Learned

Development of a Home Visitation Model

In the beginning, Project Ujima staff attempted a clinic-based model of care for the youth and families enrolled in the program. Intake occurred in the ED, with Community Liaisons describing the program and offering support. Although many families consented for enrollment in the program, very few kept the appointments in the Project Ujima clinic, which was located in a central city neighborhood and was free of charge. In speaking with many of the families regarding use of the clinic, staff found that families did not value a follow-up visit, particularly if the injuries had healed. Some were concerned about cost, while others had difficulty in taking off from work to accompany their child to the clinic. In addition, many were concerned that their child would have to miss school or sports activities in order to visit the clinic. Attempts were then made to make the clinic hours later in the day and on Saturday mornings to address these barriers. Despite these attempts, families and youth rarely utilized the clinic model. Subsequently, Project Ujima began operating under a "home visitation model." According to this model, the Community Liaison who met the family in the ED, a Milwaukee Health Department nurse, and a Volunteer Peer Liaison comprised the home visitation team. The team approach, with appointments at convenient times for families, met with improved success and provision of services. At that point, mental health counseling was provided at a community agency located within the central city. Referrals for these services were made by the Liaison following consultation with the medical and program directors.

Development of In-Home Mental Health Counseling

As Project Ujima continued providing services, it was apparent that mental health services were being underutilized. Although the agency providing these services was located in Milwaukee's central city, and in the neighborhood of many of the victims, few individuals took advantage of the services. It was apparent that, much like medical services, mental health counseling services were not viewed as a priority by families. We then designed, in conjunction with the Department of Psychology at the University of Wisconsin-Milwaukee, a mental health delivery team that could provide in-home consultation and counseling services to both youth and their families. The mental health therapists became part of the home visitation team, which allowed them to meet all of the families participating in Project Ujima and to make a determination regarding the need for mental health services. Due to the sensitive nature of the services, the therapists sought private areas in the home where youth and other family members could receive counseling.

Issues Facing Emergency Department Staff

Another difficulty encountered by Project Ujima was the perception among hospital staff regarding the worthiness and needs of youth assault victims. Some viewed the youth as perpetrators rather than victims; others were concerned that the parental supervision of the youth was deficient and an underlying cause of the injury. Often times these perceptions were bolstered by the attitudes of police officers who accompanied youth to the ED. In some cases, the perceived need of ED staff to be efficient in their care competed with the time needed for social service and Project Ujima staff to support and evaluate the victim and their family. This made some staff members reluctant to consult social services and Project Ujima staff because the ED was already "backed up" in seeing patients. Addressing these issues has become easier as we streamlined the referral process in triage and as procurement of a "Project Ujima consult" became more routine in the work patterns of the ED staff. In addition, ED staff began to appreciate the value that the Project Ujima Community Liaison brought to the patient's medical experience as well as to the family's support during a critical time.

Maintaining Confidentiality While Providing Multidisciplinary Services

At the point of identifying patients to be referred to Project Ujima, these youth are patients at CHW. Because several agencies are involved in providing subsequent services, we needed to develop a mechanism to be able to share information in a confidential manner among staff from the different agencies. Because the issue of violence is particularly sensitive, we also needed to assure that confidentiality is maintained. Therefore, we developed a consent form, which is discussed at the time of the ED visit with parents and which allows for release of information tailored to the youth's needs, as well as granting permission to participate in Project Ujima activities. One difficulty with this strategy was that many parents were not present at the time of the youth's ED visit. In these cases, consent was attempted by telephone or by mail. However, lack of parental presence at the time of the ED visit remains a significant barrier to enrolling youth in the program.

Another related issue is obtaining consent for participation in research activities associated with the evaluation of Project Ujima services. Because this type of consent requires both the assent of the youth and the consent of the parent, many opportunities for enrollment into research activities have been missed. In some cases, the parent was not present in the ED; in others, Project

Ujima staff members were reluctant to seek consent for participation in research because they feared that families would be more apt to refuse program services. This fear was based on the negative impact of studies, such as those conducted with the Tuskegee airmen, that may dissuade youth and their families from entering into a research study (Freimuth, Quinn, and Thomas, 2001, p. 797; Shavers, Lynch, and Burmeister, 2001, p. 563). We have subsequently found that obtaining consent for research participation is best done after the initial ED visit, when families are not under the duress of the acute event.

Maintenance of Safety for Project Ujima Staff

Community violence raises a significant challenge in providing in-home services, since many of the youth served by Project Ujima live in the most violent neighborhoods in Milwaukee. In order to insure the safety of our staff, multiple staff members attend home visits. Because many youth are in school during the day and many of their parents are at work, many home visits are scheduled in the late afternoon and early evening hours at a time when, unfortunately, safety may be at question. By building rapport with the family at the time of their ED visit and by assessing neighborhood safety through telephone contact with the family, Project Ujima Community Liaisons lay the groundwork for a safe visit. In a few cases, when safety around the home of the family cannot be assured, meetings are arranged at public community places such as libraries, schools, and restaurants. Taking the opportunity to meet the youth and family during medical clinic appointments is another strategy utilized to build rapport, support the youth and family, and to assure good medical follow-up.

Support of Staff

Support of staff in this highly stressful program is integral to its success and the long-term commitment of its staff. Staff members enjoy extremely flexible schedules that allow them to meet the needs of clients and still meet their own families' needs as well. A staff retreat is conducted at least once a year to reenergize and wind down from a long and intense period of client interventions. The program manager reserves time to debrief during lunches and outings with staff, and has incorporated staff appreciation activities into all aspects of work life. In addition, staff are encouraged to take time for professional training and education to increase their skills and comfort level in dealing with youth and families in crisis. Staff are also encouraged to take an active role in program development and implementation within Project Ujima and the community in order to increase confidence in achieving positive impacts.

Value and Challenges to the Member Agencies of the Partnership

In a process evaluation of Project Ujima conducted in 1997, external evaluators from the University of Wisconsin-Madison interviewed staff from the various organizations, as well as youth and families who had received services. Their report noted that the organizers of the program were dedicated, willing to change procedures that were not effective, and willing to create partnerships with community organizations. They noted that the overwhelming majority of youth and family who were interviewed described multiple experiences with violent assaults, suggesting that the context of victim and perpetrator violence, left unchecked, may be self-perpetuating (Moberg, 1997).

Each of the partners joining together to form Project Ujima brings specific talents to the partnership. Whether it is health care, mental health services, basic community support services, or research abilities, all are necessary to pull together well-organized services to support youth victims of violence and their families. Understanding the needs of each of the partners is key to program development. For example, on a basic level, each partner has different fiscal calendars and methods of budgeting for personnel. In some years, hiring freezes meant that the program had to seek out nursing services from a different partner. Therefore, flexibility is important.

Engagement and understanding of the leadership of the partner agencies is another important organizational issue. Because each of the partner agencies had well-aligned missions and goals for their own agency and because positive youth development was central to each of their missions, Project Ujima is able to thrive. In fact, because of the support of key leaders in each of the agencies, the program has continued to grow in scope of services as well as in the size of its staff. Continued communication among agency leaders, sharing of successes among partners, coordinated release of program press releases, and collaboration of the direct serve staff are key to a successful program.

Issues Related to Youth Services

Another pertinent issue was the perceived needs of youth victims and their families. In general, staff sought psychosocial solutions for the violent experiences while youth reported that they needed a job or job training. As Project Ujima has evolved, programs and services have integrated mental health counseling with the employment needs of the youth by providing group experiences. During these experiences, mental health therapists and Community Liaisons build on strengths and assets of each youth while developing job readiness skills and career exploration. During the group experiences, youth are able to express themselves and support other youth who have been victimized through similar violent experiences.

Future Directions

Through our psychosocial support program, we have devised strategies to engage and support the youth victim of violence and his/her family. In considering why a certain youth becomes victimized while other youth living in the same environment do not, there may be risk and protective factors that play a part in the outcome. By studying potential risk and protective factors among victimized youth, as well as healthy youth from the same community, we hope to advance our psychosocial interventions and violence prevention efforts. Although we informally build on strengths of a given youth-parent dyad, we plan to further develop a treatment plan individualized to each family unit based on that family's strengths.

Another initiative is to further develop our primary violence prevention activities targeting children in elementary and middle schools (American Academy of Pediatrics Task Force on Violence, 1999; Borg, 1999; Nolin, 1996; Powell and Hawkins, 1996). Although we currently participate in programs to provide violence prevention to youth in Milwaukee schools, these programs are usually limited to a single assembly at the school. In utilizing the approach that Olweus took in Norway, we are planning a violence prevention coalition with an elementary and middle school as the centerpiece organization (Olweus, 1993). By working with all constituencies in this neighborhood, we hope to prevent bullying and interpersonal violence among youth. Proposed community partners include an elementary school, YMCA, housing authority and Resident Council for a Milwaukee housing development, day care center, and community block watch group. It is our hope that by using an organized, community approach, we may improve youth and family nonviolent communication skills as well as foster peaceful attitudes.

For many of the families seen by Project Ujima, there exists a culture of violence and retaliation that exists as part of the culture of survival in urban areas. Some parents train their children to fight, to make the first strike, so that they do not get a reputation for weakness in their community. For many families this has become a point of honor. For these families, education and intervention are important in order to disrupt the cycle of violence. Parents need assistance in order to understand that violence towards another will not restore honor to the family.

Many of our youth victims have been eager to share their stories in order to prevent future violent injuries in their communities. Although they have had opportunities to address medical and other professional groups regarding their injuries and recovery, we hope to develop an ongoing platform for them to speak to other youth and families, set in a school-based violence prevention curriculum. It is our hope that we can provide both primary and secondary prevention through this program.

Summary

Through the support of many community partners and the leadership of each of these partners, Project Ujima has grown to be able to provide cost-effective, culturally sensitive, and family-centered care to violently injured youth and their families. By designing the services through the dedicated teamwork of a multidisciplinary group of professionals in the community, we are able to support these victims and prevent future violent injuries in our community. Project Ujima is truly "working together to make things right."

References

Achenbach, T.M. (1991). *Manual for the Child Behavior Check-List/4-18 and 1991 Profile.* Burlington, University of Vermont, Department of Psychiatry.

American Academy of Pediatrics (1996). Adolescent assault victim needs. A review of issues and model protocol. *Pediatrics.* 98: 991-1001.

American Academy of Pediatrics Task Force on Violence. (1999). The role of the pediatrician in youth violence prevention in clinical practice and at the community level. *Pediatrics.* 103: 173-181.

American Psychiatric Association. (2000). *Diagnostic and Statistical Manual of Mental Disorders* (4th ed., text rev.). Washington, DC: Author.

Barber, C.C., et al. (2002). The Target Symptom Rating: A brief clinical measure of acute psychiatric symptoms in children and adolescents. *Journal of Clinical Child and Adolescent Psychology, 31,* 181-192.

Barkley, R.A., Edwards, G.H., and Robin, A.L. (1999). *Defiant Teens: A Clinician's Manual for Assessment and Family Intervention.* New York, Guilford Press.

Becker, M.G., Hall, J.S., Ursic, C.M., Jain, S., Calhoun, D. (2004). Caught in the Crossfire: The effects of a peer-based intervention program for violently injured youth. *Journal of Adolescent Health.* 34:177-183.

Borg, M.G. (1999). The extent and nature of bullying among primary and secondary schoolchildren. *Educational Research. 41,* 137-153.

Briere, J. (1996). *Trauma Symptom Checklist for Children: Professional Manual.* Odessa, FL: Psychological Assessment Resources.

Briere, J. (1995). *Trauma Symptom Inventory Professional Manual.* Odessa, FL, Psychological Assessment Resources.

Centers for Disease Control and Prevention. (1994). Homicides among 15-19 year-old males: United States, 1963-1991. *Morbidity and Mortality Weekly Report,* 43: 725-727.

Cicchetti, D., and Toth, S.L., (1997a). *Developmental Perspectives on Trauma: Theory, Research, and Intervention.* Rochester, NY, University of Rochester Press.

Cicchetti, D., and Toth, S.L. (1997b). Transactional ecological systems in developmental psychopathology. In S. S. Luthar, J. A. Burack, et al. (Eds.), *Developmental Psychopathology: Perspectives on Adjustment, Risk, and Disorder.* New York, Cambridge University Press: 317-349.

Coll, C.G., Akerman, A., and Cicchetti, D. (2000). Cultural influences on developmental processes and outcomes: Implications for the study of development and psychopathology. *Development and Psychopathology.* 12: 333-356.

Compton, K., Snyder, J., Schrepferman, L., Bank, L., and Shortt, J.W. (2003). The contributions of parents and siblings to antisocial and depressive behavior in adolescents: A double jeopardy coercion model. *Developmental Psychopathology.* 15: 163-182.

Crick, N.R., and Dodge, K.A. (1994). A review and reformulation of social information-processing mechanisms in children's social adjustment. *Psychological Bulletin.* 115: 74-101.

de Castro, B.O., Veerman, J.W., Koops, W., Bosch, J.D., and Monshouwer, H.J. (2002). Hostile attribution of intent and aggressive behavior: A meta-analysis. *Child Development.* 73: 916-934.

Dishion, T.J., and Andrews, D.W. (1995). Preventing escalation in problem behaviors with high-risk young adolescents: Immediate and 1-year outcomes. *Journal of Consulting and Clinical Psychology.* 63: 538-548.

Dolins, J.C., and Christoffel, K. (1994). Reducing violent injuries: Priorities for pediatrician advocacy. *Pediatrics.* 94: 638-645.

DuRant, R.H., Cadenhead, C., Pendergrast, R.A., Slavens, G., and Linder, C.W. (1994). Factors associated with the use of violence among urban Black adolescents. *AJPH,* 84: 612-627.

Feldman, R.A., Caplinger, T.E., and Wodarski, J.S. (1983). *The St. Louis Conundrum: The Effective Treatment of Antisocial Youth.* Englewood Cliffs, NJ, Prentice Hall.

Fingernut, L. (1993). Firearm mortality among children, youth and young adults 1-34 years of age, trends and current status: United States 1985-1990. National Center for Health Statistics, Advance Data, 231: 1-20.

First, M.B., Spitzer, R., Gibbon, M., and Williams, J.B.W. (1996). *Structured Clinical Interview for DSM-IV Axis I Disorders (SCID-I), Clinical Version.* American Psychiatric Press, Washington, DC.

Fitzpatrick, K.M. (1997). Aggression and environmental risk among low-income African-American youth. *Journal of Adolescent Health,* 21: 172-178.

Freimuth, V., Quinn. S.C., Thomas, S.B. (2001). African American's views on research and the Tuskegee syphillis study, *Social Science and Medicine* 52: 797-808.

Garbarino, D., et al. (1992). *Children in Danger.* San Francisco: Jossey Bass.

Griffith, E., and Bell, C. (1989). Recent trends in suicide and homicide among Blacks. *JAMA,* 262: 2265-2269.

Grundle, T.J. (2002). Wraparound care. In D.T. Marsh and M.A. Fristad (Eds.), *Handbook of Serious Emotional Disturbance in Children and Adolescents.* New York, Wiley: 323-333.

Haddon, W. (1980). Advances in the epidemiology of injuries as a basis for public policy, *Public Health Reports.* 95: 411.

Hammond, W.R., and Yung, B. (1993). Psychology's role in the public health response to assaultive violence among young African-American men. *American Psychologist.* 48: 142-154.

Hastings, T.L., and Kelley, M.L. (1997). Development and validation of the Screen for Adolescent Violence Exposure (SAVE). *Journal of Abnormal Child Psychology,* 25: 511-520.

Hausman A., Spivak, H., Roeber, J.F., Prothrow-Stith, D. (1989). Adolescent interpersonal assault injury admissions in an urban municipal hospital. *Pediatric Emergency Care.* 5: 275-280.

Hennes, H. (1998). A review of violence statistics among children and adolescents in the United States. *Pediatric Clinics of North America.* 45: 269-280.

Hodges, K. (1998). Use of the Child and Adolescent Functional Assessment Scale (CAFAS) as an outcome measure in clinical settings. *Journal of Behavioral Health Services and Research.* 25: 325-336.

Kaufman, J., Birmaher, B., Brent, D.A., Rao, U., and Ryna, N. (1996). *Revised Schedule for Affective Disorders and Schizophrenia for School Aged Children: Present and Lifetime version (K-SADS-PL).* Pittsburgh: Western Psychiatric Institute and Clinic.

Kaufman, A.S., and Kaufman, N.L. (1990). *Kaufman Brief Intelligence Test: Professional Manual.* Circle Pines, MN, American Guidance Services.

Kazdin, A.E., Holland, L., and Crowley, M. (1997). Family experience of barriers to treatment and premature termination from child therapy. *Journal of Consulting and Clinical Psychology.* 65: 453-463.

Kazak, A., et al. (2004). Posttraumatic stress symptoms (PTSS) and posttraumatic stress disorder (PTSD) in families of adolescent childhood cancer survivors. *J. Ped. Psychology.* 29:211-219.

Kazdin, A.E., Siegel, T.C., and Bass, D. (1992). Cognitive problem-solving skills training and parent management training in the treatment of antisocial behavior in children. *Journal of Consulting and Clinical Psychology.* 60: 733-747.

Koop, C.E., and Lundberg, G.D. (1992) Violence in America: A public health emergency. *JAMA (Editorial).* 267: 3075-3076.

Landolt, M.A., et al. (2002). Brief report: posttraumatic stress disorder in parents of children with newly-diagnosed Type 1 diabetes. *J. of Ped. Psychology.* 27:647-652.

Lewis, M. (2000). Toward a development of psychopathology: Models, definitions, and predictions. In. A.J. Sameroff, M. Lewis, and S.M. Miller (Eds.), *Handbook of Developmental Psychopathology* (2nd ed.), New York, NY, Kluwer: 3-22.

Lochman, J.E., and Dodge, K.A. (1994) Social cognitive processes of severely violent, moderately aggressive, and nonaggressive boys. *Journal of Consulting and Clinical Psychology.* 62: 366-374.

Lochman, J.E., Whidby, J.M., and FitzGerald, D.P. (2000). Cognitive-behavioral assessment and treatment with aggressive children. In P.C. Kendall (Ed.), *Child and Adolescent Therapy: Cognitive-Behavioral Procedures* (2nd ed.) . New York, NY, Guilford Press: 32-87.

Marcelle, D.R., and Melzer-Lange, M.D. (2001). Project UJIMA: Working together to make things right. *Wisconsin Medical Journal.* 100: 22-25.

McCart, M.R., Davies, W.H., Harris, R., Wincek, J., Calhoun, A.D., and Melzer-Lange, M. D. (2005). Assessment of trauma symptoms among adolescent assault victims. *Journal of Adolescent Health.* 36(1): *70–77.*

McCart, M.R., Davies, W.H., Phelps, L.F., Heuermann, W., and Melzer-Lange, M.D. (2004). Contextual assessment of challenges to coping among adolescent assault victims. Manuscript submitted for publication.

McClosskey, L.A., and Walken, M. (1999). Posttraumatic stress in children exposed to family violence and single event trauma. *Journal of the American Academy of Child and Adolescent Psychiatry.* 38: 385-92.

Melzer-Lange, M., Lye, P.S., and Calhoun, A.D. (1998). Advised follow-up after emergency treatment of adolescents with violence-related injuries. *Pediatric Emerg. Care.* 14(15): 334-337.

Moberg, P.F. (1997). A process evaluation of Project Ujima, *University of Wisconsin Evaluations.* 1: 1-35.

Morrissey, T.B., Byrd, R., and Deitch, E.A. (1991). The incidence of recurrent penetrating trauma in an urban trauma center. *Journal of Trauma.* 31: 1536-1538.

National Center for Health Statistics (NCHS) Vital Statistics System. 1998 leading causes of death. Retrieved November 03, 2001, from http://www.cdc.gov

National Committee for Injury Prevention and Control. (1989) *Injury Prevention: Meeting the Challenge.* Oxford England, Oxford University Press; 1989: 23-24. (Published as supplement [no.3] to *American Journal Preventive Medicine.*

Nolin, M.J. (1996). Victimization at school. *Journal of School Health.* 66: 216-222.

Olweus, D. (1993). *Bullying at School. What We Know and What We Can Do.* Cambridge, MA, Blackwell Publishers.

Patterson, G.R. (2002). The early development of coercive family process. In J.B. Reid, G.R. Patterson, and J. Snyder (Eds.), *Antisocial Behavior in Children and Adolescents: A Developmental Analysis and Model for Intervention.* Washington, DC: American Psychological Association: 25-44

Phelps, L.F., Davies, W.H., McCart, M.R., Klein-Tasman, B.P., Melzer-Lange, M.D., and Heuermann, W. (2004). Concerns and coping of African-American mothers after youth assault requiring emergency medical treatment. *Journal of Pediatric Psychology.*

Poole, G.V., Griswold, J.A., Thaggard, K., and Rhodes, R.S.(1993). Trauma is a recurrent disease. *Surgery,* 113: 608-11.

Powell, K.E., and Hawkins, D.F., (1996) Youth violence prevention: descriptions and baseline data from thirteen (13) evaluation projects. *American Journal Preventive Medicine.* 12 (5 Suppl.).

Reynolds, C.R., and Kamphaus, R.W. (1998). *Behavior Assessment System for Children.* Circle Pines, MN, American Guidance Service.

Shavers, V.L, Lynch, C.F., Burmeister, L.F. (2001). Knowledge of the Tuskegee study and its impact on the willingness to participate in medical research studies. *Journal of the National Medical Association.* 92: 563-72.

Skiba, K.M. (December 13, 1998). Homicide rates drop in Milwaukee and U.S. Officials hope that decline is a long-term trend and not a blip. *Milwaukee Journal Sentinel.* p. 1 and 11A.

Thomas, S.B., Leite, B., and Duncan, T. (1998). Breaking the cycle of violence among youth living in metropolitan Atlanta: A case history of kids alive and loved. *Health Education and Behavior.* 25, 160-174.

Thornton, T.N., Craft, C.A., Dahlberg, L.L., Lynch, B.S., and Baer, K. (2002). *Best Practices of Youth Violence Prevention: A Sourcebook for Community Action* (Rev.). Atlanta. Centers for Disease Control and Prevention, National Center for Injury Prevention and Control.

Tolan, P.H., and Gorman-Smith, D. (1997). Families and the development of urban children. In H.J. Walberg, and O. Reyes, (Eds.), *Children and Youth: Interdisciplinary Perspectives. Issues in Children's and Family's Lives,* Thousand Oaks, CA, Sage Publications: 67-91.

Tolan, P.H., and Loeber, R.L. (1993). Antisocial behavior. In P.H. Tolan and B.J. Cohler (Eds.), *Handbook of Clinical Research and Clinical Practice with Adolescents.* New York: Wiley: 307–331

U.S. Department of Justice, Office of Juvenile Justice and Delinquency Prevention. (2001). The growth of youth gang problems in the United States: 1970-98. *OJJDP Report.* 11-18.

Van Emmerik, A.A.P., Kamphuis, J.H., Hulsbosch, A.M., and Emmelkamp, P.M.G. (2002). Single session debriefing after psychological trauma: A meta-analysis. *Lancet,* 766-771.

Walsh-Kelly C.M., and Strait R. (1998). Impact of violence and the emergency department response to victims and perpetrator: issues and protocols. In H. Hennes and A.D. Calhoun (Eds.) *Pediatric Clinics of North America.* New York, NY, Elsevier, 45:449-458.

Webster-Stratton, C., and Herbert, M. (1994). *Troubled Families-Problem Children. Working with Parents: A Collaborative Process.* Chichester, England, Wiley.

Yung, B.R., and Hammond, W.R. (1995). *Positive Adolescent Choices Training: A Model for Violence Prevention Groups with African American Youth (Program Guide).* Champaign, IL, Research Press.

Chapter 6

Caught in the Crossfire: Closing the Revolving Door of Youth Violence

Deane Calhoun, MA, and Marla Becker, MPH

Introduction

At the height of the crack-cocaine gun wars in East Oakland, California, in the late 1980s, Deane Calhoun, the founder of Youth ALIVE! developed the *Teens on Target (TNT)* violence prevention peer leadership program to help highly at-risk, East Oakland high school students draw on their own strengths and experiences to prevent and reduce the lethal violence in their schools, neighborhoods, and community. TNT members developed and began presenting violence prevention workshops for middle school students and presented policy recommendations to the city council and county board of supervisors. But that was not enough to stem the rising violence.

The students involved in these workshops later identified the urgent need to help violently injured youth being treated in local hospital trauma units so that they and their family members would have positive alternatives to retaliation. The number of youth being treated at the Alameda County Medical Center's Highland Hospital Trauma Unit—mostly for gunshot wounds—had reached epidemic proportions, particularly among young African American men.

The hospital was discharging these young men and women to the same set of violent conditions in their same neighborhoods, with no "prescription" for how to stay safe or support to find non-violent solutions. Nor was there support for family and friends in how to stop the violence. A heart attack victim might be discharged with a diet and exercise plan and with prescribed medication, but young patients injured by violence were discharged empty-handed. Too often, family and friends felt that the way that they could "help" their child or friend was to retaliate against the perpetrator in the name of the recovering victim. This set up a "revolving door" of violence, as many were being reinjured and injuring others to prove their loyalty. Reinjury rates soared and East Oakland, where many of the shootings were taking place, was renamed "the killing fields" by the local police.

An Alameda County Medical Center (ACMC) social worker, a surgeon, and a young man who had been injured by violence were desperately searching for ways to prevent reinjuries and, to stop the killings. At the same time, the Youth ALIVE! Executive Director, inspired by the students involved in Youth ALIVE! *Teens on Target* workshops, started gathering statistics from the hospital trauma coordinator on the rising number of injured youth being treated for violence-related injuries and looking for help in providing counseling to injured youth and their families.

The hospital social worker, Karen West, and Youth ALIVE! Executive Director, Deane Calhoun, worked together to involve older youth, from neighborhoods similar to the youth being injured, to provide bedside services to talk the youth and their families out of retaliation. Ms. West described how Dr. Henderson, Chief of ACMC Trauma Services, and one of his patients, a young adult survivor named Sherman Spears who had been recently paralyzed as a result of a gunshot wound, were thinking along the same lines. Mr. Spears had been discharged back to his neighborhood after being treated at ACMC. He had told Dr. Henderson that he wanted to help stop the violence in his community and that he had developed a service plan, based on his own experience, outlining what recovering youth needed to prevent further violence.

Ms. Calhoun immediately called Mr. Spears, interviewed him, and hired him to develop a peer intervention program at ACMC. Dr. Henderson and Ms. West agreed to work with them on staff training, referral protocol, follow-up, and whatever it took to make the program happen. *Caught in the Crossfire* was born! The team spent many months with hospital administrators, working out the details involved in establishing *Caught in the Crossfire* as a collaborative program between the ACMC's Trauma Unit and Youth ALIVE! They successfully resolved issues of confidentiality and liability and developed and pilot-tested protocols for referral and treatment. And then Mr. Spears began working with his first client.

The Public Health Approach

The *Caught in the Crossfire* model is framed in the public health approach to youth violence. Through the public health lens, violent injury is seen as a health problem that grows out of conditions in the broader community, which in turn generate risk factors in the neighborhood, the family, and for individuals. Reducing violent injury among youth requires a comprehensive approach, identifying the risk factors most closely associated with the violence, building resilience among potential victims to those risk factors and, as much as possible, eliminating those factors.

Research on youth violence has identified the major risk factors for violence as follows: ready access to guns and alcohol and drugs, inadequate education, economic inequality, few positive peer role models, and family violence (U.S. Department of Health and Human Services, 2001).

The research on best practices to prevent youth violence demonstrates that one effective approach involves guiding young people to *enhance* the protective factors they need to *overcome* the risk factors associated with violence to build their resilience (Catalano and Hawkins, 1995; Catalano, Loeber, and McKinney, 1999; Catalano et al., 1998; Masten and Coatsworth, 1998). These protective factors include peer groups, schools, and communities that emphasize positive social norms; warm, supportive relationships and bonding with adults; opportunities to become involved in positive activities; recognition and support for participating in positive activities; and cognitive, social, and emotional competence.

Caught in the Crossfire provides opportunities for pro-social behavior through positive peer role-modeling, conflict resolution, anger management, and life skills training with the intent of fostering resilience to the risk factors associated with violence.

A February 2002 research bulletin produced by the federal Office of Juvenile Justice and Delinquency Prevention and the Centers for Disease Control and Prevention concludes that "violent victimization during adolescence has a pervasive effect on problem outcomes in adulthood" (Menard, 2002). This analysis of the research found that being a victim of violence during adolescence "increased the odds of being a perpetrator or victim of violence in adulthood, including felony assault perpetration and victimization and domestic violence perpetration and victimization." The author also concludes that the frequency of adolescent violent victimization is a "risk factor for failure to make a successful transition from adolescence to adulthood." The effect of violent victimization is an even greater risk factor than others that have been identified such as "minority race/ethnicity, lower socioeconomic background, adolescent violent offending, and adolescent drug use." According to the author, these outcomes "strongly suggest the need for interventions to reduce violent victimization during adolescence." Others have reached similar conclusions (Dobrin and Brusk 2003).

Literature Review of Similar Programs

In spite of the rising violent injury rate among youth, effective hospital-based or hospital-linked intervention services for these youth remain rare, although the number of programs are growing (Belcher, Deforge, and Jani, 2005; Zun, Downey, et al., 2006). A 2001 study by the federal Office of Victims of Crime reported that "there are fewer than a dozen hospital centers nationwide that offer *comprehensive* [emphasis in original] counseling, intervention, and inpatient treatment programs to victims of gun violence (U.S. Department of Health and Human Services, 2001). Oakland's *Caught in the Crossfire* program, which was developed in the early 1990s at Alameda County Medical Center/Highland Hospital, Project Ujima at Children's Hospital of Wisconsin, Project Ujima at Children's Hospital of Wisconsin in Milwaukee and the *Support, Mentoring and Advocacy Resources for Trauma Recovery (SMARTR)* program in Tempe, Arizona, were among the first to involve peers in the in-hospital rehabilitation process and in transitioning patients back into the community. In 2007, Youth ALIVE! replicated *Caught in the Crossfire* at the University of Southern California Medical Center in Los Angeles. In summary, hospital-based or hospital-linked programs are known to be currently operating in Oakland, Los Angeles, Boston, Philadelphia, Milwaukee, San Francisco, and Chicago.

Effective long-term violence prevention requires multidisciplinary approaches that not only address the day-to-day manifestations of the problem, but also address the underlying roots of the problem. Models that involve families and communities as part of an interconnected mentoring system show promise (Henggeler, Cunningham, Pickret, et al. 1996). Nontraditional interventions offer positive alternatives to the current ways of handling the varied problems of violence victims who wind up in the ED. Approaches that appear more effective require collaboration between hospital departments and outside agencies, such as community-based programs, the courts, and probation departments (Cornwell, Chang, Phillips, and Campbell, 2003; Belcher, Deforge, and Jani, 2005; Zun, Downey, et al., 2006).

One ED-based program located in Chicago, *Within Our Reach*, utilized psychosocial, emotional, and spiritual support among violently injured youth aged 10–24 years with services provided both for the victims and their families (Zun, Downey, et al., 2006). Services offered included primary and dental care, gang-related tattoo removal, services provided by the Boys and Girls Clubs of Chicago, and a variety of other referrals, if needed, such as legal assistance, alternative education, financial assistance, and spiritual counseling. After six months of case management in the program, their outcomes were compared to a matched control group who only received a written list of referral services. Self-reported reinjury rates were significantly different with the treatment group reporting reduced rates compared to the controls, although no differences between the groups in self-reported arrests, state-reported reinjuries, or state-reported incarcerations were found.

Another hospital-based violence prevention program in Boston involved a six-step intervention based on the health beliefs' model, self-efficacy, the theory of reasoned action, and mediation theory. Working with 12–17 year olds who are violence victims, a trauma department violence prevention team: 1) reviews and assesses the incident with the patient, 2) reviews the patient's conflict resolution strategies and offers nonviolent alternatives, 3) provides prevalence information on violence/homicide and the patient's risk status, 4) explores their coping skills and support system, 5) develops a safety plan, and 6) refers the patient to follow-up services. To date, no statistically significant differences between intervention and non-intervention controls have been found regarding reinjury recidivism.

Caught in the Crossfire Program Description

Caught in the Crossfire was originally designed to serve youth between the ages of 12 and 20 who are hospitalized for interpersonal violence-related injuries. The intervention is a part of the broader community-based youth violence intervention program Youth ALIVE! that works to close the "revolving door" of violence.[1] *Caught in the Crossfire* recruits, trains, and employs young

[1] Since its incorporation in 1991, Youth ALIVE! has developed its programs based on the understanding that the complex root causes of violence demand a comprehensive approach, guided by those most directly affected by violence in the community. This is the foundation for Youth ALIVE!'s mission: *to prevent youth violence and build youth leadership in California communities.* To this end, Youth ALIVE! hires and trains staff who have grown up in violent conditions to be educators, case managers, and role models for their peers and builds vital partnerships with the public and private agencies working with the same communities.

adults who are community residents who have experienced and overcome violence in their own lives. They act as peer mentors (in that they are from the same environment, rather than being the same age) and provide case management, support, and access to services to young people for up to one year after the youth leaves the hospital.

Caught in the Crossfire can also be adapted for other populations at risk for violence and their family members, specifically students facing suspension for violence, youth on probation for violence, and youth detained, but not arrested, by local police.

Three ingredients have made this program successful:

1) Close partnerships with public and private agencies offering a broad spectrum of concrete services;
2) Staff recruited from the communities served;
3) Work with the family members of youth clients.

The program's goals are to:

- Provide trained crisis intervention and long-term case management and mentoring, home visits and follow-up assistance to youth who are hospitalized for violent injuries, as well as to their family and friends.
- Prevent retaliatory violence and reduce the total number of youth injured by interpersonal violence.
- Reduce re-entry into the hospital and the criminal justice system.
- Link youth with local resources that help them live nonviolent lifestyles.
- Provide positive peer role models and promote positive alternatives to violence.

Program Participants

Caught in the Crossfire serves youth between the ages of 12 and 20 who are hospitalized for interpersonal violence-related injuries. In order to reach as many young people as possible, every violently injured person under 21 years of age being treated at the Alameda County Medical Center's Highland Hospital Trauma Unit is eligible for *Caught in the Crossfire* services. At Children's Hospital Oakland, which serves a younger population, the minimum age is set at 12 because of legal constraints related to serving a younger population.

Since its inception, *Caught in the Crossfire* has worked with over 700 injured youth being treated at these two local hospitals and an estimated 1,400 of their family members. The program expanded to work with other populations that are at particularly high risk of being victims or perpetrators of violence. In Oakland, California, we have worked with 180 middle school and high school students suspended pending an expulsion hearing or on the verge of being suspended for violence, and another 120 youth on probation for violent offenses.

The Role of Family Members and Other Caretakers

Assessing the capacity of family members and other caretakers to play an active role and, if so, at what level of involvement, is a major responsibility of the Intervention Specialists. Family/caretaker involvement in the development and implementation of the case plan can be crucial. Family members can provide vital support and reinforcement.

Tragically, many family members of even the youngest participants are unable and/or unwilling to play an active role. Some are grappling with poverty, serious substance abuse, or domestic violence issues. Others may be in prison or jail. Also, older youth may be at a developmental level where active involvement of family members, even those who are willing and able to engage, may be unwelcome. However, when family members do become involved, they can help in the following ways:

- Consent for participation from parents/guardians is required if *Caught in the Crossfire* is to serve any youth under 18.
- Involving family members and close friends early on in conversations about what *Caught in the Crossfire* can provide frequently dissipates the anger and frustration that can lead to retaliation. Bringing family members and close friends into the needs assessment and case planning process refocuses them on healing instead of retribution.
- Involvement of family members and other caretakers, particularly of younger participants, is crucial to ensuring that these participants are able to follow the case plans they work out with *Caught in the Crossfire's* Intervention Specialists. Involved family members can help a participant remember to attend appointments and follow-up on treatment plans.
- Regular interaction between family members/close friends and the Intervention Specialist also increases the chances that the Intervention Specialist can identify and help work out family issues that may have contributed to the precipitating violent injury, for example, family member substance abuse, domestic violence, or lack of adequate housing.

Program Staff

Caught in the Crossfire's peer mentors/case managers, called Intervention Specialists, are from similar neighborhoods as the youth they work with and all have experienced violence in their lives. Many are former victims of violence and/or have family members or close friends who are victims of violence. Also, some were involved in criminal and/or gang activities as teenagers or young adults.

Young people, who are recovering from violent injury, particularly youth growing up in low-income neighborhoods, need to immediately trust those working with them so they can begin to make the kinds of changes in their lives that prevent re-injury and find clear paths toward building productive lives. *Caught in the Crossfire's* Intervention Specialists are able to quickly establish trusting relationships with these injured youth, connect with their family members and caretakers to shape a strong system of support, and help them heal physically, psychologically, and socially.

In addition, all Intervention Specialists are committed to improving their communities. The program recruits, hires, and trains staff to ensure that the program is closely linked to the target community (an organizational chart and sample job descriptions are included in Appendices B and C of this chapter).

Caught in the Crossfire's Program Director and Program Coordinator require additional skills and experience. These positions require well-developed program development skills, ability to lead a staff who may have significant "street experience" but limited professional experience, and an understanding of social work principles and practices. It is crucial that the people in these positions understand on a deep level the nature of the communities that *Caught in the Crossfire* participants live in. They also must be able to work effectively with the hospitals, other public agencies, and community-based agencies that are essential to the success of the program.

Overview of Staff and Job Responsibilities

A peer intervention program like *Caught in the Crossfire* requires basically two different types of staff, but staff who also embody similar qualities. (See Appendix C for sample job descriptions.) One type, the Intervention Specialist, must bring to the program the experience gained from growing up in similar neighborhoods as the youth they work with and also be able to grasp clinical concepts such as confidentiality, mandated reporting, etcetera. The other type, the Program Director and Program Coordinator, must bring to the program well-developed organizational and leadership skills as well as a solid knowledge of social work principles and practices. However, all staff must share qualities. For example, the Intervention Specialist must not only be able to quickly develop the trust of clients and navigate through their world, but also keep track of countless details and provide services of the highest standards. Similarly, the Program Director and Program Coordinator must not only know how to lead staff and implement programs, but also be able to communicate effectively with people from a variety of cultural backgrounds and have an excellent understanding of different cultural frameworks.

When jobs become available, in addition to traditional listing sources, it is essential to get the word to the community you serve by talking with colleagues and former patients/clients, making announcements at meetings, etc.

The following is a summary of job responsibilities for Intervention Services staff for hospital and other clients based on the job description and the basic requirements of Youth ALIVE! Intervention Services staff.

For Patients in the Hospital

After receiving a new hospital patient referral from the Coordinator, Director, or hospital Medical Social Worker (MSW), arrive at the hospital within 20 minutes. When you get the call ask:

- How old is the patient?
- Will the patient be admitted and for how long?
- What is the injury?
- Are their family/friends there?
- What room is the patient in?
- Has the hospital social worker seen the patient?

During the initial interview focus on the following:

- Establishing a connection with the patient.
- Addressing any immediate needs the patient might have (i.e. understanding what is going on, making them as comfortable as possible, helping them follow-up on contacting family, etc.).
- Introducing the program's benefits to the patient (be simple and brief).
- Reviewing the incident and any needs.
- Learn how long the patient expects to be in the hospital.
- Establish a plan for follow-up.
- Give program information, including your card, to the patient and any friend or family member there.
- Complete the initial interview documents as thoroughly as possible immediately after every initial visit with a patient.

Follow-Up (Hospital)

No more than five days after leaving the hospital contact the patient and set up a home visit. Coordinate initial home visits with the Program Coordinator. Be prepared and on time for all home visits. (Bring extra descriptions of the program, business cards, pens, paper and your planner/calendar.) Establish a "service plan" with the participant and hospital MSW, if possible.

Revise the service plan as often as needed.

For All Referrals

After receiving a referral from the Coordinator, you must attempt to contact that person within *48 hours*. Continue to attempt contact at least weekly for four weeks. If still unsuccessful, refer the case to the Coordinator. Once contact has been made, explain the program, your role, the participant's role, and answer any questions. Begin developing a "service plan" to ensure the participant stays safe, healthy, and out of trouble. Be sure to include the Public Health Nurse and her services as part of the "service plan."

Be sure to ask parent/child if there are any other community-based organizations (CBOs) working with the family. After getting the consent form signed retrieve the class schedule and attendance record from school.

You must physically go to the participant's school at least once per week; meet with the participant, teacher, counselor, etcetera. (We have a letter for teachers requesting a meeting or telephone call to discuss the participant.) Maintain contact with parents at least once per week. Contact CBOs and discuss your role, concerns, etcetera. Visit the participant at least once per week (this could be at school). Call the participant at least twice per week. Prepare the participant for the closure of their case *before* the 12th month of their participation in the program. Consult with the Coordinator as to whether to keep the case for longer than a year.

Meetings

Attend weekly Intervention Services staff meetings (mandatory) on time and prepared. These meetings will include:

- Reviewing appointments/responsibilities for the week.
- Brainstorming on participant issues/needs.
- Sharing information on referral sources.
- Sharing information on relevant current events.
- Bringing up any other issues/ideas and concerns.

Attend weekly supervision meetings (mandatory, time and day flexible) with the Coordinator on time and prepared. These meetings will include:

- A general check-in.
- Discussing any part of your job responsibilities that you are having difficulty meeting.
- Bringing up any other issues/ideas and concerns.

Attend biweekly Youth Alive! staff meetings (mandatory) on time and prepared. Intervention Services staff will present a case at this meeting. Prepare to discuss difficulties, successes, challenges, and even fears with our staff. Expect to get feedback, others' outlook, and suggestions. Attend meetings with committees and other organizations as needed.

Presentations

Consult with the Director when you receive requests to present on behalf of Youth ALIVE!, TNT, or Intervention Services, to both prioritize and prepare your workload and the presentation itself. Prepare all materials needed for presentations in advance, including handouts. Complete the presentation record form after every presentation.

Documentation

Document immediately, consistently and briefly any attempts that you make to get in contact with each participant and the results of those attempts (i.e., left message, phone disconnect, spoke with sister). Keep daily tally of ALL phone calls, in-person contacts, and time spent with participants or service providers. Maintain accurate and up-to-date case notes on your interactions with participants or service providers. Document, prioritize, and respond to all messages received on your phone and your voicemail within a 24-hour period. Maintain accurate and up-to-date time sheets and mileage records. Turn in mileage forms (by the 7th of each month), check requests, and time sheets on time.

Dependability

"Check in" with the Coordinator daily at the beginning of your workday. Be prepared to discuss your planned activities. Your workday should start and end at the office, unless you have early morning or late afternoon appointments. If you are starting your day outside of the office, you must call the Coordinator by 8:30 a.m. If you will be outside of the office for more than two hours you must call every two hours. It is not the Coordinator's responsibility to check in with you.

On days that you will not be able to come to work or will be late to work, you must call and leave a message on the Coordinator's voice mail at least one hour before you are scheduled to start. If you have appointments that need to be covered and you cannot reach the Coordinator or Director, you should discuss it directly with the Associate or Executive Director (exceptions will be made for emergencies).

Keep your Nextel on during the day (except when in a meeting or such) for easy two-way communication. Return all messages as soon as possible. Check your inbox, e-mail, and voice mail regularly. Notify the Coordinator of all changes in your schedule as soon as you know of them.

Petty Cash

Intervention Services staff have a petty cash fund to be used for the following:

- Emergency food for participants.
- Purchasing legal documents (birth certificates, identification, police reports, etc.).
- Emergency transportation (bus tickets, bus passes).
- Parking reimbursement for staff.
- Emergency reimbursements.

You must sign for any money you get from petty cash and return a receipt for all money used. Reimbursement or cash withdrawn from petty cash cannot exceed $25.00. Any reimbursement exceeding $25.00 must be submitted via check request. Requests must be turned in by Wednesday and a check will be issued on the following Thursday.

Open-Door Policy

Intervention Services offices should be open at all times, unless you are meeting with program participants including participant family members. During these meetings, you should post a note on your door warning the rest of the staff that a meeting is in progress (and if you can or can't be disturbed). The Coordinator's door will be closed during supervision with all staff for respect and privacy. Having our doors open helps foster a sense of team, sharing, and openness that is important in a work environment. If music or discussion is too loud, deal with it without closing your door.

Emergency

In case of emergency and you need assistance, the Director is available by Nextel 24 hours a day.

Staff Training

Staff training involves initial orientation and ongoing training with a mix of agency and outside trainers. In addition to the basic agency and program orientation sessions, new staff should receive training in the following areas within the first month of employment and periodically thereafter:

- Anger management/conflict resolution.
- Casework.
- Community social work.
- CPR training.
- Cultural competency.
- Effective communication.
- Orientation from your major institutional partner(s), e.g., hospital confidentiality guidelines and other special requirements of working in the institution.
- Resource identification.
- Sexual assault.
- Staff counseling skills development.
- The theoretical frameworks of counseling.
- Working with Lesbian, Gay, Bisexual, Transgender and Questioning (LGBTQ) youth.
- Youth development principles and practices.

Orientation

Caught in the Crossfire provides intensive training for all new staff members as they are hired, and ongoing staff development training to build the professional skills of all staff regardless of their length of employment.

Newly hired Intervention Specialists "shadow" a more experienced Intervention Specialist for at least the first two weeks. Through this process, they take part in every phase of the program and get a better handle on the meaning of the work. Within the first week, the new employee participates in and receives an orientation that covers the following areas and is facilitated by the following staff members:

- The agency's history, mission, public health approach to violence prevention (Executive Director).
- Gunshot's video (contact Youth ALIVE! office).
- *Day in the Life* or description of a typical day of work (Intervention Specialist).
- Office management (Administrative Assistant).
- Agency structure, performance standards, reviews (Program Director).

Caught in the Crossfire program details:

- History (Program Director).
- Program description including referral sources, population served, services provided (Program Coordinator).
- Protocols, forms, and meetings (Program Coordinator).
- Shadowing plan, including introduction to other service providers (Program Coordinator).

Ongoing Training

Ongoing professional development training is provided monthly. *Caught in the Crossfire* facilitated the following training in 2002 for staff and volunteers involved in the program:

- Hospital orientation, e.g., hospital do's and don'ts, hospital paging system, safety, and confidentiality (hospital staff).
- Documentation, theoretical framework, counseling skills (Program Director).
- How to work with the media (Berkeley Media Studies Group).
- Human resources, including payroll, benefits, policies, insurance, etcetera (Agency Director of Human Resources).
- Working With Lesbian, Gay, Bisexual, Transgender, and Questioning Youth (Representative of local agency).
- Highland Hospital Sexual Assault Advocacy (hospital sexual assault staff/Department of Medical Social Services).

- Youth Development Principles and Practices (local trainer).
- Minors Involved in Prostitution (Representative of Child and Protective Services Agency).
- School District Disciplinary Hearing Panel (Panel Members).
- Anger management/conflict resolution (certified facilitators).
- Cultural competency (certified trainer).
- CPR (hospital).
- Alameda County Public Health Department—Confidentiality/HIPPA (Program Coordinator).
- Alameda County District Attorney's Office—Navigating the Courts (informal).

In addition to receiving training in the areas above, the Program Director and Program Coordinator receive training in the following areas:

- Supervision: Helping People Achieve Results (local trainer).
- Resolving Conflict with Employees (local trainer).
- Writing skills development (local trainer).
- Public speaking (local trainer).
- Database software (local trainer).

Program Services

The steps that *Caught in the Crossfire* staff use to help participants heal and reduce their risk for further violence are as follows:

Step 1: Youth treated at hospital for injury.
Step 2: Youth seen by hospital social worker and/or other liaison and referred to *Caught in the Crossfire* if appropriate.
Step 3: Intervention Specialist meets with youth and family at bedside within 12 hours of receiving referral and obtains consent for participation (participation is voluntary).
Step 4: Intervention Specialist conducts intake assessment and develops an individualized case plan. Intervention Specialist also assesses threat of retaliatory violence by youth's family and friends and takes necessary steps to prevent retaliation.
Step 5: Intervention Specialist guides youth in process of implementing case plan through frequent phone and in-person contacts for up to one year (average is 60). They amend case plan as needed.
Step 6: Intervention Specialist and youth complete exit interview.

Referral Protocol

When a young person is admitted to the hospital as a result of violent injury, she/he is seen by a social worker who completes a referral form and delivers it to the *Caught in the Crossfire* Program Coordinator by cell phone and/or fax during normal business hours (evening and weekend referrals are received the following business morning). When *Caught in the Crossfire* receives a referral, the Program Coordinator asks the following questions:

1) How old is the patient?
2) Will the patient be admitted to the hospital and for how long?
3) What is the injury?
4) Are their family/friends at the hospital?
5) What room is the patient in?
6) Has the hospital social worker seen the patient?

The Program Coordinator assigns the patient to an Intervention Specialist who meets with the injured youth within 30 minutes (when the referral is received during business hours) to provide immediate intervention and describe the program's ongoing support services for the youth and his/her family and friends. If the patient is no longer at the hospital by the time the referral is made to the Program Coordinator, an Intervention Specialist will call the youth within 48 hours of receiving the referral to introduce the program and schedule an initial visit.

If a youth chooses to work with *Caught in the Crossfire* (98% of youth approached by an Intervention Specialist do), the Intervention Specialist talks with the youth's parent(s)/guardian(s) about the program services and secures consent for services if the youth is under 18 years of age.

Hospital Bedside Visit

The Intervention Specialist first assesses the threat of retaliatory violence by the youth's family and friends and takes any necessary steps to prevent retaliation. This initial meeting often lasts for close to two hours, and serves as the foundation for building a trusting relationship with the youth and his/her family.

Since building a trusting relationship is central to *Caught in the Crossfire's* success, this is a major focus of the initial meeting. To facilitate the building of trust and to gather all the information needed to begin providing services, during the initial meeting the Intervention Specialist completes an intake assessment, which includes such areas as health, housing, probation status, school registration, employment, etcetera. Using an intake assessment form to guide the interview process is essential to ensure that every Intervention Specialist, regardless of their level of experience, gathers the same essential information. The Intervention Specialist and the young person also review the circumstances that triggered the referral and explore alternative strategies for dealing with conflicts and violence. Since participation in *Caught in the Crossfire* is voluntary, the client often needs to be convinced that there is great benefit in becoming involved in the program and that the program is there to support them. As the Intervention Specialist describes "what's in it for them," the benefits become remarkably clear.

Intake Assessment

The Intervention Specialist then conducts a formal intake assessment. During the assessment there is a review of the violent incident, and, if necessary, the Intervention Specialist develops a plan for preventing any retaliation that may be planned by friends or family. The Intervention Specialist attempts to address any immediate medical or social needs the patient might have, helps them understand hospital procedures, helps make them as comfortable as possible, and helps them follow-up on contacting family. At this time the Intervention Specialist explains how the program works, what it offers, and what is expected of the youth and his/her family members. The Intervention Specialist also learns how long the youth expects to be in the hospital and establishes a plan for a follow-up meeting with the patient within five days. At the end of the assessment the Intervention Specialist gives the patient and any friend or family member program contact information, including the Intervention Specialist's business card. Depending on the emotional and physical health status of the youth, the intake assessment sometimes needs to be completed at another time.

Case Plan and Ongoing Case Management/Peer Mentoring

The Intervention Specialist continues to work with the youth and, when appropriate, his/her family members after the youth leaves the hospital to ensure that the injured youth takes the steps required to heal sufficiently and begin a new way of living. Intervention Specialists average weekly contact with the youth and their families and monitor their program participation for up to one year. All contacts with participants, including updates on progress and difficulties, are recorded in case notes in the participants' files.

Building on the intake assessment, the Intervention Specialist establishes an individualized case plan in conjunction with the injured youth and, whenever possible, his/her family members based on the initial information given. This usually takes place at the youth's home within five days after the youth leaves the hospital. Often the hospital social worker is part of the development of the plan.

The case plan usually focuses on enrolling in school or job training and/or finding employment. Housing, medical, substance abuse treatment, and transportation needs are often part of each plan. Also, the plan may include ways of supporting each youth's strengths or assets such as athletic, artistic, or other gifts and establishes a network of support that can continue after the service period ends. The case plan incorporates the development of relationships, skills, and opportunities that are core to leading a nonviolent lifestyle, such as:

- Peer groups, schools, and communities that emphasize positive social norms.
- Warm, supportive relationships and bonding with adults.
- Opportunities to become involved in positive activities.

- Recognition and support for participating in positive activities.
- Cognitive, social, and emotional competence.

Over the subsequent months, the Intervention Specialist communicates at least weekly with the injured youth and/or his/her family members to facilitate and monitor progress in meeting the objectives of the case plan. Usually this communication is a mix of telephone conversations and face-to-face meetings. Case plans are periodically reviewed to ensure that the participant is meeting objectives as planned and to make adjustments as issues surface. For example, if the Intervention Specialist discovers serious domestic violence issues in the family after working with the youth for several months, the Intervention Specialist will work with the youth (and possibly family members) to plan and develop ways of reducing the violence.

The Intervention Specialist determines the frequency and nature of contact based on his/her assessment of the injured youth's ability to follow his/her case plan. Usually the Intervention Specialist and injured youth (and possibly family members) need less frequent contact as they make progress on the case plan and the level of trust between them develops.

Caught in the Crossfire staff directly provides the following services to participants.[2]

- Employment assistance (job seeking, interview preparation, resume writing).
- Educational assistance (advocacy, enrollment/re-enrollment in school, tutoring programs, GED preparation classes, and ESL classes).
- Mentoring (regular contact between the young adult Intervention Specialist and the youth).
- Housing assistance (advocacy, shelter/transitional housing).
- Legal aid (court advocacy, assistance with paperwork and identification).
- Transportation (by Intervention Specialist or free bus tickets).
- Information and referrals.

Caught in the Crossfire also offers all of these services to family members of the participants as needed. In order to change behavior and address external factors that may have a critical impact on a young person's decisions, it is often necessary and of great importance to incorporate the closest members of that person's support system into the service plan.

Details about the participant and his/her environment emerge as their trust in the Specialist grows. The services listed above are promoted within the context of constant support, encouragement, and leadership. Intervention Specialists regularly revisit a participant's coping skills and emotional well-

[2] All services are available in Spanish as well as English. The few clients who cannot communicate in English or Spanish are linked with appropriate local providers.

being, and short- and long-term goals are constantly spelled out and/or reorganized. Intervention Specialists remain in constant contact with the participants and their families, visiting frequently, and are available any time via cell phones. They also oversee each youth's participation in services to which they are referred.

All too often, successful progress toward meeting the objectives laid out in a case plan require that we are able to meet immediate and concrete needs of clients, e.g., food, clothing, emergency shelter, or transportation. If these needs cannot be met through other providers, we draw on emergency funds set up specifically to pay for these concrete needs.

Services Provided by Other Organizations

When, during the development or implementation of the case plan, the Intervention Specialist identifies an area of need that cannot be addressed with *Caught in the Crossfire* core services (e.g., mentoring or advocacy), the Intervention Specialist usually refers the youth and/or his/her family members to other service agencies.

For example, a public health nurse from the local health department conducts numerous home health exams for some of the youth and family members who *Caught in the Crossfire* works with. She also served for several years on the oversight board of our school-based services.

Over the years, *Caught in the Crossfire* Intervention Specialists have assembled a local resource guide. The guide lists organizations` and individuals throughout the community that can provide a broad array of services from residential drug/alcohol treatment to tattoo removal to free clothing. The resource guide includes basic location and contact information as well as a detailed description of the services available and how to most efficiently access them.

The resource guide is routinely updated in order to ensure that all contact information is up to date, that new resources are added, and that resources that have provided inferior services to clients are removed.

In addition, when *Caught in the Crossfire* has specific funding, we have been able to contract with an agency for services that we use for many clients such as family counseling or job training. This arrangement significantly reduces the time between referral and actual provision of services.

If and when a need arises that is out of an Intervention Specialist's scope of expertise, clients are referred to organizations that make up *Caught in the Crossfire*'s network. The most commonly used services are in the areas of education, job training, and mental health and counseling services, specifically:

- Physical health exam by a public health nurse, wound care, sexually transmitted infection testing and treatment, inoculations, and referrals to specialists.
- Substance abuse counseling.
- Mental health evaluation and counseling.
- Life skills classes.

- Job readiness workshops for interview skills and resumé assistance.
- Job training and job retention programs.
- After-school tutorial programs.
- GED preparation classes.
- Anger management classes.
- Emergency shelter and clothing.

Partnerships

Building partnerships is essential to this type of peer intervention program. Partnerships lay the groundwork required to eventually institutionalize or make the program an ongoing part of the public health, juvenile justice, or public school systems. Partnerships ensure more comprehensive services for participants, better quality planning, and stronger outcomes. Partnerships can help leverage needed systems or policy changes. They also require a lot of hard work and careful attention to detail while always keeping the bigger picture in mind.

Caught in the Crossfire's key institutional partners over the years have included local hospitals, schools, juvenile probation, and the local police department. Our work with hospital partners is our most successful and long-term effort. Our work with local school systems has focused on providing peer intervention for middle school and high school students suspended for violence and, in some cases, facing expulsion, as well as students identified by their teachers or counselors as being at high risk for violence. That effort fell victim to California's huge budget deficit. We have also worked with youth on probation for violent offenses. We worked closely with the local police department at one point, providing peer intervention services for young people stopped by police, but not arrested. Sustaining our services with these partners depends on maintaining close relationships with the leadership in each agency. A planner from the county's inter-agency committee focused on children and youth served for several years on the oversight board of our school-based services and helped to institutionalize parts of the effort.

Community partners over the years have taken two forms: individuals and community-based agencies. Our partnerships with community-based agencies (CBOs) usually involve exchanging in-kind services or other forms of support. Occasionally we are able to secure funds to allow us to contract with other CBOs for specific services such as family counseling or cultural competency trainings. Individuals from the community usually serve on program advisory boards and provide advice about how to overcome specific challenges. We have drawn on these partners to help guide us in implementing *Caught in the Crossfire* services with a new population. Their combined experience not only helps us do a better job implementing the program, but also securing resources to continue the work beyond the initial start-up grant.

Concluding the Case Management Process

Most case plans take six to nine months to complete, although services are available for up to one year. Several conditions trigger the conclusion of *Caught in the Crossfire's* case management process. One is when a participant meets all of the objectives of his/her case plan. At that point, the Intervention Specialist and youth complete an exit interview, focusing on accomplishments over the preceding months and on concrete plans for the future. Another is when a participant chooses to discontinue working with the program, by not responding in a timely way to efforts by the Intervention Specialist to contact him/her via telephone, in person, or by letter.

By the successful conclusion of the case management process, a supportive network is in place to sustain progress made. This network may include a link with a responsible adult in the community who can serve as an ongoing mentor. It often includes the array of support that a solid job training program can provide. Connections with the Narcotics Anonymous or Alcoholics Anonymous support groups are another aspect of many of these networks.

In every case, each network expresses the individual strengths and limitations of the participating youth. The network fosters the participating youth's continued healing and growth for months and years after they are no longer working with *Caught in the Crossfire.*

Program Results

Effectiveness of Caught in the Crossfire

An evaluation of the *Caught in the Crossfire* program covering the period from 1998 to 2001 examined the effect of the program on three key outcomes: 1) rate of entry/re-entry into the criminal justice system; 2) rate of re-hospitalization for violent injuries; and 3) rate of violence-related deaths (Becker, Hall, Ursic, et al., 2004). These outcomes are directly related to the primary goals of the program: 1) prevent retaliatory violence; 2) reduce entry and re-entry into the criminal justice system; 3) reduce the total number of youth injured and killed by interpersonal violence; 4) promote alternatives to violence for youth; and 5) provide positive peer role models.

To minimize selection bias, this retrospective case-control study matched clients who participated in the intervention to youth who did not receive the intervention by age and injury severity. For ethical reasons, the intervention was not withheld from any violently injured youth during the intervention period.

The findings revealed that hospitalized youth who participated in *Caught in the Crossfire* were 70% less likely to be arrested and 60% less likely to have any criminal involvement (placement on probation, violation of probation or arrest) during the six-month post-injury period versus hospitalized youth who did not participate in the program. Furthermore, violent retaliation was reduced among 100% of hospitalized youth served and 78% of youth on probation successfully completed their sentences (compared with 28% of nonparticipants on probation).

A small proportion (1.8%) of the youth were rehospitalized for a violent injury during the evaluation period. A total of two youth (one in the treatment group and one in the control group) were rehospitalized owing to another injury. The difference in rehospitalization of the two groups was insignificant and no youth died as a result of violence-related injury in either group.

An expanded evaluation with a larger sample size and longer follow-up period has since been conducted and demonstrated similar results (Shibru, Zahnd, Becker, Bekaert, and Calhoun, 2007). The sample included 77 patients ages 12–20 years with an 18-month follow-up period and a matched cohort of hospital-based youth who did not participate in the program. Program participation lowered the risk of criminal justice involvement as well as subsequent violent criminal behaviors. The program was also found to be more effective with younger patients and was cost-effective. The sample was still too small to assess reinjury and death.

While the quantitative findings provide evidence for the effectiveness of the intervention, *Caught in the Crossfire* is best illustrated through reviewing a few past cases that highlight the program's effects on both the youth and their family members. In the next section we present several case studies of youth who participated in the intervention. Individuals' names have been changed for purposes of confidentiality.

Case Studies

Three case studies are presented to illustrate the characteristics of youth who participate in *Caught in the Crossfire.*

"Rick" and "Rob"

Two brothers, Rick, 14, and Rob, 13, were referred to *Caught in the Crossfire* after one of their frequent sibling fights got out of hand. Both were seen at Children's Hospital Oakland for facial lacerations and other bumps and bruises sustained while fighting each other. *Caught in the Crossfire* Intervention Specialist Gregory received the referral and immediately contacted Rick and Rob's mother, Chrissy. She notified Gregory that Rob refused to return home after being released from the hospital. He was placed at a local youth crisis shelter and was due to be released within the next couple of days. Gregory accompanied Chrissy to the shelter to meet Rob. En route to the shelter Chrissy shared that Rick was truant in school and Rob had been dropped from his school because he had not attended school in months. Chrissy also disclosed that she needed assistance with her nine-year-old daughter who had been sexually molested, and was frustrated that Rob would leave home for days without permission. Adding to the family's problems was the fact that Chrissy was also a recovering drug addict with only three months' sobriety.

Gregory was quick to establish a relationship with both brothers. They talked openly about their frustrations with each other that always led to physical altercations. Gregory, who is certified in anger management facilitation, helped the brothers learn to communicate with each other without fighting. Program Coordinator Kesha Turner assisted Chrissy with finding supportive services for her daughter. The daughter started receiving psychological counseling and also began attending support groups at Girls, Inc., a local youth service organization.

Gregory contacted school officials to begin the tedious process of getting a dropped student re-enrolled in school. The school principal was pleased to see that Youth ALIVE! was providing services to the brothers and felt that a positive male role model was precisely what the brothers needed in their lives. Because Gregory agreed to monitor the brothers daily, they were allowed back in school.

Rick's attendance and grades improved and he was promoted to the 11th grade. He is now attending job readiness workshops and is in line for employment within the next couple of weeks. Rob, on the other hand, has taken steps toward changing his behavior, but his progress is slower. He has continued to stay away from home and does not attend school consistently. He remains angry and aggressive but knows he needs to change his behavior. Rob maintains contact with Gregory, however, who repeatedly assures him that he will be ready to assist him whenever he is ready to accept help. Chrissy, Rick and Chrissy's daughter are now in family counseling working to strengthen their family. Gregory continues to work with Rick and Rob and their family, recognizing that long-term change takes time and persistence.

"Raul"

Raul, age 15, was shot several times due to mistaken identity. As a result, he was paralyzed from the waist down. After receiving months of physical therapy, he was ready to return home. His house was in no way equipped for a wheelchair-bound person and he only had the wheelchair that was given to him by the hospital. *Caught in the Crossfire* researched and located an agency in San Francisco that would donate a wheelchair and a fully functional hospital bed. The family was elated. There was only one problem: the items had to be picked up the next day and the family would have to provide their own movers and their own truck. The family was unable to pay for the truck and had no one available to assist with the actual move. *Caught in the Crossfire* was able to pay for the U-Haul truck *and* the movers! In addition, Intervention Specialist Emilio also assisted the family with securing funds through the City of Oakland to pay for widening doorways, adding a ramp, and installing railings in the bathrooms and around the front porch. Emilio also worked relentlessly to secure funding from the Victim and Witness Assistance Division of the Office of the District Attorney in Alameda County that resulted in the purchase of a brand new van for Raul equipped with hand controls. With the help of Emilio and other *Caught in the Crossfire* staff, Raul returned to school (he currently attends Laney Community College) and plays basketball in a league for people with disabilities.

"Marcel"

One evening, Marcel was hanging out with his homeboys, looking for something to get into. Unfortunately that something turned out to be a fight with rival gang members. Marcel was assaulted and was rushed to Highland Hospital's Trauma Center. He was treated and released that evening and a referral was sent to *Caught in the Crossfire.* Intervention Specialist Emilio made contact the next day. Marcel had recently been released from juvenile camp; he still had restitution to pay and no job. *Caught in the Crossfire* managed to make contact with his Probation Officer and was able to get his restitution modified. Sadly, shortly thereafter, Marcel was again assaulted, this time with a baseball bat. *Caught in the Crossfire* assisted Marcel with filling out a Victim's of Crime application and gathering the necessary paperwork to have his medical bills covered.

After a vigorous search, *Caught in the Crossfire* was able to find employment for Marcel at a local restaurant. With Emilio's help, Marcel began to realize it was time to make some changes in his life. His employment was steady and his performance was outstanding. He was soon promoted to shift manager. Marcel saved his money and paid his restitution in full. Emilio talked to Marcel about the importance of education. Marcel decided to take his General Equivalency Diploma (GED) examination. As a show of support *Caught in the Crossfire* paid the fee for the exam. During the same period, Marcel asked to attend meetings and groups dealing with violence prevention. His first meeting was at Youth ALIVE! He discussed the services he had received from *Caught in the Crossfire* and how Emilio had encouraged him to further his education and leave gang life behind. Not only had he decided to leave gang life behind, he wanted to prevent others from entering a destructive lifestyle. Emilio encouraged Marcel to apply for a youth violence prevention position. Marcel now works for the City of Oakland's Safe Passages Program as a Youth Ambassador. He works with city officials developing programs for young people. Marcel stays in touch almost daily. He is excited about his new job and his suddenly more promising future.

Recognition and Replication

Youth ALIVE! has been widely recognized for its creative and consistent work to prevent and reduce violence. In 2002, the Fetzer Institute awarded *Caught in the Crossfire* the Norman Cousins prize for our outstanding work with violently injured youth in a health care setting.

In the late 1990s, former Attorney General Janet Reno visited the *Caught in the Crossfire* program in Oakland and then worked to disseminate the model nationwide. In 1997, the federal Justice Department identified Youth ALIVE! as one of four sites nationwide to implement a gun violence reduction initiative. Two years later, a Youth ALIVE! staff member received the "Spirit of Youth Award" by the national Coalition for Juvenile Justice. In 2000, the federal Substance Abuse and Mental Health Services Administration awarded Youth ALIVE! a two-year grant to support peer intervention services for students facing expulsion for violence. Our intervention work with youth on probation was cited as a model program in a 2001 federal publication (Bonderman, 2001). In 2002, Youth ALIVE! was one of six sites in California awarded a California Justice Department grant to lead a collaborative effort that provides prevention and intervention services in East Oakland middle and high schools.

Over the past five years, Youth ALIVE!'s *Caught in the Crossfire* staff have provided technical assistance to several hospitals and other agencies that were establishing similar programs. We worked closely with Family Services of Milwaukee (Wisconsin) and the city health department to replicate the program there as Project UJIMA.

Technical assistance provided to the John Muir Medical Center in Walnut Creek, California, helped launch a program in the late 1990s, and *Caught in the Crossfire* staff assisted San Francisco General Hospital in launching a peer intervention program in 2002. We helped launch the Arizona State University-associated program, *Support, Mentoring and Advocacy Resources for Trauma Recovery (SMARTR).* Youth ALIVE! replicated the *Caught in the Crossfire* program in Los Angeles County in 2007. Most recently, *Caught in the Crossfire* staff have provided technical assistance to representatives of Carolinas Medical Center in Charlotte, North Carolina, Jefferson Hospital in Philadelphia, Pennsylvania, and Boston Medical Center in Massachusetts (the program has since been replicated at six sites throughout Massachusetts and Youth ALIVE! staff provide ongoing technical assistance).

Conclusion

This concludes the description of the *Caught in the Crossfire* program. As noted above, the program has been recognized as an effective youth violence prevention program and has been or is in the process of being replicated around the country. At the end of this chapter we have included a variety of materials to facilitate further replication of the program. The materials include a sample plan for designing a peer intervention program (Appendix A), the *Caught in the Crossfire* Program Organizational Chart (Appendix B), and sample Job Descriptions (Appendix C). We have also included the following forms used by *Caught in the Crossfire* staff:

- Appendix D: *Caught in the Crossfire* Referral Form.
- Appendix E: *Caught in the Crossfire* Initial Intake Interview Form.
- Appendix F: *Caught in the Crossfire* Case Plan Form.
- Appendix G: *Caught in the Crossfire* Follow-up and Progress Form.
- Appendix H: *Caught in the Crossfire* Monthly Services Tracking Form for Data Intake.

All of the material included in the appendices can be obtained from the chapter authors.

Appendix A: Eleven step plan to design and implement a successful peer intervention program.

To get started on creating a peer intervention program, the most important elements required are:

- A clear mission you are committed to carrying out;
- The capacity to be persistent and practical;
- The appropriate partners; and
- The time to do careful planning and to lead a solid start-up phase.

The 11 key steps in implementing a successful peer intervention program follow.

Step 1. Identify Partners

List the institutional and community partners that are most likely to make the program work well. Think about components of institutions that may function as almost separate partners-for example, not just the local hospital, but also the hospital trauma center and the hospital social work department. Include representatives of all of the parts of the institution which are likely to be in contact with the youth you plan to provide services to.

Research and identify potential community-based partners that have an outstanding service reputation with the population you have selected; include influential community leaders and representatives of organizations doing similar work.

The most important partners are the ones you must enlist in working with you to get the program off the ground. A planning group of three or four is usually sufficient during the initial planning phase. You can add others at a later period.

Before you have selected your "team," meet with each person individually to talk about the program and assess whether s/he can bring essential resources to the effort. Invite those individuals to join the planning group whom you feel confident about working with over several years. Each one should share your vision, know how to work well with others, and bring key skills and connections to the process. A sense of humor is very helpful.

Step 2. Conduct a Needs Assessment

A needs assessment is essential not only to document the problem you plan to address, but also to inspire the resources you will need, such as administrators and funders. A typical needs assessment includes information about the population to be served, including demographic information on the youth and the communities they live in. Analyze the data with your partners. Look for trends over several years and/or see if there are differences among potential clients if the data are divided by race/ethnicity, age level, gender, etcetera. Use this data to develop the program plans and add planning partners, if necessary.

Steps Involved in Conducting a Needs Assessment

1	Community Conditions and Characteristics	Local hospital admissions for violent injuries, e.g. number per year for the past ten years and re-admissions, if possible. (NOTE: It may only be possible to secure admission data for the past four or five years, but the longer the period of time covered, the better.) Demographic characteristics of patients admitted, e.g. age, race/ethnicity, gender, nature of injuries. Demographic characteristics of community served by hospital, e.g. rates of assaults and homicides, income levels, racial/ethnic diversity.
2	Other Agencies	Public and private agencies involved in providing services to violently injured patients either at the hospital or by referral from hospital staff including name of agency, key contact person, description of type of services and population served. Public and private agencies serving youth at high risk for violence in the community and their family members including name of agency, key contact person, description of type of services and population served.
3	Data Analysis	Determine changes in rate of admissions and characteristics of those admitted over time by age, race/ethnicity, gender, nature of injuries.
4	Report	Determine changes in re-admission rates, if possible, by age, race/ethnicity, gender, nature of injuries. Prepare a report about the data and findings for partners and for potential funders and other supporters.

Step 3. Map Out a Plan

Develop a plan that includes the following:

- Overall program vision and how it fits in with the mission of the program.
- Definition of the population to be reached.
- Problems to be addressed by the program.
- Actions to take over a two year period to address the problems.
- Develop a timeline that also details the major activities, start and completion dates and who will be responsible for each activity.
- An evaluation plan with clear and measurable objectives.

Preparing a logic model can help program developers understand the overall plan. A logic model depicts how the assumptions and principles underlying your program are linked to specific objectives, activities, and intended outcomes. As the baseball great, Yogi Berra, once said, "If you don't know where you're going, how are you gonna' know when you get there." Information about designing a logic model is available on the Internet and at many libraries. The W.K. Kellogg Foundation produced an excellent manual for developing logic models: Logic Model Development Guide (Available through their website at: www.wkkf.org).

Step 4. Secure Funding

If you and those you are partnering with are passionate and informed about your mission, securing funding for a needs assessment, planning, and implementation may be easier than you think. In the beginning, some people may be willing to provide in-kind services or volunteer. There may be resources within your own agency. Be sure to stay in open communication with the agency/hospital you are partnering with about your findings. Then look for government sources and private foundations that are interested in assisting this population.

The Internet and libraries have information about foundations and government funding programs. Gather as much information as you can about the specific types of programs each source is willing to support, the geographical restrictions, and the amount they are likely to give. When you have selected a prospect, find out the process for requesting funding, the deadlines, and what information they need in order to review a request. Although it's normally a good idea to allow a year from your first contact with a potential funder to receiving a decision, some sources may have a quicker response time, especially for start-up funding. If you are not already familiar with grant writing, information is available on the Internet, in many public libraries, and, in some communities, through nonprofit agencies that provide training.

Step 5. Address Legal/Liability/Confidentiality/Client Protection Issues

All hospitals and other community-based agencies involved in direct services require attention to specific legal, liability, and client protection issues.

These must be addressed as part of the program planning phase and also before seeking funding.

Step 6. Identify a Central Referral Source at the Hospital

Whether the lead partner is a hospital or a non-hospital provider, designating a specific hospital staff member to serve as the primary liaison is crucial. This could be you, or a social worker, the trauma coordinator, a trauma surgeon, an Emergency Department nurse, or a triage clerk. Hospital medical and/or social work staff are essential to ensuring that appropriate program clients are identified and referred for peer intervention services in a timely manner.

A designated Program Liaison also facilitates the smoothest possible interaction between other hospital staff involved in the program and non-hospital, community-based agency staff. They can troubleshoot barriers to effective communication and sort out other problems. It is essential that they believe in the program and want to see it succeed.

Step 7. Identify Referral Resources in the Community

Unless your organization already has a resource guide that you use with a similar population, you will need to create a format. Your resource guide can be stored in a computer database or in a three-ring notebook format. Each are easy to update and distribute, which is essential. If you already have a resource guide, you should identify potential resources that will allow your peer intervention specialists to meet client needs that are not met by your agency. Program staff can take responsibility for contacting several potential resources and visiting their site. They should gather written materials about the program services, intake procedures, costs for services, and so on.

Once a listing of essential resources is established, your staff should continue to look for new resources. They should also listen closely to clients' reports about the quality of services and note any limitations in the resource guide. Any resources that do not meet the standards of your agency for quality service should be dropped immediately. Also, through a process of trial and error, you can weed out providers that are no longer providing services.

Step 8. Hire and Train Staff (Internal Agency Training and External Training)

The program's staff is the most important part of your program. Selecting people who have the capacity and passion to do the job and providing them with ongoing training and support are crucial.

Step 9. Pilot Period and Full Program Implementation

Start off by serving a smaller number of clients than is indicated by the needs assessment. A pilot phase, which can last two years or more, provides the opportunity to test the program design in your community and get a clearer sense of what it will take the program to scale in terms of effort, coordination, staffing levels, access to services, additional resources, and whether you can move into full program implementation. When you decide to go ahead, you should begin the planning and resource development needed for full implementation.

Step 10. Evaluation

Collecting data about clients, how you are working with them, and the outcomes of your efforts is vital. In addition to providing information for funders and other supporters, it provides a means to periodically check your progress. For example, even though it may feel as though you are making little or no progress, a report about how many people you have linked to community services in the past month can often be encouraging. Similarly, reports from your database can also show areas that need improvement such as paying more attention to linking female clients to gender-specific services.

There are several data collection forms or instruments on which data are entered by hand.[3] One is a referral form that the hospital social worker or other primary referral source completes to gather basic information about the injured youth and to inform the *Caught in the Crossfire* Coordinator that the injured youth needs to be contacted.[4] The information on this form gives the Intervention Specialist the basic information s/he needs to initiate the first meeting with the injured youth.

After the injured youth and/or his/her parent/guardian have consented to work with *Caught in the Crossfire,* the Intervention Specialist gathers additional information on an initial intake/assessment form. This information serves as the basis of the case plan. It includes information about the participant's support system, the nature of the injury, notes about the subjects covered in the interview, and notation about the date and time of the next planned meeting.

At the next meeting, the Intervention Specialist fills out as much of the case plan form as possible. This form indicates areas of attention (e.g., education, employment, health) and specific subcategories related to each area (e.g., under "education" the listings include enrolling in school and taking part in a tutoring program). It also ensures that the injured youth and Intervention Specialist agree on what date a specific activity will be completed. The injured youth and Intervention Specialist periodically review the case plan form and make changes as new issues arise, barriers that require extending deadlines, and so on. The Program Coordinator should also periodically review this form with the Intervention Specialist during weekly supervision meetings in order to insure that the Specialist is staying on task in accomplishing the goals that have been set. A second form, the case notes form, provides a way to chronological-

[3] Some agencies have the resources to provide laptop computers that their field staff use to input data as they work with program participants. These data are then transferred to a central database every week or every month.

[4] Relevant hospital staff receive training in completing and transmitting the form.

ly document contacts made between the injured youth and Intervention Specialist. It shows the date of contact, the method of contact (e.g., telephone, mail, face-to-face), the issues discussed, progress made and/or outcomes, and next steps. This form should also be reviewed periodically during weekly supervision meetings with the Program Coordinator.

Each month, the Intervention Specialist completes a monthly report form. This form, which serves as the basic charting form, ensures that the Intervention Specialist conveys specific information about services provided and changes in participant status (e.g., enrolled in job training) during the preceding month. When a participant is no longer involved in the program, the Intervention Specialist notes that on the form.

The Program Coordinator reviews each Intervention Specialist's client folder on a monthly basis in order to insure that services are being provided in the most effective and efficient manner possible.

How data get entered (database)

Whenever a referral form is received at the office, the agency's Administrative Assistant immediately enters the data into *Caught in the Crossfire's* database.[5] Also, the Administrative Assistant enters the data from the monthly report forms each month. Periodically, the Administrative Assistant and the Program Coordinator review the database files for current clients and look for possible errors.

How data get reported

The Administrative Assistant generates data reports. The database includes specific "queries" that produce reports such as the number of newly injured youth who were referred the previous month or the previous quarter. Because of limitations with the database, more complex data reports must often be hand-counted. For example, a report of the number of African American females referred in the previous six months from one of the two local hospitals might require a hand-count of a printout of all referrals from that hospital.

How data inform the program

As highlighted above, data collection and reports can serve many useful purposes. One purpose is to identify programmatic issues that need to be addressed and conveying that information back to staff, usually as part of week-

[5] Caught in the Crossfire hired a consultant to develop its database, using the Microsoft Access program. There are many database programs available. Key to the development process is to plan as carefully as possible before you develop your database. Know what data fields you absolutely require and what fields you would like. Think about the kinds of questions or queries you would like to have answered using the database. You can almost always add or delete fields, but those changes mean that you will have missing data for the clients already entered in the database unless you can find the data in case files and have the human resources to update your database with this information.

ly staff meetings. Another is to highlight program progress for current and potential funders as well as the news media. A third purpose is to provide information that can be used in research and publication of findings as part of the building of the knowledge base about what works, what doesn't work, and why.

Process and impact evaluation and ongoing training

Evaluating your program will keep it alive. To do this, you must define specific, measurable, achievable, reachable, and time-bound (S.M.A.R.T.) objectives. Some should capture the most essential expectations about the processes involved in the program, for example providing intervention services for a certain number of people. Others should capture the most important impacts you expect the program will have for example reducing recurrence of violent injuries among those served by a certain percentage compared with the baseline data of the rate of recurring injury before the program started. Records of progress toward meeting those objectives should include not only the quantitative information from the program database, but also qualitative information such as records of meetings, staff and client satisfaction surveys, and interviews with selected staff and/or clients. Then the evaluator, either a designated staff member or an outside consultant, should compile a report based on an analysis of those data.

Evaluation reports can be produced monthly, quarterly, annually, and/or at the end of a grant period. Most organizations periodically produce reports about clients served or results of surveys throughout the year and then a final evaluation at the end of a grant period.

Step 11. Public Relations

Getting media attention about the program helps to inform your community that the program is in place and working to address a serious problem. Media coverage can alert potential funders, particularly individual donors, and acknowledge current funders. It is a good way to celebrate the launching of the program or its successes after several years. Reporting about a particularly effective staff member is a great way to encourage his/her work in the field. For assistance and obtaining additional materials, go to the Berkeley Media Studies Group website, www.bmsg.org.

Steps For Reaching the Media

1	Define your message so that you can speak clearly and concisely about the purpose and value of the program.	Determine what is newsworthy; Specify the ways it most directly affects the news audience. Identify 2-3 key messages. Produce a list of brief talking points that will grab the attention of reporters.
2	Focus your outreach so that you can reach the media sources most likely to respond.	Produce a list of the print and electronic media you want to reach, including contact information for reporters most likely to report on your program. Produce and distribute a news release of two pages or less that covers your program's key messages.
3	Follow up so that your message isn't lost in the flood of information media sources receive.	Within two days after sending out the news release, call your contacts (this is called "pitching"). The best time to pitch a story to print reporters is between 10:00 a.m. and 1:00 p.m. Most television stations change shifts between 11:30 a.m. and 1:00 p.m., so call them at other times.

Appendix B: Caught in the Crossfire Program Organizational Chart

Program Director

Ensure that all services are provided.

Supervise Program Coordinator.

Ensure proper program documentation.

Research, develop new, and maintain current relationships with community leaders, public agency representatives, and community service providers securing additional resources to address participant and family needs, as well as represent Caught in the Crossfire at committees and presentations.

Program Coordinator

Supervise Crisis Intervention Specialists (CISs) including orientation and ongoing training.

Ensure proper program documentation.

Support Director in developing and maintaining relationships with community.

Administrative Assistant (8 hours/week)

Enter intake, service, and exit data into program database.
Provide other program support.

Intervention Specialist
(Number determined by average caseload = 17 active clients)

Provide emotional and crisis support, mentoring and advocacy to youth participating in the program.

Provide support to family and friends of youth.

Provide client referrals to community service providers.

Maintain intensive follow-up contact with clients, family, friends, and service providers.

Document consistently and accurately in records.

Appendix C: *Caught in the Crossfire* Job Descriptions

***Caught in the Crossfire* Program Director**

Caught in the Crossfire is a program of Youth ALIVE!, a nonprofit public health organization dedicated to reducing violent injuries and deaths to youth in California by involving youth in developing solutions to violence. *Caught in the Crossfire* is a youth violence prevention/intervention peer-based program providing trained support, mentoring, advocacy, and case management to violence-involved youth and their families. *Caught in the Crossfire* pairs youth with trained peer mentors called Intervention Specialists. Intervention Specialists come from the same communities as the population they serve and have experienced violence in their own lives, and work in collaboration with an extensive resource network to provide wrap-around support services. *Caught in the Crossfire* works closely with public service providers (including Highland Hospital/Alameda County Medical Center, the Alameda County Department of Probation, Children's Hospital Oakland, and the Oakland Unified School District).

Job Description:

The Program Director of *Caught in the Crossfire* is responsible for program management, development, and expansion; oversight of case management of clients and their families; staff support, training, and supervision; and representing and presenting the *Caught in the Crossfire* public health model for violence intervention to the public.

Job Responsibilities:

Manage daily activities of *Caught in the Crossfire*.

Supervise *Caught in the Crossfire* Program Coordinator.
Oversee supervision, training, and support of *Caught in the Crossfire* program staff.
Serve as liaison to public agencies/officials (e.g., Alameda County Medical Center/Highland Hospital, Alameda County Probation Department, Oakland Unified School District, Alameda Public Health Department) and community-based organizations.
Expand the services of *Caught in the Crossfire* to other sites/agencies and departments.
Plan and implement hospital and school staff training to facilitate client referral process.
Participate as a member of the *Caught in the Crossfire* Evaluation Team.
Provide leadership/participate in appropriate collaborations/efforts to reduce violence.
Oversee program compliance with funding commitments.
Provide technical assistance ansd training to other sites interested in program replication/ adaptation.
Develop youth violence prevention policies and strategies with Youth ALIVE! management team.
Coordinate and/or deliver local and national presentations in order to increase awareness of *Caught in the Crossfire.*
Prepare reports consistent with requirement of funders and Youth ALIVE!.
Other responsibilities as assigned.

Qualifications:
Extensive program management and supervisory experience (five + years preferred).
Program development experience.
Experience working with youth and families from "high risk" communities.
Committed to improving the health and well-being of youth.
Effective public speaker.
Experience working with public agencies (e.g., hospitals, schools, juvenile justice).
Ability to work well in a team environment.
Ability to provide team leadership.
Experience working with multiple collaboratives.
Understanding of public health approach to violence prevention.
Well-organized and demonstrated ability to prioritize and delegate.
Computer skills (proficiency in Word, Access and Excel preferred).
Strong written and verbal communication skills.
Must be able to present self and program in a highly professional manner.
Ability to work in stressful situations.
Ability to work well with people from varying backgrounds.
Ability to work some evenings and weekends as needed.
Must have reliable transportation.
MSW/MPP/MPH or Master's Degree in related field preferred; Bachelor's Degree required.
Flexible, good sense of humor.

Caught in the Crossfire Program Coordinator

Job Description: The Program Coordinator

This position is responsible for the coordination and administration of crisis intervention and follow-up services provided by *Caught in the Crossfire*, a program of Youth ALIVE!. Youth ALIVE! is a nonprofit organization dedicated to reducing violent injuries and deaths to youth in California by involving youth in developing solutions to violence. *Caught in the Crossfire* is a youth violence prevention program providing trained peer support, information, and referrals to youth hospitalized for violent injuries, juvenile violent offenders, and other Oakland youth involved in violence. This position is supervised by the *Caught in the Crossfire* Program Director.

Responsibilities:

Supervise all Crisis Intervention Specialists (CISs).
Coordinate and oversee case assignment, follow-up, and continuity of services for all referred participants.
Accompany CISs on field work as needed.
Oversee necessary documentation.
Collect program data and compile into reports.
Assist Program Director with compiling funders' reports and program evaluations.
Research, develop new, and maintain current relationships with community service providers to secure additional resources for program participants.
Represent *Caught in the Crossfire* at committees and network meetings.
Assist *Teens on Target (TNT)*, under TNT Program Director's supervision, if needed.
Assume other responsibilities as assigned by Program Director.

Qualifications:

Program management/coordination experience preferred.
Violence prevention policy and media experience preferred.
Experience and commitment to working with at-risk youth.
Strong written and verbal communication skills.
Well-organized and demonstrated ability to prioritize.
Ability to present self and program in a professional manner.
Ability to work well in a team environment.
Ability to work well with many different kinds of people.
Must have reliable transportation and be insurable as a driver.
Ability to work some evenings and weekends as needed.
Ability to work in stressful situations.
Computer skills (proficiency in Word, Access and Excel preferred).
High School Diploma or GED required; BA or BS preferred.
Applicants with personal experience in overcoming violence/ violence-related injuries/ the criminal justice system are encouraged to apply.

Caught in the Crossfire Intervention Specialist

Job Description: Intervention Specialist

This position is responsible for the provision of crisis intervention and follow-up services provided by *Caught in the Crossfire,* a youth violence prevention program providing trained support, information, and referrals to youth involved in violence. *Caught in the Crossfire* is a program of Youth ALIVE!, a nonprofit organization dedicated to reducing violent injuries and deaths to youth in California by involving youth in developing solutions to violence. *Caught in the Crossfire* is a collaborative effort between Youth ALIVE! (the lead agency), Alameda County Medical Center at Highland Hospital, Children's Hospital Oakland, and the Oakland Unified School District.

Job Responsibilities:

Provide emotional and crisis support, mentoring, and advocacy to violence-involved youth who are hospitalized for gunshot wounds and other forms of violent injuries, on probation for violent offenses, and/or suspended or at risk for suspension from school for violence.

Provide support to family and friends of youth.

Provide client referrals to community service providers.

Maintain intensive follow-up contact with clients, family, friends and service providers through home visits and telephone contact.

Document consistently and accurately in records all contacts with clients.

Attend weekly staff meetings.

Other responsibilities as assigned by Program Director.

Qualifications:

Must be bilingual in English/Spanish.

Demonstrated commitment to working with youth.

Knowledge of urban youth issues, specifically youth violence.

Demonstrated ability to work independently and as part of a team.

Ability to take constructive criticism and work well with supervision.

Ability to work well with diverse populations.

Punctual and extremely reliable.

Highly organized and detail-oriented.

Must be able to present self and program in a professional manner.

Flexibility to work some evenings and weekends.

Ability to work in stressful situations;

High School Diploma or GED required; BA or BS preferred.

Must have reliable, insured car and DMV clearance.

Applicants with personal experience in overcoming violence/ violence-related injuries/ the criminal justice system are encouraged to apply.

Appendix D: Caught in the Crossfire Referral Form

Attention: Kesha Turner, Program Coordinator
3300 Elm Street Oakland, CA 94607; Phone 510.594.2588 x.303 / Fax 510.594.0667

Referral Contact:	Date of referral:

Referral source:	Alameda County Department of Probation (Unit___________)
	Oakland Unified School District Discipline Hearing Panel (DHP)
	Caught in the Crossfire
	Alameda County Office of Education (ACOE)
	Highland Hospital
	Children's Hospital
	Other (specify

Reason for referral (check appropriate reason and circle the mechanism):	
Weapons-related offense— gun/knife/other _______	History/experience with weapon- gun/knife/other _______
Victim of violent injury- gun/knife/other _______	Other (please specify)

Referral Name:			
Address:			Phone:
Age:	DOB:	Sex: M F	English fluency? Y N
Race/Ethnicity (circle1): African American Latino/Hispanic Asian/Pacific Islander White Native American other			

Other Contacts: include name/phone #/relationship to the Referral:
1.
2.
3.

What school/alternative programs is the participant currently involved?
1.
2.

Areas of concern (check all that apply):			
Physical health ___	Mental health ___	Peer group ____	Parenting ____
Support system___	Job training ____	Housing/food ___	GED Preparation ____
Participation in school ___	Anger management ___	Conflict resolution ___	Substance use/abuse ____

Parental/ Legal Guardian consent (if appropriate)

I understand and consent to refer ______________________ to the *Caught in the Crossfire* program for information and referral services.

____
Parent/Legal Guardian Signature

Appendix E: Caught in the Crossfire Initial Intake Interview Form

Date of Referral: **Date of first contact:** **Intervention Specialist:**

Participant Name:	Social Security #:
Address:	English fluency? Y N
Phone #s (include name/relationship to the Participant): Participant living with:	

Age:	DOB:	Sex: M F	Race: AA L A/PI W NA other:

Referred from: HH CHO Probation OUSD DOJ other:

Current school status:	Current employment status:
Any previous violent injuries? N Y How many? Resulted in medical treatment? N Y	
On Probation? N Y For what? How many? Violent? N Y	List previous offenses: Gun involved? N Y
Date of last health physical: Have immunizations card? N Y	Date of last dental check:
Substance abuse? N Y Which?	Other concerns:

IF HOSPITAL REFERRAL

Referred by:	MSW other:	Medical record #:
Date admitted:	Seen in the hospital: N Y (date) Room #:	
Type of injury: GSW SW Assault 261 other		Location of wound:

IF PROBATION REFERRAL

Referred by:	P.O. other:	Case pending? Y N

Is Participant interested in program? Y N

Follow-up date/time/location:____
Additional information: ____
____

Appendix F: *Caught in the Crossfire* Case Plan Form

Participant Name:	Crisis Intervention Specialist name:

Date Case received:	Initial Contact date:
Referral Source: HH CHO Probation OUSD-DHP Advocates other:	

GOALS/OBJECTIVES		WHERE, WHY, WHAT, DETAILS...	DATE COMPLETED
EDUCATION			
Reconnect w/ school system			
GED program			
Tutoring program			
High School diploma			
Assist w/DHP			
College classes			
Other			
EMPLOYMENT			
Clothes/tools for job			
Job training			
Computer training			
Other vocational training			
Resume/cover letters			
Job interview			
Maintain current employment			
Obtain employment			
Other			

HEALTH (PHYSICAL AND EMOTIONAL)			
Physical therapy			
Medical/hygiene supplies			
Medical/dental appointment			
Drug/alcohol rehab./counseling			
Counseling (specify)			
Anger management			
Conflict resolution			
Pre-natal care			
SSI/MEDI-Cal/other			
Other			
LEGAL			
Driver's License			
ID card			
Social security			
Government assistance			
Court advocacy			
Legal aid/lawyer			
Report to probation			
Naturalization			
Victims of crime			
GOALS/OBJECTIVES		WHERE, WHY, WHAT, DETAILS…	DATE COMPLETED
HOUSING/SHELTER			
Obtain housing			
Utility assistance			
Housing advocacy			

Shelter/Temporary housing			
Other			
NUTRITION/FAMILY			
Emergency food			
Food stamps			
Parenting classes			
Child care			
Family planning/sex education			
Other			
SOCIAL/RECREATIONAL			
After school program			
Support group			
Link w/community center			
Mentor			
Church/faith-based connection			
Sports			
Improve communication skills			
TNT			
Volunteer work			
Other			
OTHER			

Appendix G: *Caught in the Crossfire* Follow-up and Progress Form

CIS:________________ Participant:______________

Date	Contact By	NOTES Include issues discussed, progress/outcomes, and next steps

Monthly Update Tracking Form for Data Intake

Referral Source: Probation Highland OUSD Advocates FIRST CHO TNT P2C

MONTHLY ONLY

Reporting Period: _____ ________
month *year*

Was the youth employed for this month? Y N

Was the youth enrolled in school this month? Y N

Was the youth arrested for a new offense? Y N

Was the youth hospitalized for a violence-related injury? (If this is a new hospital case, answer no) Y N

Number of phone calls made: _____

Number of in-person contacts made: _____

Number of family/friends served for the first time: _____

What is the youth's probation status? _____

On probation _____

Not on probation _____

Completed probation _____

Please provide in some detail your impression of how this youth is progressing, as well as any new/critical incidents.

INTAKE ONLY

Client's Name ____________________
Age _____ DOB _________
Address ____________________
City ____________ Zip __________

Race: AA W L API O

Gender: Male Female

Is the youth enrolled in school?
Enrolled Not Enrolled N/A

Is the youth employed?
Employed Not Employed N/A

Is the youth on probation?
On probation Not on probation

Who is the youth living with?
Both parents Independent
Father Only Incarcerated
Mother Only Significant Other
Legal Guardian Homeless

HOSPITAL USE ONLY

Date Admitted ___/___/___
Did the youth get a bedside visit? Yes No
Type of Injury
GSW SW
FTF DV
BBB PA
261 Other

Appendix H: *Caught in the Crossfire* Monthly Services Tracking Form for Data Intake

1) Did the youth participate in non-traditional educational programs? YES NO
   If yes, please identify:
   - GED Preparation
   - Adult School
   - ESL Courses
   - Job Corps
   - Other (please note)

2) Was the youth placed in a job by Intervention Specialist YES NO

3) Was a family/friend placed in job by Intervention Specialist? YES NO

4) Was the youth placed in job by other placement program? YES NO

5) Did the youth receive vocational assistance from the IS? YES NO

6) Did a family/friend receive vocational assistance? YES NO

7) Did the youth participate in an outside vocational program? YES NO

8) Did the youth receive counseling from an outside agency? YES NO
   If yes, please identify:
   - Substance Abuse
   - Anger Management
   - Life Skills
   - Other (please note)

9) Did the youth participate in a life skills program? YES NO
   If yes, please identify:
   - Job Corps
   - Support Groups taught by Youth ALIVE!
   - Other (please note)

10) Did the IS provide the youth with mentoring services? YES NO
    (This question is just so that we may keep track of services)

11) Did the youth receive rides from the Intervention Specialist? YES NO

12) Did the youth receive bus passes or other transportation passes? YES NO

13) Did the youth receive advocacy services by the Intervention Specialist? YES NO

If yes, please identify:

Legal Advocacy

Educational Advocacy

Vocational Advocacy

Other (please note)

14) Did the youth receive advocacy services by another program? YES NO

15) Did the youth receive assistance with documentation gathering and completion by Intervention Specialist? YES NO

16) How many times was the client seen by the public health nurse? ____

References

Becker, M.G., Hall, J.S., Ursic, C.M., et al. (2004). Caught in the Crossfire: The effects of a peer-based intervention program for violently injured youth. *Journal of Adolescent Health.* 34(3):March.

Belcher, J.R., Deforge, B.R., and Jani, J.S. (2005). Inner-city victims of violence and trauma care. The importance of trauma-center discharge and aftercare planning and violence prevention programs. *J. Health, Soc. Polic.*, 21(2):17–34.

Bonderman, J. (2001). *Working with Victims of Gun Violence.* Washington, DC: U.S. Department of Justice, Office for Victims of Crime.

Catalano, R.F., Loeber, R., and McKinney, K.C. (1999). *School and Community Interventions to Prevent Serious and Violent Offending.* Washington, DC: Office of Juvenile Justice and Delinquency Prevention.

Catalano, R.F., M.W. Arthur, J.D. Hawkins, L. Berglund, and J.J. Olson (1998). Comprehensive community- and school-based interventions to prevent antisocial behavior, in *Serious and Violent Juvenile Offenders: Risk Factors and Successful Interventions,* ed. R. Loeber and D.P. Farrington. Thousand Oaks, CA: Sage Publications: 248–283.

Catalano, R.F., and J.D. Hawkins. (1995). *Communities That Care: Risk-Focused Prevention Using the Social Development Strategy.* Seattle, WA: Developmental Research and Programs, Inc.

Cornwell, E.E., Chang, D.C., Phillips, J., and Campbell, K.A. (2003). Enhanced trauma program commitment at a level I trauma center: Effect on the process and outcome of care. *Arch. Surg.*, 138(8):838–843.

Dobrin, A,, and Brusk, J.J. (2003). The risk of offending on homicide victimization: A public health concern. *Am. J. Health Behav.* 27(6):603–12.

Henggeler, S.W., Cunningham, P.S., Pickret, S.G., et al. (1996). Multisystemic therapy: An effective violence prevention approach for serious juvenile offenders. *J. Adolescent Health.* 9:47–61.

Masten, A.S., and Coatsworth, J.D. (1998). The development of competence in favorable and unfavorable environments: Lessons from research on successful children. *American Psychologist.* 53(2):205–220.

Menard, S., 2002. *Youth Violence Research Bulletin,* Washington, DC: Office of Juvenile Justice and Delinquency Prevention.

Shibru, D., Zahnd, E., Becker, M., Bekaert, N., and Calhoun D. (2007). Benefits of a hospital- based peer intervention program for violently injured youth. *J. of the Amer. College of Surgeons.* 205(5):684–689.

U.S. Department of Health and Human Services (2001). Youth Violence: A Report of the Surgeon General. Rockville, MD: U.S. Department of Health and Human Services, Centers for Disease Control and Prevention, National Center for Injury Prevention and Cotnrol, Substance Abuse and Mental Health Services Administration, Center for Mental Health Services, and National Institutes of Health, National Institute of Mental Health. www.surgeongeneral.gov/library/youthviolence/. 2001. Accessed September 2006.

Zun, L., Downey, L., et al. (2006). The effectiveness of an ED-based violence prevention program. *Amer. J. of Emergency Med.* 24(1):8–13.

Chapter 7

Summary and Recommendations for Programs and Research

Robert D. Ketterlinus, PhD

Summary

Throughout its history, the United States has been preoccupied with attempts to understand and control violence in its many forms (Reiss and Roth, 1994). Despite the steady decrease in U.S. violent crime rates over the past decade, violence remains a topic of great concern among citizens, policymakers, and the scientific community. As discussed in Chapter 1, exposure to violence creates a potential cascade of negative outcomes that affects victims, perpetrators, and their families and communities. The effects of interpersonal violence also have enormous economic impact that affects Americans' quality of life and interferes with efforts to create a more equalitarian society.

As demonstrated in numerous public opinion polls, youth crime and violence continue to be of great concern to Americans (Moeller, 2001). For example, 90% of voters polled agreed that youth crime is a major problem in communities, but only 35% say they believe that the juvenile justice system is effective in getting youth to stop committing violent and nonviolent crime (National Council on Crime and Delinquency, 2007). Violence in schools is viewed as a particularly worrisome problem. For example, a recent poll by *Time* magazine and the Discovery Channel, in conjunction with the National Campaign Against Youth Violence, revealed that fewer teens feel "very safe from violence" in schools today (33%) than shortly after the Columbine killings (42%). Parents are also concerned. A poll by *USA Today*, CNN, and Gallup found that 63% of adults feel that an incident like Columbine could happen in their community. As a result of the school shootings, many parents (40%) feel much more concerned about their child's safety.

This book provides information about promising approaches to preventing youth violence in hospital-based settings with a focus on hospital emergency departments (EDs) that have the potential to address the public's concerns about this ongoing, and in some communities, growing problem. While Philadelphia HealthCare Collaborative (HCC) programs are no longer working together, they, and other programs described in this book, provide valuable lessons about how other hospitals and their EDs could approach violence prevention in their city.

There is a large volume of literature about the prevalence, causes, consequences, and prevention of violence in general and about intentional youth violence in particular (see Chapter 1). The findings have helped inform the development of a systematic process called the public health approach to youth violence. This approach has four steps: define the problem, identify risk and protective factors, develop and test prevention strategies, and assure widespread adoption of prevention principles and strategies. The chapters in this book together reflect a public health approach to understanding intentional youth violence within the context of hospital-based settings (with a focus on emergency departments), especially those located in poor urban areas.

The focus of this book on youth violence in *urban areas* is appropriate because these areas include high numbers of persons at greatest risk of violence victimization such as young males, minorities, persons with a history of delinquent or criminal behavior or of violence victimization, and persons living in poor urban communities (Department of Health and Human Services, 1986; Fingerhut, et al., 1992; Gladstein, et al., 1992; Rosenberg, et al., 1987; Smith and Brewer, 1992). Young African Americans are at especially high risk for violent injury, homicide is the leading cause of death in black men and women aged 15–24 (Kochanek and Hudson, 1995), and these violently injured youth have a significant need for educational support, employment assistance, mental health services, and gang intervention services (Zun and Rosen, 2003).

Despite the fact that medical professionals have been viewing this problem as a public health issue for almost 20 years, the published literature on intentional youth violence intervention in hospital settings is relatively small. A compelling reason for calls for ED-based intentional violence prevention interventions is research that suggests that patients with ED visits for assault, firearm injuries, and substance abuse are at increased risk for homicide and often have an escalating number of visits leading up to the homicide event. For example, it has been estimated that the recurrence rate for repeat violence is between 6 and 44 percent with a five-year mortality of 20 percent (Zun, Downey, and Rosen, 2006). Furthermore, many adolescents who use the ED as their usual source of care and end up in EDs as the result of intentional violence are often from vulnerable populations. Many have special mental or physical needs that are unlikely to be met with ED visits only, and they are likely to have missed care they needed. Creating linkages between EDs and other services could help at-risk adolescents identify and use more appropriate sources of primary and other health and mental health care (Wilson and Klein, 2000). Therefore, it is appropriate and desirable that ED-based identification and social services referral programs should be considered for this high-risk population (Crandall, et al. 2004; McCart, et al., 2006).

The book's focus on hospital-based, and in particular ED-based youth violence interventions, will hopefully re-energize calls for action in these settings that have appeared since the early 1990s (for example, see Prothrow-Stith, 1992; American Academy of Pediatrics, 1996; American Academy of Pediatrics

Task Force on Violence, 1999; Anglin, 1997; Christoffel, Spivak, and Witner, 2000; Shepherd, Sivarajaingam, and Rivara, 2000). There is little published information about hospital-based programs, and even fewer descriptive or effectiveness studies of ED or trauma-department-based programs. Exceptions include published research on four programs included in this book, two from the Philadelphia HealthCare Collaborative (HCC) and two from programs in other cities (Milwaukee, WI, and Oakland, CA), and several other surveillance and prevention programs in other cities (see Chapter 1, Part II). At the end of this chapter a brief description is provided of a new youth violence surveillance and intervention/prevention program being implemented in three trauma centers in Philadelphia, PA.

Chapter 2 includes a description of *The Violence Intervention Project (VIP) of The University of Pennsylvania* that was part of the Philadelphia HCC, and summarizes what the authors have learned about the relationship between youth exposure to violence and Acute Stress Disorder and Post-Traumatic Stress Disorder and its implications for emergency room physicians. Their chapter fits into an expanding literature on the causes and consequences of child and adolescent trauma, and on the identification and treatment of trauma resulting from exposure to violence (and other causes) in health care and other settings (e.g., see Mabanglo, 2002). Since the initiation of the Philadelphia HCC programs in the mid-1990s, there has been a heightened awareness about the importance of providing children and youth exposed to violence with trauma-informed programs and services, and there are many evidence-based and promising programs available that can be adapted in hospital and other settings (see, for example, the federal government funded National Child Traumatic Stress Network at www.nctsnet.org).

In Chapter 3, the focus of the book turns to Ginsburg's description of the development of a theoretical framework for assessing behavioral change grounded in developmental and behavioral change. theory, and operationalized and fine-tuned during his consultations with the staff of the VIP at the University of Pennsylvania (see Chapter 2). While this framework can be applied in any hospital-based setting, Ginsburg also provides guidelines for using this framework to create a process for assessing the needs, resources, and potential to change behaviors for young, violently injured patients, using examples of methods he and his colleagues at the VIP have used to help youth change behaviors that could lead to violent outcomes.

In Chapter 4, Corbin and colleagues describe their experience designing and implementing an ED faith-based approach to the care of violently injured youth that was incorporated into the Thomas Jefferson University (TJU) Hospital ED-based "*Jefferson Community Violence Prevention Program (JCVPP),*" which was also part of the Philadelphia HCC program. This multidisciplinary collaboration of physicians, nurses, social workers, and chaplains illustrates some of the challenges hospitals face developing a cross-disciplinary approach (especially regarding collaboration with hospital chaplaincy programs), and the advantages of the approach to providing support to violently injured youth. Because of the largely insular nature of major departments within large urban hospitals, especially academic-based hospital centers, cross-disciplinary collaboration is not a natural occurrence (Liedtka and Whitten, 1998). Case studies have suggested that shared values, trust, and personal engagement can lead to participants' perceptions of successful collaboration. However, this does not guarantee improvement in the collaborative's outcomes, in part because different professional groups can have differing views of each other's roles and responsibilities (Thomas, Sexton, and Helmreich, 2003). Action research studies have suggested that effective inter-disciplinary health care collaboration requires effective communication, teamwork, and the commitment to deliver integrated care, and that integrated documentation is a key strategy for enhancing interprofessional collaboration and reducing the isolation of professionals (Atwal and Caldwell, 2002; Dechario-Marino, Jordan-Marash, Traiger, and Saulo, 2001). Research also suggests that multidisciplinary interventions can improve communication and collaboration between critical care nurses and physicians (Vazirani, Hays, Shapiro and Cowan, 2005), and can reduce patients' length of stay in the hospital as well as reduce hospital costs (Cowan, Shapiro, et al., 2006).

Finally, descriptions of and findings from research on Project Ujima in Milwaukee, WI (see Chapter 5), and Caught in the Crossfire in Oakland, CA (see Chapter 6) provide support for the idea that hospital-based youth violence prevention programs can achieve the goal of reducing the incidence and effects of youth violence. Both chapters include detailed descriptions of the respective programs' content and materials, and lessons learned. Both chapters also include case studies of program participants that permit readers a rich contextualized understanding of the nature of youth violence and the impact of different types of hospital-based prevention programs (also see case studies from the Philadelphia VIP in Chapter 2). It is important to note that at the time this book was published, both of these programs continued to operate and expand, and therefore provide good resources for those interested in learning how to promote the long-term sustainability of hospital-based youth violence prevention programs.

Looking Forward: Recommendations for Programs and Research

In this final section we present a selection of topics and issues that illustrate new directions in programs and research related to the major focus of the chapters in this book. While there are many other topics and issues that could have been addressed, we believe that the ones we chose to discuss are among the most important ones for the broad field of youth violence prevention, and are relevant to a wide range of health care and allied professionals involved in (or interested in becoming more involved in) the prevention and treatment of youth intentional violence.

We begin with a description of a new youth violence surveillance and intervention/prevention program being implemented in three-university hospital trauma centers in Philadelphia (a brief introduction to this program can be found in Chapter 1). This is followed with a brief overview of a developmental perspective on research and prevention and treatment practice related to youth intentional violence. We then present selected information about training in youth violence prevention that is available to health care workers in settings where formal violence prevention programs have not yet been implemented. Finally, we discuss the problem of vicarious trauma and related conditions that affect health care and allied professionals who work on a daily basis with youth victims of violence.

Pennsylvania Injury Reporting and Intervention System (PIRIS)

At the time of the publication of this book there was only one published experimental study of the effectiveness of an ED-based youth violence prevention program. The Boston Violence Prevention Project, described in Chapter 1, Part II, found differences between program and the control groups in their service utilization and in self-reported revictimization, but the groups did not differ in arrest and state-reported incarceration and reinjury rates 6 and 12 months after their intake into the study. This research suggests that referring young victims of violence from the ED to psychosocial services can be successful if a case management model is utilized.

In this section we discuss a new youth violence surveillance and intervention/prevention program—the Pennsylvania Injury Reporting and Intervention System (PIRIS)—being implemented in three university hospital trauma centers in Philadelphia, PA. (A brief introduction to this program is presented in Chapter 1.) PIRIS is the only initiative of its kind in the nation that combines surveillance with intervention as a means to directly control and prevent the impact of gun violence on youth. The system is built on a public health model, which is a science-based approach.

The unique features of this new program include identification of youth victims of intentional gunshots by trauma center social workers, and referral to case managers (dedicated to this population) who conduct intensive needs assessments, referrals to social services, and follow-up services. The program also includes a surveillance component designed to identify characteristics of youth gunshot victims and to determine the types of victims who agree or refuse to participate in the program. The goal of the program is to reduce repeat violence among young victims ages 15–25 years old of intentional gunshots. Funded by the Pennsylvania Department of Health, a long-term goal is to have trauma centers in other cities in the commonwealth adopt the PIRIS program.

The PIRIS System Includes Two Key Components:

Surveillance. Involves the collection of information by the hospitals on injuries, specifically firearm-related injuries. This information can be used by state and local agencies and community partnerships to target activities, develop new programs, and evaluate current violence reduction efforts.

Intervention. The multi-system case management intervention for the victim and family provide specific services designed to prevent future violence. Referrals to community services, such as drug and alcohol treatment, job training, education programs (general education diploma and vocational education), and mental health treatment and services will address the victim and family members of both the victim and the offender. The intervention component is customized to address the specific situation, such as domestic violence, gang violence, attempted suicide, or accidental shooting. Intervention strategies build on existing community- and school-based violence prevention services and programs, when appropriate.

Program Structure

PIRIS involves a partnership between three university hospital trauma centers, a large public health organization, a community-based street outreach organization, the state trauma center foundation, and a university-based firearms research center, all under the leadership of and funding from the Pennsylvania Department of Health. A list of the PIRIS partners and their major roles and responsibilities is presented in Table 1 below.

Table 1. PIRS: Partner Roles and Responsibilities

PIRIS Partner	Partner Roles and Responsibilities
Pennsylvania Department of Health	Project funding (grant); Overall project oversight.
Philadelphia Health Management Corporation (PHMC)	Project management and administration; Case management intervention and MIS; Intervention quality control evaluation
Philadelphia Anti-Violence/Anti-Drug Network (PAAN)	Community Outreach and Organizing
The University of Pennsylvania Hospital Trauma Center	Participant screening and recruitment; Referral to Case Managers (PHMC)
Temple University Trauma Center	Participant screening and recruitment; Referral to Case Managers (PHMC)
Albert Einstein Medical Center Trauma Center	Participant screening and recruitment; Referral to Case Managers (PHMC)
Firearms Injury Center at The University of Pennsylvania	Surveillance and other data systems management and analysis; Technical Support
Pennsylvania Trauma Foundation	Surveillance data collection

Participant Identification and Recruitment

The current participant selection criterion for the PIRIS program includes youth ages 15 to 25. After a gunshot victim enters any of the three PIRIS project hospital trauma centers and is medically stabilized, a trauma center staff member dedicated to the project (usually a trauma center social worker) determines if the person meets the project inclusion criteria, that is, a person 15–25 years old who is a victim of intentional gunshots. The victim may have been shot during an altercation in which he or she was involved or simply because they were in the line of fire (e.g., random drive-by shooting). At an appropriate time determined by the hospital staff, the social worker then describes the PIRIS program to the patient (and his or her parents or guardians if the patient is under age 18), and asks the patient for permission to make a referral to a PIRIS case manager to pursue the possibility of participation in the program. If the patient assents to the referral the social worker obtains contact information that is recorded on a referral form that includes basic demographic information about the clients, and faxes the referral form to the PIRIS case management supervisor within several hours. The case is assigned to a case manager who contacts the patient (and his or her parents if appropriate) within 24 hours, either at the hospital or at their home if they have been discharged from the hospital. During this first contact the case manager begins to learn about the patient's situation and describes the PIRIS program and asks if the patient would be interested in participating. The patient may agree at that time to participate (or decline) or the recruitment process may be extended to give the patient and his parents time to make a decision.

Patients who decline to participate are no longer contacted, but they are given a phone number to call if they change their mind. Case managers make initial appointments to meet with patients who agree to participate at their homes or other mutually agreed upon locations. A typical first meeting between the case manager and patient and parents involves learning more about the patient's current medical, social, and economic situation and needs, as well as learning about the participant's safety concerns. The case manager then typically meets once a week with the participant to develop a more structured and formal case management plan that specifies needed services and appropriate referral agencies, and in some cases, sources of financial and transportation support. A formal biopsychosocial assessment is administered around the third visit to the participant, using the Global Appraisal of Individual Needs (Quick version) developed by Chestnut Health Systems in Bloomington, IL (www.chestnut.org), and a follow-up GAIN-Q assessment is administered every three months thereafter to help track the participant's progress.

While the basic intervention model is applied consistently to all participants, the details of the case management service plans and schedule of contacts and follow-up are highly individualized. Also there is no standard for how long participants should or can stay in the program; instead, participant's work with their case managers to decide how long they will participate and at what intensity. Some participants cease participating in the program for some length of time because of personal or other reasons, but they are permitted to re-enter the program at any time if appropriate.

In the first year of the program approximately 130 youth ages 15–25 (mean age 19.7) were recruited by the program, 92% male and 92% African-American (7% Hispanic). The participants who were currently active or had been active and were discharged from the program had identified a total of 364 problems or needs that they told case managers they would like help with (mean of 3.5 per participant). The most common problems/needs involved health (29%), education (23%), and employment (13%). Less than 10% of the problems involved legal issues (7%), mental health (7%), finances (4%), housing (4%), and relationships, parenting, and substance abuse (between 2% and 3% each), and the remaining 7% involved "other" problems or needs.

During the first year of the program PIRIS case managers reported minimal difficulties identifying and helping participants link to basic services and resources to address their problems and needs. Over time the intervention team continued to learn more about resources that they were not previously aware of, for example, financial support services available through the Philadelphia School District. There has also been an increase in referrals to behavioral health services, in part due to case managers' intensified focus on identifying participants' behavioral health problems and case managers' discovery of behavioral health resources of which they were not previously aware.

Because the PIRIS program did not include a formal evaluation, it is difficult to determine whether the program was successful in terms of either preventing further involvement in gunshot incidents or other violence or with regards to achieving participants' other goals. However, because the program tracks these outcomes in the Management Information System (MIS) and through anecdotal evidence, it is possible to provide some evidence for the success of the program.

During the first year of the program, only one participant was the victim of a repeat gunshot, although this was a fatal, drug-related incident. This participant had been on probation for weapons and other felonies and had been involved in a previous gunshot incident. On the other hand, there have been many success stories among participants that had a variety of risk factors, including dysfunctional family environment, educational failure, previous involvement with the police, and involvement of family members in drug trade and violence.

Because the PIRIS MIS records the outcomes of goals identified by participants, it is possible to estimate the degree to which the program has been successful, and how the program can improve its efforts to help participants. For example, in the first year of the program, 62 participants who had been discharged from the program had identified a total of 162 problems or needs (mean of 2.7 per participant). Data from the MIS indicated that 22% of the goals associated with these problems/needs had been met, 41% were "in progress" (that is, participants started working on these during the program and were continuing to work on them at the time they left the program), 9% were "discontinued" (that is, the participant/case manager decided that this was not a problem or need to be addressed at this time), and 28% of the goals were not met at the time the participants were discharged from the program. These findings suggest that while some of the participants' goals are not being met, a majority of the discharged participants made progress towards their goals as a result of their participation in the program.

At the time this chapter was prepared the PIRIS was still in operation and it was anticipated that it would receive further funding to continue into the future, and that based on lessons learned, would be expanded to other cities in Pennsylvania. While the PIRIS program illustrates a promising approach to youth violence prevention in a trauma center setting, it is currently being refined to better address the needs of a wide variety of youth who are victims of intentional gunshots. It is hoped that as the model matures funding will become available to conduct a formal observational and experimental study of the effectiveness and efficacy of the program.

Developmental Perspective on Research and Prevention and Treatment Practice: Developmental Pathways, Risk and Protective Factors, Brain Development and Individual Differences

Over the past several decades, developmental science has revealed new ways of understanding the development of complex human behaviors like those involved in aggression and violence, and the challenges faced when attempting to change these behaviors. Contemporary developmental science focuses on the basic processes of development, recognizing its multi-level and multi-trajectory nature (Valsiner, 2005). As explained in Chapter 1, developmental researchers have demonstrated that the causes of aggression and violence have influences at the individual, family, community and wider societal level, and have identified discrete developmental pathways that can lead to serious violence and delinquent behavior during adolescence and young adulthood. Developmental scientists have also demonstrated the importance of examining individual, family, and community level risk and protective factors when attempting to understand the causes and prevention of aggression and violence. As explained in Chapter 1, much less attention has been paid to protective factors, that is, factors that reduce the probability of leading to violence, than risk factors that increase the probability of violence. Recently, developmental science has begun to specify the effect that exposure to violence has on brain development and the resulting cascading effects on long-term involvement in violence and other negative behaviors and outcomes.

What, then, are the practical implications for hospital-based prevention and intervention programs of these findings from developmental science? We suggest two, but there are potentially many others.

First, emergency department, trauma center, and allied hospital staff involved in violence intervention and prevention initiatives need to pay special attention to understanding individual differences in the risk and protective factor profiles of intentionally injured youth. While ED and trauma center staff are able to spend little time with youth (and a majority of this time is focused appropriately on dealing with medical issues), they can play a role in setting the stage for increasing the effectiveness of longer term work with these youth (for example, case management as in the PIRIS program) by sharing with social workers information they may learn about risk and protective factors, and by supporting patients' expressions of trying to change negative aspects of their life to avoid a repetition of the violent incident.

Second, in order to get as much information about risk and protective factors as possible, hospital staff who work with intentionally injured youth should attempt to incorporate evidence-based screening and assessment tools into their standard clinical protocols. An example of a family of screening and assessment tools developed specifically to be used with youth is the Global Appraisal of Individual Needs (developed and supported by Chestnut Health Systems in Bloomington, IL) used in the Philadelphia PIRIS project discussed earlier in this chapter.

Training in Youth Violence Prevention

Because of the potential high costs and difficulty implementing a formal violence prevention program like the ones surveyed in this book, not every hospital will have the ability, or desire, to implement a formal program. An alternative is to provide hospital staff with training in the state-of-the art theory and practice of youth violence prevention, and, if possible, make this training mandatory and part of standard hospital staff training protocols, especially for staff working in emergency departments, trauma centers, and associated outpatient clinics.

A potential barrier to this approach is that there are few resources available for training ED and trauma center staff in violence prevention. Despite the fact that ED physicians and nurses frequently medically manage victims of violent assault, there are few courses on youth violence prevention framed from the viewpoint of emergency health care providers, and ED staff remain relatively uneducated as a specialty on the identification, assessment, and referral resources available for early intervention and prevention (Cunningham, Vaidya, Walton, and Maio, 2005). While there are published resources that describe core competencies in violence prevention for health care professionals (Knox, 2001; Commission for the Prevention of Youth Violence, 2000; American Journal of Preventive Medicine, 2005), EDs and trauma center staff report a variety of barriers to becoming involved in injury prevention activities, including a lack of time and dedicated funding (McDonald et al., 2007), and, at some hospitals, a lack of clarity about the ED's role in identification of mental health concerns (e.g., Reder and Quan, 2004).

We recommend that hospital staff interested in receiving training in youth violence prevention lobby hospital administrators to support expansion of hospital training programs and resources to develop a training program that would focus on ensuring that all hospital staff who come into contact with intentionally injured youth develop the core competencies necessary to provide positive, proactive support to youth suffering the consequences of exposure to violence. Funding for this training may be available from local foundations, or from insurance providers who view the investment in the training program a cost-

effective method of reducing long-term health care costs by reducing violence and related recidivism.

The Problem of Vicarious Trauma and Related Conditions: Treating the Healers

The focus of this book has been on describing and suggesting various hospital-based approaches to preventing intentional injuries among youth and to reducing the negative social, psychological, and economic consequences associated with these injuries. While the programs presented in this book differ in several ways in how they approach prevention and intervention, they all share the fact that those who implement the programs are health care professionals who are themselves exposed to violence and the trauma associated with violence, in very real and often times graphic ways. Emergency room and trauma center physicians and nurses view first hand, daily in urban areas, the physical devastation of violence, especially gun-related violence, suffered by young victims, and are exposed to the psychological trauma suffered by their patients and family members when dealing with the immediate aftermath of their injuries. Hospital social workers and case managers that work with victims after they are discharged from the hospital can also be traumatized with repeated observation of and exposure to victims' long-term physical and mental consequences.

All of these experiences are a formula for vicarious traumatization among hospital and social work staff. Vicarious trauma, and the related conditions (secondary traumatic stress, traumatic countertransference, burnout and compassion fatigue), have potential adverse consequences for health care workers who strive to help people who are traumatized (Collins and Long, 2003). Vicarious traumatization involves the cumulative impact of human services consumer trauma experiences on behavioral health and other human services providers working with these individuals, as well as direct trauma suffered by providers in the course of working in violent communities. Vicarious traumatization is often expressed as provider "burn-out" and PTSD-like symptoms (Brady, Guy, Poelstra, and Brokaw, 1999), which can result in high staff turnover and reductions in the quality of services provided to consumers. The potential for vicarious traumatization is highest for providers working in the areas of domestic and sexual violence, child abuse and neglect, and in criminal justice settings where trauma is common (Way, VanDeusen, Martin, Applegate, and Jandle, 2004). Also, people who work with trauma victims and who have a personal trauma history show more negative effects from their work than people without a personal trauma history (Pearlman and Mac Ian, 1995).

While some researchers have questioned the degree to which health care workers experience vicarious traumatization (Sabin-Farrell and Turpin, 2003), the consequences of ignoring the possible effects of close and prolonged work with victims of trauma and abuse may have high costs in terms of health care workers' own health, mental health, and job performance. For example, psychological consequences can include development of anxiety, depression, intrusive thoughts, alienation, dissociative episodes, feeling of helplessness, paranoia,

hypervigilance, and disrupted personal relationships (Blair and Ramones, 1996).

Fortunately, research suggests that certain protective factors can mediate the effect professionals' work with victims of violence. For example, Lerias and Byrne (2003) found that a history of previous trauma, previous psychological well-being, social support, age, gender, educational achievement, socioeconomic status, and styles of coping can mediate the effects of indirect exposure to a traumatic incident.

Furthermore, there is a rather substantial literature describing theory- and evidence-based approaches to minimizing or preventing vicarious traumatization and related conditions, some of it derived from the disaster medicine literature. For example, the concepts of cognitive processing models and investigation into memory dynamics has provided an understanding of vicarious traumatization that may help define preventive measures and treatment options for this condition (Blair and Ramones, 1996). An example of one of the most well-known treatment programs that has a published practice manual is the Accelerated Recovery Program (ARP), a brief treatment (five sessions) protocol for professionals who are suffering the effects of Compassion Fatigue (Gentry, Baranowsky, and Dunning, 1997; Gentry, 2002). Also, there are published guidelines to assist organizations in preventing vicarious trauma among staff susceptible to this condition (Bell, Kulkarni, and Dalton, 2003), as well as treatment for professionals who treat those suffering from vicarious trauma and related conditions (Figley, 1995).

Finally, Ai and Park (2005) have suggested that the effects of trauma and violence may be better understood by taking a broader perspective that includes resilience and recovery as well as damage and symptomatology. This groundbreaking article integrates three interrelated trends in mental health research: 1) the positive psychology movement, 2) the recognition of the role of spirituality and religion in health and well-being, and 3) stress-related growth to provide a counterbalance to the predominant orientation of victimization and pathology evidenced in the literature. This promising new approach to thinking about violence and trauma has implications for both young victims of intentional violence as well as for those who work with these youth and their families.

References

Ai, A.L., and Park, C.L. (2005). Possibilities of the positive following violence and trauma. *J. of Interpersonal Violence.* 20(2): 242-250

American Academy of Pediatrics (1996). Task force on adolescent assault victims needs a review of issues and a model protocol. *Pediatrics.* 98: 991-1001.

American Academy of Pediatrics Taskforce on Violence. (1999). The role of the pediatrician in youth violence prevention in clinical practice and at the community level. *Pediatrics.* 103: 173-181.

American Journal of Preventive Medicine. (2005). Training health care professional in the prevention of youth violence. *American J. of Preventive Medicine.* 29 (Supplement 2).

Anglin, T. (1997). The medical clinician's roles in preventing adolescent involvement in violence. *Adolescent Medicine.* 9: 501-515.

Atwal, A., & Caldwell, K. (2002). Do multidisciplinary integrated care pathways improve

interprofessional collaboration? *Scandinavian J. Of Caring Sciences.* 16 (4): 360-367.

Bell, H., Kulkarni, S., and Dalton, L. (2003). Organizational prevention of vicarious trauma. *Families in Society.* 84(4): 463-470

Blair, D.T., and Ramones, V.A. (1996). Understanding vicarious traumatization. *Journal of Psychosocial Nursing and Mental Health Services.* 34(11): 24-30.

Brady, J. D., Giu, J. L., Poelstra, P. L., & Brokaw, B. F. (1999). *Vicarious Traumatization, Spirituality, and the Treatment of Sexual Abuse Survivors: A National Survey of Women Psychotherapists.* Washington, D.C. American Psychological Association.

Christoffel, K., Spivak, H, and Witner, M. (2000). Youth violence prevention: the physician's role. *JAMA.* 283: 1202-1203.

Collins, S., and Long, A. (2003). Working with the psychological effects of trauma: consequences for mental health-care workers—a literature review. *Journal of Psychiatric and Mental Health Nursing.* 10(4): 417–424.

Commission for the Prevention of Youth Violence. (2000). *Youth and Violence: Medicine, Nursing and Public Health: Connecting the Dots to Prevent Violence.* Chicago, IL, American Medical Association.

Cowan, M.J., Shapiro, M., Hays, R.D., Afifi, A., Vazirani, S., Ward, C.R., and Ettner, S.L. (2006). The effect of a multidisciplinary hospitalist/physician and advanced practice nurse collaboration on hospital costs. *Journal of Nursing Administration.* 36 (2), 79–85.

Crandall, C.S., Jost, P.F., Broidy, L.M., Daday, G., Skalr, D.P. (2004). Previous emergency department use among homicide victims and offenders: a case-control study. *Annals of Emergency Medicine.* 44 (6): 646–655.

Cunningham, R.M., Vaidya, R.S., Walton, M., and Maio, R.F. (2005). Training emergency medicine nurses and physicians in youth violence prevention. *American Journal of Preventive Medicine.* 29(Supplement 2): 220-225.

Dechario-Marino, A.E., Jordan-Marash, M., Traiger, G., and Saulo, M. (2001). Nurse/physician collaboration: action research and the lessons learned. *Journal of Nursing Administration.* 31(5): 223-232.

Department of Health and Human Services. (1986). *Report of the Secretary's Task Force on Black and Minority Health. Volume V. Homicide, Suicide, and Unintentional Injuries.* Washington D.C., Government Printing Office.

Figley, C.R. (Ed.) (1995). *Compassion Fatigue: Coping with Secondary Stress Disorder in Those who Treat the Traumatized.* New York, NY: Brunner/Mazel.

Fingerhut, L.A., Ingram, D.D., & Feldman, J.J.. (1992). Firearm and nonfirearm homicide among persons 15 through 19 years of age. Differences by level of urbanization, United States, 1979 through 1989. *JAMA.* 267, 3048–3053.

Gentry, J.E., Baranowsky, A.B. and Dunning K. (1997). *Accelerated Recovery Program (ARP) For Compassion Fatigue.* Presented at the Thirteenth International Society For Traumatic Stress Studies Conference, Montreal, Canada, November 9, 1997.

Gentry, J.E. (2002). Compassion fatigue: A crucible of transformation. *Journal of Trauma Practice.* 1(3/4): 37-61.

Gladstein, J., Slater Rusonis, E.J., & Heald, F.P. (1992). A comparison of inner city and upper-middle class youths' exposure to violence. *J. of Adolescent Health.* 13: 275–280.

Knox, L. (2001). *Youth Violence and the Health Professions: Core Competencies for Effective Practice.* Alhambra, CA, Southern California Center for Youth Violence Prevention.

Kochanek, K.D., & Hudson, B.L. (1995). *Advance Report of Final Mortality Statistics, 1992.* Monthly vital statistics report; Volume 43, No. 6 (Suppl). Hyattsville, MD, National Center for Health Statistics.

Lerias, D., and Byrne, M.K. (2003). Vicarious traumatization: Symptoms and predictors. *Stress and Health.* 19(3): 129–138.

Liedtka, J.M., & Whitten, E. (1998). Enhancing care delivery through cross-disciplinary collaboration: a case study. *Journal of Healthcare Management.* 43(2): 185–203.

Mabanglo, M. (2002). Trauma and the effects of violence exposure and abuse on children: A review of the literature. *Smith College Studies in Social Work.* 72(2): 231–251.

McCart, M.R., Davies, W.H., Phelps, L.F., Heuermann, W. & Melzer-Lange, M.D. (2006). Psychosocial needs of African American youth presenting to a pediatric emergency department with assault-related injuries. *Pediatric Emergency Care.* 22(3): 154–159.

McDonald, E.M., MacKenzie, E.J., Teitelbaum, S.D., Carlini, A.R., Teter, H., and Valenziano, C.P. (in press). Injury prevention activities in U.S. trauma centers: Are we doing enough? *Journal of Injury.*

Moeller, T.G. (2001). *Youth Violence and Aggression: A Psychological Approach.* Mahway, NJ, Lawrence Erlbaum Associates, Inc.

National Council on Crime and Delinquency. (2007). Attitudes of U.S. voters toward youth crime and the justice system. *Focus: National Council on Crime and Delinquency.* (February 2007).

Pearlman, L., & Mac Ian, P. S. (1995). Vicarious traumatization: An empirical study of the effects of trauma work on trauma therapists. *Professional Psychology: Research ad Practice.* 26: 558–565.

Prothrow-Stith, D. (1992). Can physicians help curb adolescent violence? *Hospital Practice.* 27: 193–207.

Reder, S., and Quan, L. (2004). Emergency mental health care for youth in Washington State: qualitative research addressing hospital emergency departments' identification and referral of youth facing mental health issues. *Pediatric Emergency Care.* 20(11): 242–248.

Reiss, A.J., Jr. and Roth, J.A. (Eds.), (1994). *Understanding and Preventing Violence.* Washington, D.C., National Academy Press.

Rosenberg M.L., Gelles R.J., Holinger, P.C, (1987). Violence: Homicide, assault, and suicide. In: Amler, R.W. and Dull, D.H. (Eds.). *Closing the Gap: The Burden of Unnecessary Illness.* New York, Oxford University Press: 164–178.

Sabin-Farrell, R., and Turpin, G. (2003). Vicarious traumatization: implications for the mental health of health workers? *Clinical Psychology Review.* 23 (3): 449–480.

Shepherd, J., Sivarajaingam, V., and Rivara, F.P. (2000). Using injury data for violence prevention. *British Medical Journal.* 321: 1481–1482.

Smith, M.D., & Brewer, V.E.. (1992). A sex-specific analysis of correlates of homicide victimization in United States cities. *Violent Victimization.* 7: 279–286.

Thomas, E.J., Sexton, J.B., & Helmreich, R.L. (2003). Discrepant attitudes about teamwork among critical care nurses and physicians. *Critical Care Medicine.* 31 (3): 956–959.

Valsiner, J. (Ed.) (2005). *Heinz Warner and Developmental Science.* New York, NY, Springer.

Vazirani, S., Hays, R.D., Shapiro, M.F. & Cowan, M. (2005). Effect of a multidisciplinary intervention on communication and collaboration among physicians and nurses. *American Journal of Critical Care.* 14(1): 71–77.

Wilson, M., and Klein, D. (2000). Adolescents who use the emergency department as their usual source of care. *Archives of Pediatric Adolescent Medicine.* 154: 361–365.

Way, I., VanDeusen, K. M., Martin, G., Applegate, B., and Jandle, D. (2004). Vicarious trauma: Comparisons of clinicians who treat survivors of sexual abuse and sexual offenders. *Journal of Interpersonal Violence.* 19(1): 49-79.

Zun, L.S. and Rosen, J.M. (2003). Psychosocial needs of young persons who are victims of interpersonal violence. *Pediatric Emergency Care.* 19(1): 15–19.

Zun, L.S., Downey, L., Rosen, J.M. (2006). The effectiveness of an ED-based violence prevention program. *Amer. J. of Emergency Med.* 24(1): 8–13.

List of Contributors

Marla G. Becker, MPH
Associate Director
Youth ALIVE!
Oakland, CA

Deane Calhoun, MA
Executive Director
Youth ALIVE!
Oakland, CA

Rose A. Cheney, PhD
Executive Director, Firearm and Injury Center at Penn (FICAP)
Adjunct Assistant Professor of Surgery
University of Pennsylvania
Philadelphia, PA

Theodore A. Christopher, MD, FACEP
Professor and Chairman
Department of Emergency Medicine
Thomas Jefferson University Hospital and Jefferson Medical College
Philadelphia, PA

Theodore J. Corbin, MD, FACEP
Assistant Professor, Department of Emergency Medicine
Director, Violence Intervention Program
Drexel University College of Medicine
Philadelphia, PA

Elizabeth M. Datner, MD
Medical Director
Associate Professor
Department of Emergency Medicine
Hospital of the University of Pennsylvania
Philadelphia, PA

W. Hobart Davies, PhD
Associate Professor
Department of Psychology
University of Wisconsin-Milwaukee
Milwaukee, WI

Linda Davis-Moon, MSN, CRNP, APRN, BC
Director for Strategic Planning and Special Projects
Thomas Jefferson University
Department of Emergency Medicine
Philadelphia, PA

Joel A. Fein, MD, MPH
Associate Professor of Pediatrics and Emergency Medicine
The University of Pennsylvania School of Medicine
Attending Physician, Emergency Medicine
The Children's Hospital of Philadelphia
Director, The Philadelphia Collaborative Violence Prevention Center
Philadelphia, PA

Kenneth R. Ginsburg, MD, MS Ed
Associate Professor of Pediatrics
The Craig-Dalsimer Division of Adolescent Medicine
The Children's Hospital of Philadelphia
The University of Pennsylvania School of Medicine
Philadelphia, PA

Wendi Heuermann, MPH
Executive Director
Community ACTION
Hudson, WI

Nancy Kassam-Adams, PhD
Associate Director for Behavioral Research,
Center for Injury Research and Prevention
Children's Hospital of Philadelphia
Philadelphia, PA

Robert D. Ketterlinus, PhD
Senior Research Associate
Public Health Management Corporation
Philadelphia, PA

Joyce Lee-Ibarra, MPH
San Diego, CA

Michael R. McCart, PhD
Assistant Professor
Family Services Research Center
Medical University of South Carolina
Charleston, SC

Marlene D. Melzer-Lange, MD
Professor of Pediatrics
Medical College of Wisconsin
Attending Physician
Emergency Department/Trauma Center
Children's Hospital of Wisconsin
Milwaukee, WI

Lori F. Phelps, MS
Department of Psychology
University of Wisconsin-Milwaukee
Milwaukee, WI

John Rich, MD, MPH
Professor and Chair, Health Management and Policy
Drexel University School of Public Health
Philadelphia, PA

Millicent West, MS
Chaplain
Philadelphia, PA

Index

Page numbers followed by *f* indicate figures; those followed by *t* indicate tables.